THE BLIND SPOT

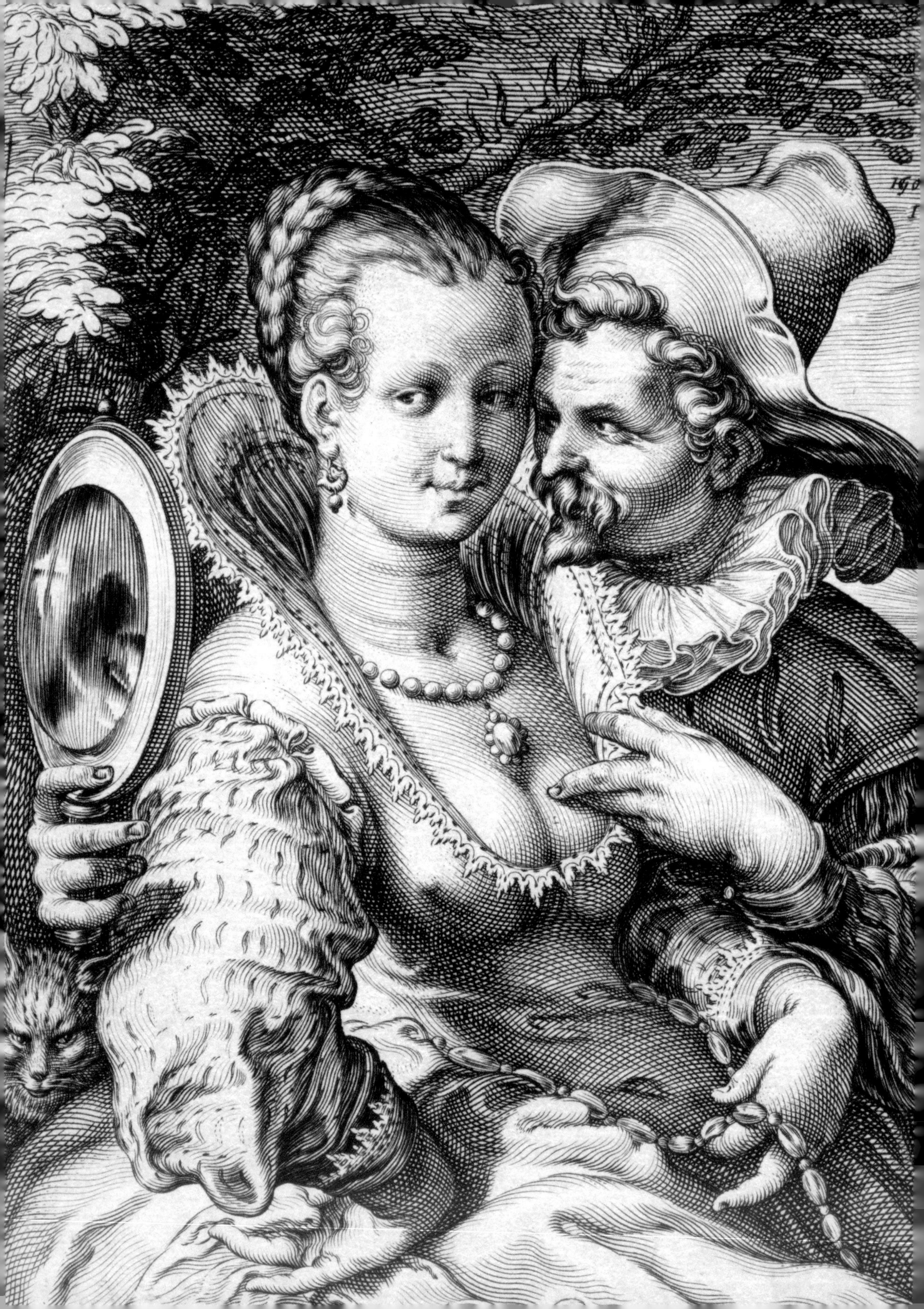

THE BLIND SPOT

An Essay on the Relations between Painting and Sculpture in the Modern Age

Jacqueline Lichtenstein
Translation by Chris Miller

Published by the Getty Research Institute

The Blind Spot: An Essay on the Relations between Painting and Sculpture in the Modern Age
Diane Mark-Walker, *Manuscript Editor*

Jacqueline Lichtenstein, *La tache aveugle: Essai sur les relations de la peinture et de la sculpture
à l'âge moderne* (Paris: Gallimard, 2003), was translated by Chris Miller

© 2008 J. Paul Getty Trust
Published by the Getty Research Institute, Los Angeles
Getty Publications
Gregory M. Britton, *Publisher*
1200 Getty Center Drive, Suite 500
Los Angeles, California 90049-1682
www.getty.edu

12 11 10 09 08   5 4 3 2 1

Cover: Jean-Antoine Houdon, *Denis Diderot (Langres, 1713–Paris, 1784), Writer* (detail), 1771. See p. 89
Frontispiece: Jan Saenredam (Dutch, 1565–1607); *Sight,* from the *Five Senses* series, ca. 1595,
engraving, 17.5 × 12.4 cm (6⅞ × 4⅞ in.); Amsterdam, Rijksmuseum. © Rijksmuseum Amsterdam
Part pages: Jacques Prou, *Sculpture Presenting Painting with the Portrait of the King* (detail), 1682. See p. 16.

Library of Congress Cataloging-in-Publication Data
Lichtenstein, Jacqueline.
  [Tache aveugle]
  The blind spot : an essay on the relations between painting and sculpture in the modern age / Jacqueline
Lichtenstein ; translation by Chris Miller.
      p. cm.
  Includes index.
  ISBN 978-0-89236-892-1 (hardcover)
  1. Sculpture, Modern—Philosophy. 2. Painting, Modern—Philosophy. I. Title.

NB1137.L5313 2008
730.1—dc22

2007044765

Contents

Foreword

To tell the story of a three-hundred-year-long conversation is the achievement of Jacqueline Lichtenstein's book *The Blind Spot: An Essay on the Relations between Painting and Sculpture in the Modern Age,* originally published in 2003 as *La tache aveugle: Essai sur les relations de la peinture et de la sculpture à l'âge moderne.* The entangled arguments that make up this discourse may seem, on the surface, familiar—arguments over the priority of painting or sculpture, sight or touch, color or design, ancients or moderns. From our vantage point, however, it can be quite difficult to understand just why so many brilliant French writers and artists remained focused for so long on these particular quarrels. What was at stake when they crossed their swords, when they championed this or that great or obscure artist, or when Charles Baudelaire famously titled an essay "Pourquoi la sculpture est ennuyeuse" ("Why Sculpture Is a Bore")? Lichtenstein's book reinvigorates the grand discourse, restores its excitement, and most importantly, shows the necessity of it.

There arose in Renaissance Italy an agon between the different arts, and it assumed the form of the famous *paragone,* a vigorous debate over whether painting or sculpture was the superior art. Imported into France in the seventeenth century, the *paragone* thrived, but Lichtenstein demonstrates that it underwent a fundamental change in the circle of the Académie royale de peinture et de sculpture. The Italian discussion had been rooted in the status of the artist and his art, and its comparative terms were the artist and the objects he created. In France, the argument turned instead on the reception of works of art, on the sensory impressions provoked by art, on the excellence of sight compared to touch. It was this aspect of her research that drew Lichtenstein to the Getty Research Institute, where she joined other scholars for a year devoted to exploring the theme "Frames of Viewing." The effect of art, the "beholder's share," became the subject of evaluation for French art criticism. The ramifications of the change in the fundamental terms of the *paragone* fueled art criticism in and out of the Académie for years to come, encompassing the issues of the mechanical versus the liberal arts, touch versus sight, ancient versus modern, color versus drawing, color and its absence, deception and reflection, the natural versus the ideal, the status and differentiation of the arts, the infirmity of painting, the death of sculpture, and the transformation of the art of the moderns into modern art. These disputes and grand themes are illuminated in *The Blind Spot.*

A professor of aesthetic philosophy, Lichtenstein not only gives an account of the discussion but also reveals the mechanisms by which it proceeds, the perfection of logical argumentation, its assertions and reversals. One of the pleasures of the book is Lichtenstein's attention to rhetorical style itself, to the individuation of the critical personalities of writers such as Roger de Piles, Denis Diderot, Baudelaire, and Joris-Karl Huysmans. Lichtenstein's rigorous analysis and deep knowledge of the evidence are accompanied by a regard for the reader. She writes with such relish and appreciation for the nuances of the rhetoric that at times her account is as vivid as if she had been eavesdropping on a centuries-old conversation.

In the past few years, the Getty Research Institute has undertaken translations of a small number of recent books, such as *The Blind Spot,* that merit a wider audience, books that ought to be accessible beyond the circle of specialists who would read it in the original language of publication. The quality of the translation is a crucial factor in this project—the translation must accurately present the technical aspects of the scholarly argument while rendering the text in a prose that conveys the voice and style of the author. We are grateful to Chris Miller for having put his skill as a translator in the service of this book.

— *Gail Feigenbaum*

Acknowledgments

I should like to express my immense gratitude to the Getty Research Institute and in particular to its former director, Thomas Crow, for enabling me to spend a year working on this book in the most intellectually stimulating conditions. Throughout my time in California, the patient, friendly, and well-informed help of my assistant, Juliana Maxim, proved invaluable. Exchanges with Charles Harrison, Deanna Petheridge, and John Hyman were especially enriching, and I thank them for their very perspicacious observations and suggestions.

I also wish to thank Christian Michel and express my gratitude to him for having taught me to look at works of art and read texts in new and different ways. This book owes a great deal to the work that we have done together over a number of years in a seminar that brings together students of philosophy and the history of art. Finally, I should like to thank Jean-François Groulier for his constant support and discerning readings. Many of the perspectives set out in this book never would have been developed without the acuity of his criticisms and the rigor of his approach.

— *Jacqueline Lichtenstein*

I would like to thank Jacqueline Lichtenstein and Kate Tunstall for their assistance in creating the present translation. Any errors are my own.

— *Chris Miller*

Vanity Reflected in the Mirror

> *One sense can sometimes inform another; however carefully fitted the garment,*
> *even the most zealous vigilance cannot avoid some slight openings through which*
> *the fingertips of sight slide home.*
>
> — Jean-Jacques Rousseau[1]

CONSIDER AN ENGRAVING after a Goltzius drawing: a man observes a woman staring at herself in a mirror (see frontispiece). He embraces the woman, his left hand caressing her breast while his right hand holds the mirror into which she stares. He presents this object to her gaze with the manifest intention of distracting her from what his other hand is doing. His forehead pressed to hers, he furtively observes her eyes to be sure that they are turned toward the mirror and that he can therefore caress her breast with impunity. Preoccupied with the direction of her gaze, he fails to see that the mirror shows not just her reflection but his too. She can observe his gaze, laugh inwardly at his device, and exploit it unbeknownst to him in an image as invisible to him as it is to us. She has not been taken in. She knows: he is using her pleasure in self-contemplation to distract her while he enjoys his sly caress. Thinking he has deceived her with the mirror, he cannot see that he is undone by his own stratagem and his vanity laid bare. Captivated by the illusory image he projects onto the whites of her averted eyes, he is blind to his real image in the mirror. If he could wrest himself from his mistress's eyes to follow her gaze, stop seeking in her eye the guarantee of his invisibility, and look in the mirror—if he could, in short, attend not to vision but the visible—he would see that she has her eye on him. And that she takes pleasure in her passivity.

The title of the engraving is *Sight*; it belongs to a series on the theme of the five senses. But this ingenious representation of the seducer's wiles and the artifice of desire might equally serve to illustrate the sense of touch. Through the interplay of hand and gaze, it enacts the subtle relation of sight and touch, such that each sense becomes a metonymy of the other. As if seeking to occupy a position

midway between sight and image, touch slides furtively into the space disclosed
by the noncoincidence of eye and gaze. While the man touches her left breast,
the woman plays with a girdle of curiously shaped beads, passing it idly between
her fingers so that it trails in the region of her sex. And just at the parting of her
breasts, slung from a necklace of pearls, hangs a medallion like a tiny mirror.
Central to the picture as a whole, it might almost be an emblem of the interplay
of sight and touch.

Note

1. Jean-Jacques Rousseau, *Julie ou la nouvelle Héloïse*
   (Paris: Garnier-Flammarion, 1967), letter 23, p. 48.

An Enduring Hierarchy of the Arts

The sculptor has no palette.

— Etienne-Maurice Falconet[1]

THE PHILOSOPHERS' VIEW of the senses of sight and touch changed dramatically during the seventeenth and eighteenth centuries. Vision had long been honored as the model and the metaphor of knowledge. Now its metaphysical and epistemological primacy was undermined by a new perspective on sensation and the relationship between our senses and ideas. It had always been recognized that sight was not reliable; though Descartes, in the first sentence of his "Dioptrique," had called it "the noblest and most universal of the senses," it was also a source of illusion and perhaps the greatest obstacle on the road to knowledge. Now came the discovery that sight acted like a form of touch and a consequent attempt to understand visual in terms of tactile experience. Over the course of the eighteenth century, touch came to preside over the empire of the senses, becoming the model of all sensation and thus of knowledge in general. In the wake of John Locke, the philosophers declared that all our ideas derived from our senses. "All senses are a form of touch," wrote Diderot in the third of his *Entretiens sur le fils naturel* (Conversations on "The natural son").[2]

Though I shall sometimes make use of the history of philosophy, I do not approach the problem of the relationship of sight and touch through the prism of philosophy. I have attempted to analyze how this problem was considered in the arts from the seventeenth century onward and to study the effect it produced. Its principal impact was on the way people thought about the hierarchy of the arts, since this had always been based on a hierarchy of the senses. In the Renaissance, as in the seventeenth century, the superiority of sight over touch was constantly invoked to justify the superiority of painting over sculpture. Unlike the painter, who, using nothing more than line and color, could imitate "on any surface," as Poussin put it, "anything visible under the sun,"[3] the sculptor sought through mass and volume to render physical solidity, the material density of bodies—in short, to imitate the reality of what we touch rather than what we see. Of course, this argument could also be made in sculpture's favor, demonstrating that its imitation was less deceitful and illusory than that of painting, which represented bodies on a flat surface. Responding to Benedetto Varchi's "poll" of Florentine artists in the sixteenth century, which asked about the relative merits of painting and sculpture, those who preferred sculpture did indeed adduce this argument.[4] Thus Benvenuto Cellini: "Painting is nothing more than the reflection in a fountain of a tree, a man or some other thing. The difference between painting and sculpture is immense; it is like the difference between a shadow and the thing that cast it."[5]

Cellini's argument is cited by Bronzino among those that "sculptors and their supporters customarily put forward.... They add that these two arts must imitate their mistress, Nature, and must resemble her. Now nature's works are made in relief and can be touched with the hand. Sculpture is an art of relief and greatly resembles nature, not only in respect of what is visible, for it is also an art of touch. Thus it is greater and more universal, since it is recognized by several senses."[6]

But painters and their supporters could easily invert this argument to show that less knowledge was needed by the sculptor than the painter precisely because sculpture was a relief art and therefore required less invention and artifice, an argument repeated by Diderot two centuries later. And they could base their demonstration on the nobility of sight as an instrument of knowledge, on the incomparable status of a sense intimately linked to the contemplative activities of the soul and to the quest for truth. The power of sight, in short, infinitely exceeded that of touch.

These debates are very familiar and have been the subject of extensive study by art historians. It is not my purpose here to analyze the development of the *paragone,* or comparison of the two arts, starting with the Renaissance and following the arguments down the centuries. Mine is a very indirect and partial approach to this theme. First, because the light in which I wish to examine it is narrowly focused and inevitably illuminates certain aspects of it at the expense of others. Second, because this light is not so much Italian as French and is cast by the theory of art, starting in the second half of the seventeenth century. The French theorists continued to relate the comparison of painting and sculpture to the comparison of sight and touch, but their arguments were somewhat different from those of their Italian predecessors. There are many reasons for this divergence, first and foremost the fact that their notion of vision was necessarily somewhat different. The new physics, developments in optics, and the philosophical trends arising from Cartesian rationalism had transformed their approach to sight and the visible and to the representation of space and the subject. The impact of these epistemological developments was felt in the domain of art, where the role and place of the spectator for the first time became the object of philosophical reflection. The nature of debate on the relative merits of painting and sculpture was similarly transformed; the issues at stake were no longer the same. In the Renaissance, these principally concerned the status of the artist and his art. The arguments on both sides of the question were rooted in the opposition between the mechanical and the liberal arts. In the *paragone,* attempts were made to show that one art was more noble and universal than the other, that it required greater intellectual abilities, that it demanded finer judgment and broader knowledge — in short, that it was by no means a manual exercise and that it required profound thought and originated in the highest faculties of the soul. The use made of the hierarchy of the senses by the Italian partisans of painting reflects this need to promote artistic activity to the ranks of the liberal arts. The superiority of sight over touch was invariably considered from the perspective of the artist, that is, in the light of the distinction thus established between the two practices. Whereas painting made demands on the eye and mind of the painter, the sculptor's efforts, as Leonardo da Vinci observed, were much more physical: "The sculptor in producing his work makes a manual effort in striking the marble or stone, whichever it is, to remove what is superfluous and extends beyond the figure shut in it. This demands a wholly mechanical exercise."[7]

The sculptor worked *per via di levare* (by removing matter); the painter, on the contrary, proceeded *per via di porre* (by addition). And, for Leonardo, this was not simply an empirical distinction. These two ways of producing a work were not of equal value. The first required "wholly mechanical exercise"; the second did not. The sculptor struggled with the resistance and durability of matter whereas the painter needed to apply but one or two touches of a delicate and subtle matter to invent forms that had only the appearance of material existence. When the sculptors continued to adduce the durability of their works, Leonardo brushed the argument aside: "The sculptor says that his art is more noble because it is more enduring, having less to fear from humidity, fire, heat and cold. One must reply to him, that this does not confer nobility on sculpture, because the capacity to last comes from the material and not from the artist."[8]

The same arguments were heard a few decades later in the response to Varchi's survey. The painters insisted on the mechanical aspect of sculpture; the sculptors on the greater permanence of their work.[9]

Attitudes changed in the seventeenth century. The comparison between painting and sculpture — sight and touch — was now made from a geometrically determined point of view: that of the spectator as subject. Of course, comparisons made from the artist's perspective did not simply vanish. The foundation of the Académie royale de peinture et de sculpture in 1648 bestowed a new social status on artists, a status justified only if their activity was demonstrably intellectual and

not manual. Thus in terms of recognition and legitimacy, the traditional criteria still applied. But a different distinction between the arts became increasingly
influential, one that concerned the spectator's mode of perception. The superiority of sight over touch remained a significant argument in painting's favor. But
that argument no longer applied primarily to the senses used to create the work,
as it had in the Renaissance; it applied to the senses employed in its reception — in
other words, to the senses to which it appealed.[10]

This change of emphasis was perceptible in the writing of most seventeenth-
century theorists but became systematic in the work of Roger de Piles and in the
colorist theory of painting. It might even be said to constitute the specificity of
that theory, which considered each art in the light of its effects; today, we might
say that it determined artistic value on the basis of aesthetic criteria. The priority
thus given to the point of view of the spectator naturally transformed the nature
and range of the comparisons. New links arose between painting and sight on
the one hand and sculpture and touch on the other, imparting an entirely new
sense to the disparity of the two arts and giving rise to new comparisons. Thus,
for de Piles, the superiority of sight over touch showed the preeminence not only
of painting over sculpture but of color over line within painting. The hierarchy
of the senses no longer simply underpinned the hierarchy of the visual arts but
affected the very definition of painting, establishing the priority of color over line.
The parallel was no longer just between the arts and the senses but between the
arts and their component parts.

Of course, the colorists were not alone in establishing a hierarchical correspondence between the visual arts and the component parts of painting, nor were
they the first to attempt it. Vasari had sought to prove the superiority of painting over sculpture in precisely this way, though he deduced it from the primacy
of line rather than color.[11] Though all visual arts are based on drawing, he said,
strictly speaking *disegno* belongs to painting: "It's ours."[12] "Il primato del disegno"
in painting in particular and in the arts in general allowed Vasari to conclude that
painting was supreme, since the principle of all other arts was contained within it.
I have shown elsewhere how de Piles used a similar argument to reach radically
different conclusions. Precisely because drawing is common to all the visual arts,
de Piles said, it cannot be thought to characterize painting. Using Aristotelian
criteria, de Piles refused to define painting in terms of line or drawing because
that definition was merely generic and did not take into account the specific difference that made painting painting rather than sculpture or architecture. That
difference was color. Completely overturning the traditional argument used by
the Renaissance theorists (and Vasari in particular), de Piles assigned drawing to
sculpture; it thus became the property of sculptors, not painters, and the latter
had to content themselves with borrowing it from their sister art. He did this by

establishing a strict term-by-term correlation between the two components of painting (drawing and color), the two visual arts (sculpture and painting), and the two senses (touch and sight).[13] His extremely rigorous analysis showed that drawing pertained to touch, not sight. It was therefore the essence of sculpture, not painting, since painting was an art of sight whereas sculpture was also an art of touch. A great deal followed from this argument. On the one hand, de Piles contrived to strip drawing of a privilege that it had held since the Renaissance: that of certifying that painting was indeed a *cosa mentale*. For him, drawing was the merely "mechanical" element in pictorial practice and not its intellectual part, which lay in the mastery of color. On the other hand, he was able to establish the supremacy of painting on new grounds by invoking the superiority of sight over touch. As we have seen, the argument itself was not new and had been widely used by Renaissance theorists. His originality did not consist in saying that painting was superior because it was an art of sight and sight alone (whereas sculpture was also an art of touch). It lay in the attribution of drawing to touch and therefore to sculpture. For him, color was to drawing what painting was to sculpture and sight was to touch. Defining painting in terms of drawing was not, in his eyes, simply a logical error, a flawed argument that made it impossible to draw a formal distinction between painting and sculpture. That definition was also ontologically false. This was a much graver error to allege, for it would ultimately make any real distinction between the two arts impossible. To prioritize drawing in painting was to subordinate painting to the model of sculpture and thus deny it any reality of its own. It also meant that a painter who was an excellent draftsman but neglected color was painting like a sculptor rather than a painter. This was the basis of de Piles's criticism of Poussin. He condemned Poussin's cold figures and his nudes in particular, which he said were "hard as marble" and resembled "painted stone." In short, he accused Poussin of producing a sculptural rather than a painterly effect. And de Piles attributed this coldness above all to the fact that Poussin's figures were modeled on ancient sculptures.[14] Too great a dependence on classical models had left Poussin painting like a sculptor; he gave flesh the appearance of stone. In this respect, Poussin was the opposite of Rubens, who always sought to imitate nature, even when copying classical statuary. Even stone, in Rubens's hands, seemed to acquire the appearance of flesh.[15]

By linking the debate about the *paragone* to the debate about color, de Piles gave a new sense to the comparison of the arts and in two ways completely redefined its scope. First, he always used the comparison for critical, not to say polemical purposes, citing it against his adversaries in defense of a colorist conception of painting and as a weapon in his dispute with the partisans of drawing. Second, he transformed the debate about sculpture into a debate about the status of antiquity. His celebration of painting—and a fortiori of color—was at one with his consistent refusal to subordinate art to the tyranny of ancient models. De Piles was not content to connect the *paragone* dispute with the *querelle du coloris* (dispute about color); the nature of his arguments meant that his critique of sculpture entered the more general quarrel of the ancients and moderns. Intersecting at certain points with the *querelle du coloris,* the quarrel of the ancients and moderns completely scrambled the traditional set of hierarchies by giving them a new basis in historical criteria.

Though it took over most of the arguments used in the sixteenth century, this approach to the *paragone* constituted a clear break with that of the Italians. And there is good reason to describe that break as "modern." The new theoretical horizon opened up by this twofold dispute — color versus line and ancients versus moderns — accounted in large measure for the new thinking about the hierarchy of the arts during the seventeenth century. It also provides the framework for my analysis of the relative status of painting and sculpture. The new perspective that developed in the theory of art during the seventeenth century made it possible to establish new correspondences between the various orders of hierarchy. By establishing an alliance between sculpture, touch, antiquity, and line on the one hand and painting, sight, the moderns, and color on the other, de Piles's theory inaugurated an account of the arts that, under various guises, continued to hold sway till the early twentieth century. It is striking that all those who defended a colorist notion of painting maintained this same system of evaluation. Whatever the date, they all had strange reservations about sculpture. Diderot clearly admired the work of his friend Falconet, as he did that of Jean-Antoine Houdon, but several times confirmed that sculpture perplexed him. It was an art that he did not understand or did not understand well and he had, he admitted, little to say about it. Baudelaire's position was rather ambiguous, and it changed over the years, but in his *Salon de 1846* he did not hesitate to describe sculpture as "only a complementary art."[16] Zola and Huysmans were both happy to announce the death of sculpture and declare its reign at an end. All of them undeniably preferred painting to sculpture. And, among the reasons given for this preference, the excessive links between sculpture and antiquity return like a leitmotif. Of course, one should not and can not confuse Huysmans's virulent attacks with Baudelaire's measured words, nor Diderot's witty arguments with de Piles's often ponderous analysis. There are perceptible differences of discourse and the differences are not simply rhetorical. All of these figures criticized sculpture in the name of a particular conception of art and that conception was based on their relationship to painting. They all thought painting an art of color, but since they did not have the same notion of color, they did not have the same notion of painting. Their idea of painting was not simply a product of abstract thought but was in a sense dictated to them by the painters themselves. By contact with certain artists and exposure to their canvases, they discovered what a great colorist was and so came to comprehend what painting was. Their idea of art was inseparable from the painting of the artists that they admired and championed.[17] De Piles, Diderot, and Huysmans all believed that the greatest painter was he whose colors were most beautiful or powerful, but the notion of a great colorist nevertheless meant different things to them. Nor did they concur about the meaning of the word *modern*. *Modernity* in Baudelaire's writings has little in common with the sense of the word *modern* in the seventeenth and eighteenth centuries. Baudelaire and his successors were defending modern art when they praised the painting of Delacroix, Manet, or Degas, whereas when de Piles or Diderot praised the paintings of Rubens or Chardin they were doing something quite different: they were praising the moderns. But if we put aside the historical and artistic differences in these ways of talking about art, we cannot help noticing that they all shared the same theoretical construct developed in the seventeenth century. Such consistency cannot easily be explained in terms of influence. Rather, it seems inherent in a certain aesthetic logic; it seems to be structurally determined by what one might call the topic of the colorist discourse, according to which the superiority of painting over sculpture follows from the superiority of color over line, and from this follows the superiority of the moderns over the ancients.

This is the topic that I have sought to analyze.[18] My inquiry (to borrow a word dear to the English philosophers) does not therefore concern the effective reality of art, meaning the history of artistic production. It focuses on neither sculpture nor painting but on the image of either as constructed in the discourse of art and as it contributed to the construction of a discourse on art. Though I have tried to be as attentive as possible to the artistic changes that occurred between the seventeenth and nineteenth centuries, it is not my intention to give even a partial account of the infinitely complex reality of art in its material existence. I am not a historian of art. The history that I have researched is that of discourses rather than works, though the analysis of these discourses has necessarily led me to speak of works and notably to measure the distance between the discourse and the work. That distance is particularly striking in the case of sculpture, where the effective reality of the art—sculptors' practices—is often at odds with the picture "painted" by the various theoretical and critical discourses. This is especially true in the second half of the eighteenth century, that is, after the writings of Winckelmann were at their most influential. If one relied exclusively on texts, one would gain a rather inaccurate picture of sculpture. The disjunction between the image of sculpture as conveyed by the discourse and the reality of the art can be explained in a number of ways, first and foremost by the fact that the sculptors did not write very much. During the Renaissance and the seventeenth century, art theory was mostly the work of painters. Artists working with the brush took up the pen more readily than those who worked with the chisel. And the tribe of writers, no doubt grateful for the homage, has tended to favor painting over sculpture.[19] But, however we explain it, that disjunction at once demonstrates the sturdiness of the theoretical construct (it went on to determine the representation of art for several centuries) and proves its relative independence from the works themselves. It also bears witness to the way in which art has always, thank goodness, resisted the conceptual frameworks to which the thinkers would like to confine it. I have not, however, sought to write what one might call a history of ideas about art any more than I have written art history. As I said, I have attempted to analyze the functioning of a topic—that is, a logic—by following its transformations from the seventeenth to the nineteenth century. I have consequently given pride of place to certain authors who seemed to me particularly representative and exemplary of this mode of thought and have necessarily schematized their positions to some degree.

I have not therefore sought to write a book on art but one on the representation of art. I have tried to show how a certain image of sculpture was created as a result of a certain idea of painting; to demonstrate how that idea of painting had itself been treated as paradigmatic in an attempt to forge a certain image of art; and thus to explain how the aesthetics of the moderns were, for several centuries, synonymous with a colorist aesthetic of painting; and thus how the idea of painting became synonymous with that of art.

Until recently, the idea of art has always been identified with that of painting. Many reasons—historical, artistic, philosophical, and theological—could be invoked to explain the astonishing priority enjoyed by painting in Western thinking. A very ancient tradition lies behind the selection of painting as the model around which the definition of art was constructed, a tradition that goes back to Plato and Aristotle. The problem of the "death of art," as set out by Hegel and restored to currency by the artists and theorists of the twentieth century, is the ultimate form of this identification of art and painting. Questions about the death of art always seem to come down to questions about the death of painting, as recent debates about contemporary art have shown. True, this identification has been more or less undone over the course of the twentieth century. Indeed, there are those who think that this constitutes one of the great novelties of our era. Today, sculptors and painters have vanished and been replaced by the general-purpose "visual artist." The traditional questions, What is painting? and What is sculpture? refer to objects with empirical and formal properties that can be described and analyzed (frame, plinth, solid matter, two- and three-dimensionality, color, relief, composition, and so on). Today they tend to be overlooked in favor of questions like "What is art?" or "When is art?" And these are not artistic but philosophic or sociological questions; they refer to an abstract category. Though painters used to make paintings and sculptors sculptures, today's artists "do" art as others "do" metaphysics or politics. In other words, what they "do" is something that cannot be "made." True, some artists continue to call themselves painters and sculptors and to make paintings and sculptures. But this more traditional aspect of contemporary art — *traditional* is not intended here in any pejorative sense — has also changed a great deal. Painting was for several centuries considered the principal vehicle of artistic modernity, but it no longer holds that status today. As Lucy Lippard noted in the catalog of an exhibition of American sculpture from the 1960s, the relationship between painting and sculpture has been transformed. Modern sculpture is often, she says, more interesting than modern painting: "Sculpture has long been considered a more or less subsidiary art, following painting's innovations and docilely translating them into three-dimensional versions.... Now the relationship is more complex. In several important ways, sculpture is gaining its independence from painting and painting, in turn, frequently finds itself its follower."[20] Right or wrong, Lippard's judgment testifies to a complete reversal of the hierarchy of the two arts established during the Renaissance and maintained over several centuries. Another of the objectives of this book is to make it possible to grasp the extent of the transformation undergone by sculpture, which is, in a sense, much more radical than the one undergone by painting. This I have sought to do by situating that transformation in the history of ideas about art, that is, by retracing the long history leading up to it.

Notes

Unless otherwise indicated, all translations are by Chris Miller.

1. Etienne-Maurice Falconet, "Observations sur la statue de Marc-Aurele," in idem, *Oeuvres complètes,* 3rd ed. (Paris: Dentu, 1808; reprint, Geneva: Slatkine, 1970), 3:63.

2. Denis Diderot, *Entretiens sur le fils naturel (Dorval et moi),* in *Oeuvres esthetiques,* ed. Paul Vernière (Paris: Éditions Garnier fréres, 1965), 167.

3. Nicolas Poussin to Fréart de Chambray, 1 March 1665; in Nicolas Poussin, *Lettres et propos sur l'art,* ed. Anthony Blunt (Paris: Hermann, 1964), 163.

4. Benedetto Varchi asked artists which was the noblest art. After conducting his survey, he gave two lectures in 1547 on the *paragone* (preceded by a lecture on Michelangelo's sonnets): "Lezione nella quale si disputa della maggioranza delle arti" and "Qual sia più nobile o la scultura o la pittura." See Lauriane Fallay d'Este, ed., *Le paragone, le parallèle des arts,* trans. Lauriane Fallay d'Este and Nathalie Bauer (Paris: Klincksieck, 1992), 96–116. For a recent scholarly Italian edition of the "Lezione," see Benedetto Varchi, "Lezione della maggioranza delle arti," in Paola Barocchi, ed., *Pittura e scultura nel cinquecento* (Livorno: Sillabe, 1998), 7–85.

5. Benvenuto Cellini to Benedetto Varchi, 28 January 1546; in Benedetto Varchi, "Lezione della maggioranza delle arti," in Paola Barocchi, ed., *Pittura e scultura nel cinquecento* (Livorno: Sillabe, 1998), 83. Michelangelo took a similar view: "Sculpture can serve to light painting's way: the difference between them is like that between the sun and the moon"; Michelangelo to Benedetto Varchi, n.d.; in Varchi, "Lezione" (this note), 84.

6. Agnolo Bronzino to Benedetto Varchi, n.d.; in Benedetto Varchi, "Lezione della maggioranza delle arti," in Paola Barocchi, ed., *Pittura e scultura nel cinquecento* (Livorno: Sillabe, 1998), 67.

7. Leonardo da Vinci, *Traité de la peinture,* trans. and ed. André Chastel (Paris: Berger-Levrault, 1987), 98. Translated by A. Philip McMahon as *Treatise on Painting (Codex urbinas latinus 1270),* 2 vols. (Princeton: Princeton Univ. Press, 1956).

8. Leonardo, *Traité* (note 7), 102.

9. "The more exercise of arm and body an art requires, the more mechanical and thus the less noble it is," Bronzino writes in his letter to Varchi; see Bronzino to Varchi, n.d. (note 6), 67. Bronzino refutes the argument from permanence in the same way as Leonardo: "This is not an attribute of the art; art cannot make marble, porphyry, and other stones, which are the work of nature"; see Bronzino to Varchi, n.d. (note 6), 67. Yet the position of the sculptors in Varchi's time was much stronger since they could cite the example of Michelangelo.

10. This way of thinking about the distinction between the senses was, it is true, already present during the Renaissance, as we see in Bronzino: he contrasts painting, whose forms can be recognized only by sight, with sculpture, which can be apprehended by more than one sense. But this use of the distinction was essentially confined to the Aristotelian problematic of recognition and was developed in Italy principally in its application to artistic practice. In Italian theory, the point of view of the spectator was mainly taken into account when presenting the more general distinction between the arts that pleased the learned and those that pleased the ignorant.

11. Vasari gives an extensive analysis of the *paragone* in the introduction to *The Lives of the Artists;* see Giorgio Vasari, *The Lives of the Artists,* trans. Julia Conaway Bondanella and Peter Bondanella (Oxford: Oxford Univ. Press, 1991). Cf. his letter to Varchi of 12 February 1547, in Benedetto Varchi, "Lezione della maggioranza delle arti," in Paola Barocchi, ed., *Pittura e scultura nel cinquecento* (Livorno: Sillabe, 1998), 61–66, in which Vasari adduces different and more traditional arguments.

12. See Giorgio Vasari, "Proemio," in *Le vite de' più eccellenti architetti, pittori, et scultori, da Cimabue insino a' tempi nostri: Nell'edizone per i tipi di Lorenzo Torrentino, Firenze 1550,* ed. Luciano Bellosi and Aldo Rossi (Turin: Giulio Einaudi, 1986), 10.

13. On this aspect of de Piles's theory, see Jacqueline Lichtenstein, *The Eloquence of Color: Rhetoric and Painting in the French Classical Age,* trans. Emily McVarish

(Berkeley: Univ. of California Press, 1993), 138–68.

14. Landscapes were almost the only paintings in Poussin's corpus to find favor with de Piles, who felt that this further confirmed the validity of his critique. After all, in painting a landscape, Poussin could not, de Piles said, rely on any ancient model; he was forced to imitate nature! See Roger de Piles, *Abregé de la vie des peintres: Avec des reflexions sur leurs ouvrages, et un traité du peintre parfait: De la connoissance des dessins: De l'utilité des estampes,* 2nd ed. (Paris: Chez Jacques Estienne, 1715), 469.

15. The power to transform stone into flesh seems at the time to have constituted one of the distinctive marks of the great colorists. Thus Molière, in his poem to the glory of Mignard, writes: "And what power you hold in your fingertips / That brings dead things to life before our eyes / A mixture of browns and of lighter tones / Makes color into mind and flesh from stones"; Molière, *La gloire du Val-de-Grâce* (Paris: Iean Ribou, 1669). The origin of this very ancient topos is in Callistratus. It recurs in Italy, for example, when people praise Michelangelo's *carnosità* (the capacity to give marble the appearance of flesh). It was to play a fundamental role in discourse on sculpture during the eighteenth century, as we shall see in our discussion of Diderot. On this subject, cf. Aline Magnien, "Callistrate et le discours sur la sculpture à l'âge moderne," in Philippe Hoff and Paul-Louis Rinuy, eds., *Antiquités imaginaires: La référence antique dans l'art moderne, de la Renaissance à nos jours* (Paris: Presses de l'École normale supérieure, 1996), 21–41.

16. Charles Baudelaire, *Salon of 1846,* in idem, *Selected Writings on Art and Artists,* trans. P. E. Charvet (Harmondsworth: Penguin, 1972), 98.

17. This is precisely what distinguishes the theory and criticism of art from a philosophical approach to art. The latter mostly starts from an abstract and general idea of art: from a concept rather than from works of art. In my view, this is the strongest philosophical objection to that approach.

18. To that extent, this volume continues the inquiry I began in *The Eloquence of Color* (note 13). It is a chronological extension in that it takes a second look at an issue that first gained currency in the seventeenth century and follows its developments through to the nineteenth century. But it also returns to certain views that I expressed therein, ones with which I am no longer wholly in accord. These are for the most part historical views. For example, I have revised my judgment about the Académie of the seventeenth century, whose workings now seem to me less rigid than they once did. But I have also revisited certain philosophical views, in particular those that relate to the distinction between imitation and illusion. The terms in which I posed this problem now seem to me inadequate and sometimes, indeed, incorrect.

19. Caylus had already noted and wondered at this injustice in the eighteenth century. His lecture on the life of the sculptor Sarrazin, given at the Académie on 1 March 1749, begins: "Gentlemen, I have never understood why the life and works of the very able sculptor-members of your Académie have been passed over in silence. A number of art lovers have celebrated our painting and done so with success. Why has none of these come forward to do justice to our sculpture?" Anne Claude Philippe Caylus, "La vie de Sarrazin" (1 March 1749), in Jacqueline Lichtenstein and Christian Michel, eds., *Les conférences de l'Académie royale de peinture et de sculpture,* vol. 4 (Paris: École nationale supérieure des beaux-arts, forthcoming).

20. Lucy R. Lippard, "As Painting Is to Sculpture: A Changing Ratio," in Maurice Tuchman, ed., *American Sculpture of the Sixties,* exh. cat. (Los Angeles: Los Angeles County Museum of Art, 1967), 31.

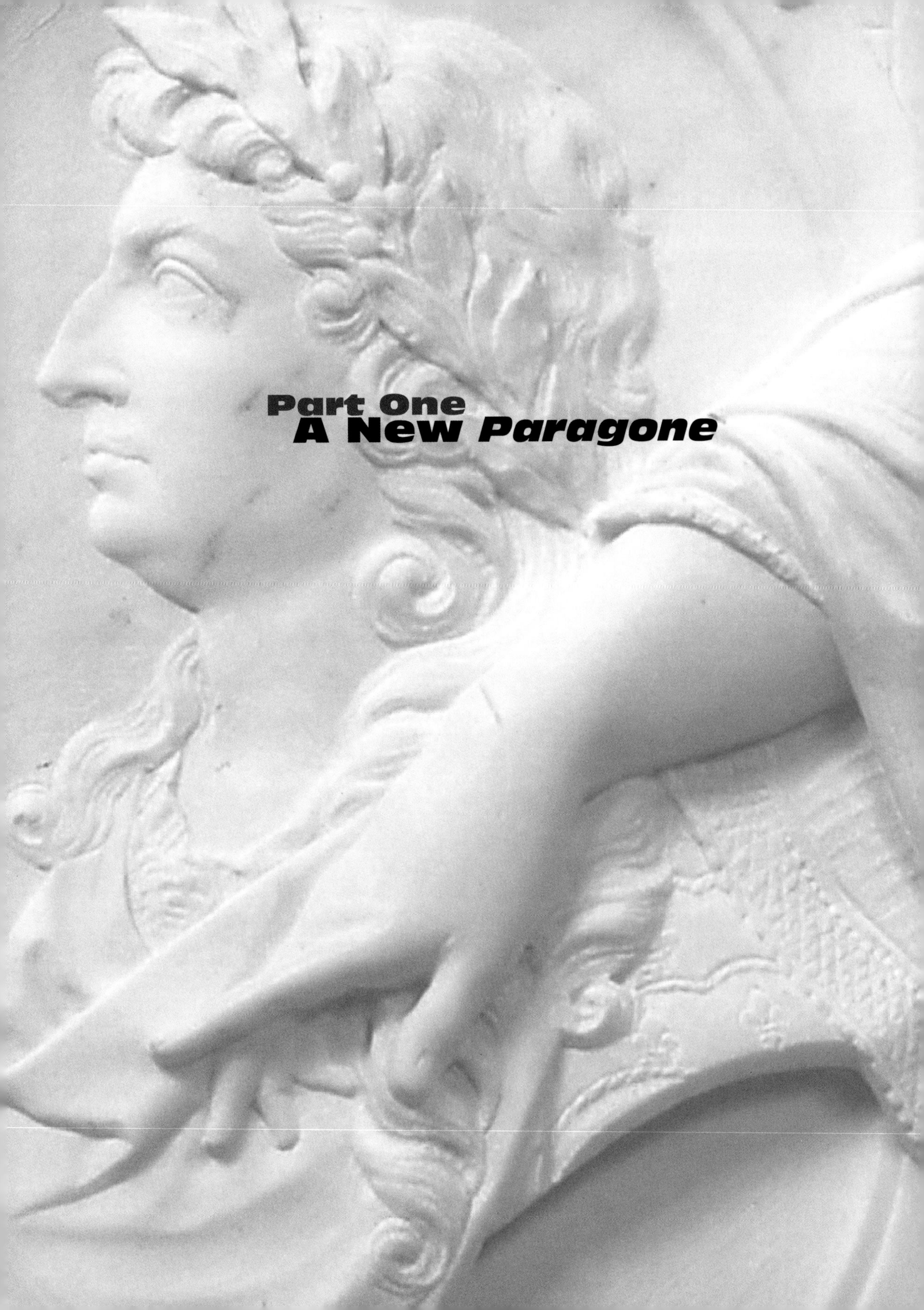

Part One
A New Paragone

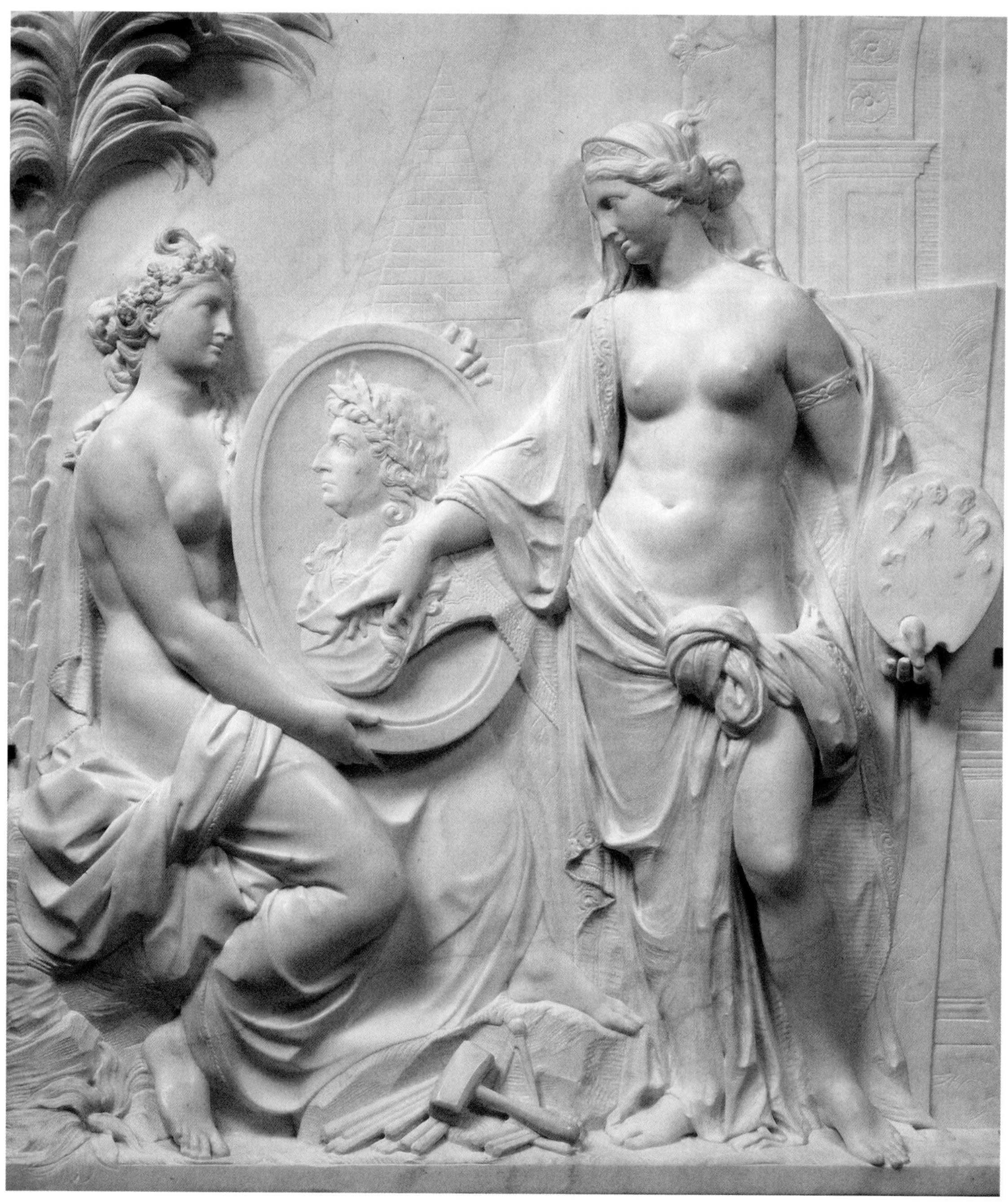

Fig. 1. Jacques Prou (French, 1655–1706)
Sculpture Presenting Painting with the Portrait of the King, 1682, marble bas-relief,
90 × 70 × 9 cm (35⅜ × 27½ × 3½ in.)
Paris, Musée du Louvre

Artistic Disputes and Pedagogical Debates in the Seventeenth Century

Sculpture at the Académie

Nature belongs to antiquity.

— Johann Wolfgang von Goethe[1]

On 5 November 1689, Guillet de Saint-Georges, the historiographer of the Académie royale de peinture et de sculpture (hereafter Académie), delivered a lecture on a bas-relief by Jacques Prou the younger representing Sculpture and Painting (fig. 1).[2] It was the first lecture on the subject of the comparison between the two arts (the *paragone*) since 1667, the date on which lectures at the Académie had begun.[3] In an earlier lecture given on 5 July 1681 about two works representing Roman Charity—a painting by Louis Boullogne the elder and a bas-relief by Jean Cornu—Guillet had given passing attention to this topic but had not attempted a comparative analysis of the two arts. He confined himself to placing a few conventional remarks on the subject of the *paragone* between his descriptions of the painting and the sculpture: "The subject is treated in the sculptor's marble and on the painter's canvas with such agreeable variety and with such different forms of expression that one cannot too highly admire the fecundity of the talents cultivated at the Académie. For the painter's brush and the sculptor's chisel take very different and ingenious roads to one and the same goal and, far from adulterating the subject, they impart new power to it and enhance its beauty."[4]

By contrast, the lecture of 1689 is entirely devoted to the comparison of the arts, since the work it sets out to analyze is itself an allegory of the *paragone*. It begins with a short description:

This bas-relief is in marble and rectangular in shape, being some two-and-a-half feet tall and two feet long. It represents Sculpture and Painting consulting each other about the portrait of the king. Sculpture appears in the figure of a handsome young woman who wears a serious look to indicate the prudence of her reflections. With both hands she holds a bust-length drawing of the king, made as a medallion. The king is crowned with laurel, which is one of the symbols of victory. He is armed and his military costume can be seen beneath his scarf, whose folds are rendered in a very natural arrangement.[5]

Prou's bas-relief was not simply a pretext for the kind of generalizations on the respective merits of painting and sculpture that one finds in many works from the Renaissance on. It was at once the object of Guillet's reflection and the source from which it sprang. In this, he was entirely at one with the Academicians' oft-expressed determination that any general artistic considerations should be based on the examination of one or more individual works. Speaking of the organization of the lectures, which took place in 1667, Testelin noted that lecturers were asked to "set about the examination of the things themselves through the consideration of individual works."[6]

Quite apart from his reflections on the *paragone,* Guillet's lecture was first and foremost a demonstration of the validity of the principles on which theorists had, since the Renaissance, founded their definition of art. It offered irrefutable proof of the fact that sculpture was indeed, like painting, an art of *disegno* or *dessein,*[7] that is, the expression of carefully worked out thoughts, the visible and material translation of a thought that the artist has inscribed in marble with his chisel. Guillet shows that everything in this bas-relief, from the figures and their attributes to the royal medallion and the architectural elements, every component of the composition and all their interrelations, answered to a precise intention on the part of the artist, testifying to the "novelty" of "his thoughts" on a subject that had already been widely treated and whose "matter" might have seemed "exhausted."[8] He highlights two aspects of the work that in his opinion showed that essential quality known in the seventeenth century as "invention," meaning the way in which the artist's ingenuity was displayed in renewing a theme and treating a subject. The first aspect concerned the arrangement of the two figures:

> Sculpture shows the drawing on the medallion to Painting, as if seeking to emphasize that this is the worthy object of their study and labors and that both must concentrate thereon with the greater exactitude and propriety because their task is to represent an august monarch, who has always favored them with particular protection and who has, to raise their art to its highest degree, founded the Académie royale that bears their name.[9]

But this arrangement also answered to another intention, to what Guillet calls "a particular thought." Indeed, it was precisely the existence of this twofold intention that constituted in his eyes the subtlety and ingenuity of Prou's invention. In this work, Guillet says, the artist sought not only to pay homage to the favor shown by the king but also to express his own personal gratitude to Charles Le Brun:

> But this arrangement, in which Sculpture presents her drawing to Painting, is also founded on a particular thought of Monsieur Prou's, who wished me to specify it here, since he is full of gratitude for the good advice and help that he has often received from Monsieur Le Brun. Here he has made a private confession of this and, knowing that the execution of the principal works of the king in both painting and sculpture has often been confided to Monsieur Le Brun, he wished to give a formal idea of it by indicating that Sculpture communicates its drawing to Painting and awaits her advice.[10]

Prou was, as Guillet tells us, perfectly aware of the ambiguity that this "particular thought" might introduce. The fact that Sculpture presents her drawing to Painting might be incorrectly understood to suggest the inferiority of sculpture and its dependence on painting. It was to avoid a hierarchical interpretation of this gesture that Prou showed Sculpture sitting down:

> But at the same time, [Prou] takes care to indicate the excellence and merit of sculpture and, remembering that works of painting executed for the king were at this time required to submit to the same inspection, he seeks to place the two talents as if in perfect counterpoise. Thus, though Sculpture asks for advice, she maintains her rank, for she sits while Painting stands; this shows that they are on familiar terms with each other, without any inferred superiority; that they are two sisters who, having their common origin in drawing, dwell forever united in close society by a praiseworthy familiarity. Nor do they ever conceive any jealousy for the particular advantages bestowed now on one, now on the other. Consequently they here consult each other in order to give reciprocal advice rather than a positive command.[11]

The fact that Sculpture was seated thus reestablished the general sense of the representation, which the existence of this "particular thought" might have disturbed. It served as a sort of "counterpoise" (Guillet's term) to Sculpture's gesture, restoring the balance between the artist's particular thought and the general thought of his work—to the advantage of the latter. For, if we are to believe Guillet, that general thought was precisely the idea of a fine balance or perfect equality between the arts.

But it is not at all clear that this notion of equality does, in fact, constitute the general thought of Prou's work. The fact that Sculpture is seated and Painting stands could easily be interpreted as bestowing a hierarchical superiority on Sculpture, whose position is royal: at the court, the king alone was seated and no one could take a seat in his presence without being expressly invited to do so. Moreover, according to the codes of the time, Sculpture occupies the place of honor, to the right of the king (on the spectator's left). Guillet begins his description there, since he analyzes the piece (from the spectator's point of view) left to right, as if reading a text. Prou may have sought to favor Sculpture, albeit discreetly, at the expense of Painting. The suggestion is by no means far-fetched; he was, after all, a sculptor. Comparison of the figures from a formal rather than an iconographic perspective might suggest further arguments in favor of that interpretation. On sculptural grounds, the left-hand figure is superior not because it is more beautiful but because it demonstrates greater virtuosity. The sculptor displays his talent in the expression of the face, the movement of the lines of the body, the play of the foreshortening, and the rendering of the shapes and volumes beneath the folds of drapery. Painting, seen in a full-frontal posture, stands as it were parallel to the plane from which she is slightly detached, with her body inscribed within a series of vertical lines (her upright position, her canvas, and the triumphal arch), whereas Sculpture sits in three-quarter profile and her position allows the sculptor to exploit all the possibilities of three-dimensionality. The self-reflexive nature of the figures is combined with extremely clever use of the figurative elements that identify and therefore differentiate them. Sculpture is not merely more sculptural, she is also, paradoxically, more pictorial, more colorist than Painting. Painting is, in turn, more linear. Inverting the properties attributed to each of the two arts, Prou made the body of Sculpture much more carnal than that of Painting, as if to show that sculpture could surpass painting on painting's own terrain and that the chisel could produce the "flesh-effects" (*effets de chair*) wrongly thought to be painting's appanage. One might say the same for the rendering of fabrics, another traditional mark of the great colorists. Their textures are clearly differentiated—smooth and brilliant, like silk, for Sculpture, matte and a bit rough, like wool, for Painting—as if the sculptor wished to show that, in this regard too, he could match painting by his skill in polishing the marble or producing a more grainy effect. Though not immediately apparent, one slightly disturbing iconographic detail is particularly significant in this respect.[12] Sculpture wears a crown of flowers. Now, according to a tradition that goes back to ancient rhetoric, flowers symbolize the art of colors. One would normally expect the flowers to crown Painting and not Sculpture.

The intent of the work seems infinitely more complex than Guillet imagines. If we begin by supposing that Prou intended to represent the superiority of sculpture over painting and not simply the pair's unity and mutual emulation, Sculpture's gesture in showing the medallion to Painting takes on a completely different meaning. The gesture may in that case be intended to restore a semblance of balance while maintaining the superiority of sculpture. Seeking to emphasize the merits and excellence of painting (the words Guillet used about sculpture),

Prou may have represented Sculpture addressing Painting and consulting her in order to hear her advice. If so, the particular thought would now "counterpoise" the general one. And this is the opposite of what Guillet had assumed. If he had perceived Prou's intentions in this light, he would undoubtedly have criticized them, since he preferred to think that the two sisters were on an equal footing. Guillet occupied the very important function of historiographer to the Académie and his interpretation presented a significant advantage: it would satisfy not just the sculptors but the painters too.

The other aspect of the work on which Guillet dwelled was the relationship of the figures in the foreground to the classical architecture in the background, the pyramid and the triumphal arch:

> We see at some distance from Painting a triumphal arch of very well-ordered architecture. In the background of the work appears a pyramid that has very little relief, touched in with those delicate and superficial strokes that are almost one with the background and which, by that device, recede into the distance. The pyramid therefore produces a handsome effect on the eye. But though he has made it a handsome ornament for his relief, he has placed it there primarily as a glorious monument to signify the solidity and permanence of the king's glory, in this way bringing it into line with the meaning of the triumphal arch and the expressions of Sculpture and Painting, who together intend to make the fame of this august monarch's heroic actions last for ever. But in seeking to proclaim the glory of a hero in a manner commensurate with his merits, the sculptor does not compare the portrait with the ancient monuments. He leaves those monuments in the distance as if to suggest that they are built in one particular place only and are therefore seen only by very few people. But he places the portrait in a dominant position in the bas-relief, as if implying that the portrait is shown to every nation and that, since it can be so multiplied as to be seen in every part of the world, by its faithful and natural features it offers to universal admiration the characteristics of the hero's soul and the greatness of his genius. Thus the sculpture vaunts with justifiable preference the advantages of sculpture and painting [over architecture].[13]

By leaving the monuments in the distance and giving them little relief, Guillet tells us, Prou meant to suggest that painting and sculpture were in his eyes superior to architecture. This interpretation must have delighted the Academicians as a whole, since there were of course no architects among them. But Guillet is unable or unwilling to see that the sculptor is not content, as he says, to praise "the advantages of painting and sculpture" over architecture; he also vaunts the advantages of sculpture over painting. Though he correctly observes that the portrait of the king occupies the central position in the work, he draws no conclusion from the fact that the portrait is a medallion, that is, a work that illustrates the art

     ARTISTIC DISPUTES AND PEDAGOGICAL DEBATES

of the sculptor rather than the painter. In an earlier version of his lecture, Guillet had given a rather different and more precise interpretation of Prou's intentions: "But it is easy to perceive that the sculptor, always zealous to defend the glory and talents of the Académie, here offers his medallion precedence over the talents of architecture, and that he rightly believes that the talents embodied in the chisel and paintbrush are better suited than others to proclaiming the great actions of a hero in a manner commensurate with his merits."[14]

Without admitting that the "dominant position" of the medallion, flanked by Painting and Sculpture, might signify anything other than the preeminence of painting and sculpture over architecture, that is, the preeminence of sculpture over painting—without, in short, saying that Prou's work accorded a preference to his own art—Guillet at least acknowledged in this initial draft that the sculptor placed "his medallion" to the fore. He eliminated the word *medallion* because, little as it says, it rather gives the game away and might have elicited undesirable reactions in his audience. This concern may also explain why he merely mentions the instruments of Sculpture lying on the ground, without saying (or without seeing) that they are, in this way, foregrounded: "Among the tools at her feet, she has a maul, a compass, and other instruments of her art."

These tools are indeed under the medallion, between the two figures, at the base of a central axis that leads to the point of the pyramid. Even if he had observed this detail, Guillet could hardly have pointed it out to his audience. In the Académie, the "dominant position," as Guillet puts it, had always been occupied by painting.

The organization of the Académie lectures bears witness to the dominance of painting. The minutes of the session of 3 May 1653 record that Academicians should "discuss the science and logic [*raisonnements*] of the arts of painting and sculpture,"[15] but less than four months later, on 30 August 1653, references to sculpture had disappeared and only "deliberations concerning the logic of painting" were required. Over the following decade, a degree of vacillation is apparent. In the minutes of the session of 7 June 1664, "lectures on the subject of painting and sculpture" again come up, but on 7 March 1665, it is resolved that "at the next assembly, the lectures on the logic of painting will be resumed." On 9 January 1666, Colbert intervened to resurrect a project still unrealized after the passage of several years. But the minutes mention only the analysis of paintings: "Monsieur Colbert proposed that every month one of the best of the paintings in the Cabinet du Roy should be explained by the duty teacher [of the month], in the presence of the assembly."[16] At the Académie, then, more was said about painting than about sculpture. The list of lectures for the period 1667–79 is particularly revealing in

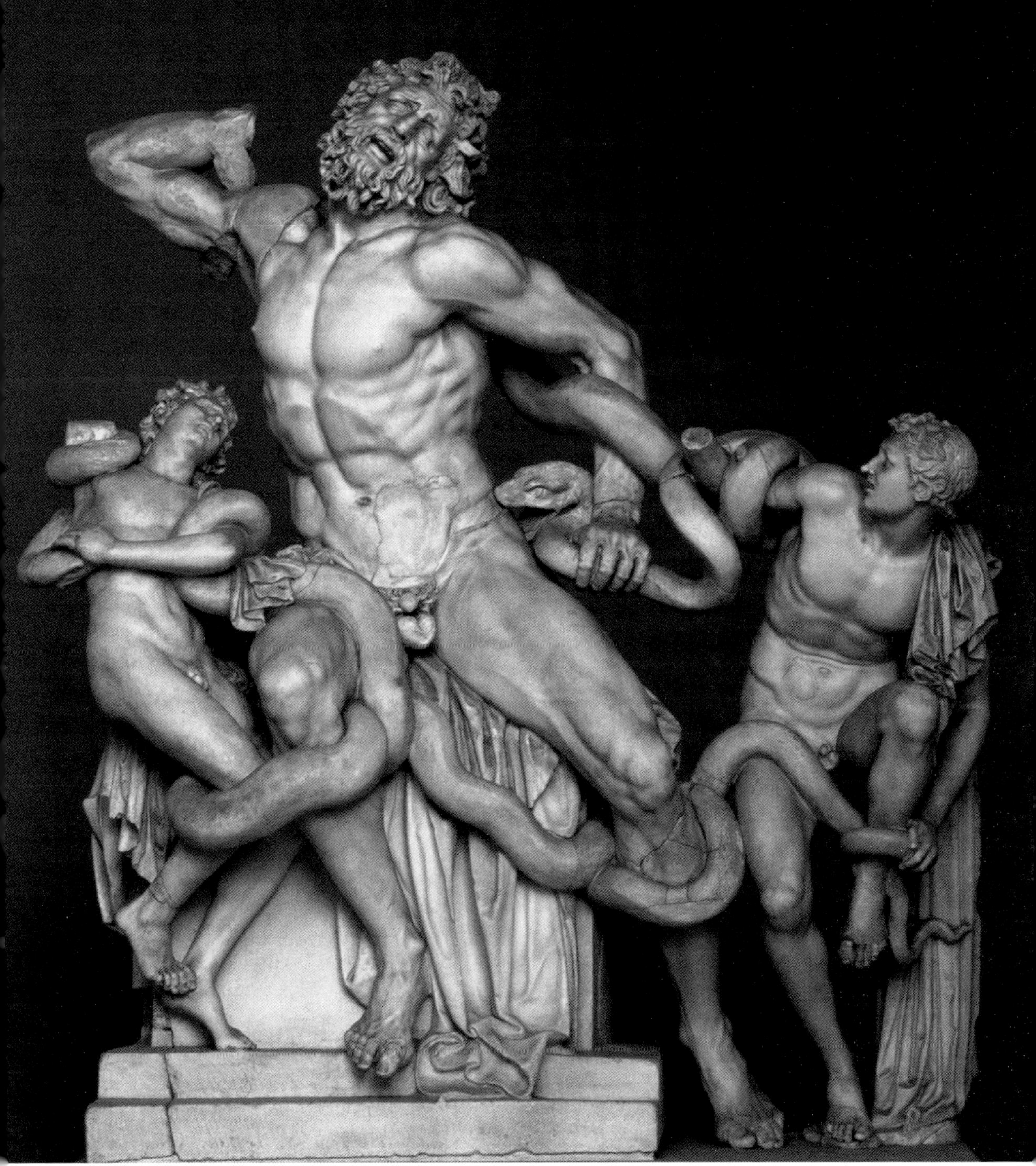

Fig. 2. **Roman copy, perhaps after Agesander, Athenodorus, and Polydorus of Rhodes (Greek, active ca. A.D. 10–20)**
The *Laokoon* group, 1st century A.D., marble, height: 210 cm (82⅝ in.)
Vatican City, Museo Pio-Clementino, Musei Vaticani

                    ARTISTIC DISPUTES AND PEDAGOGICAL DEBATES

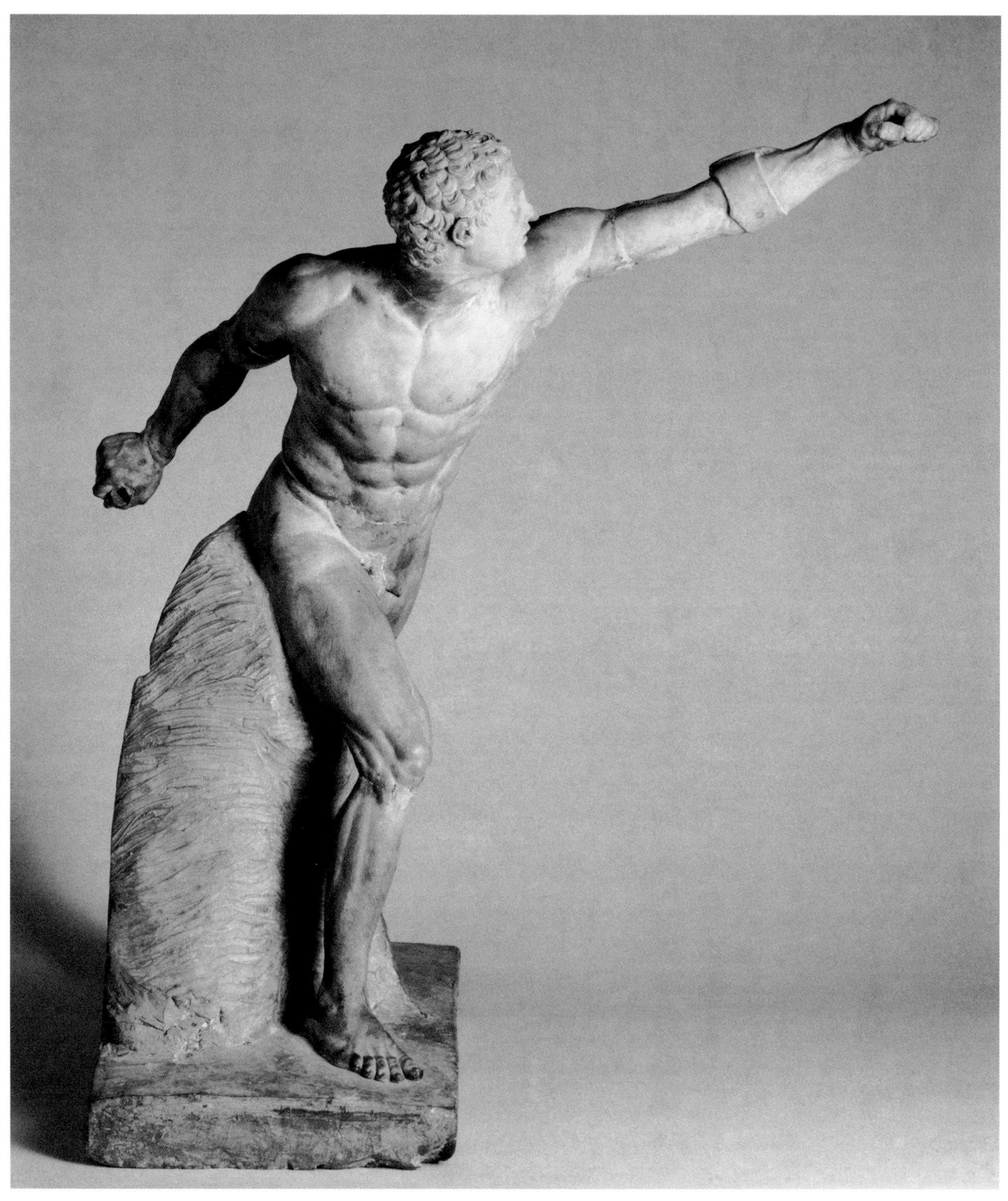

Fig. 3. Nicolas Coustou (French, 1658–1733)
Borghese Gladiator, 1683, terra-cotta, 55.5 × 40 × 45 cm (22 × 15¾ × 17¾ in.)
Paris, Musée du Louvre

this regard. Only nine lectures concerned sculptures, whereas, during the same period, twenty-eight lectures on paintings were delivered.[17] The main reason for this was practical — the works being analyzed were always present in the hall when the lecture was given and it was, of course, easier to transport a picture than a statue. On 2 July 1667, when Gerard van Opstal lectured on the *Laokoon* group (fig. 2), he brought to the hall a little plaster copy (about fifty centimeters tall) of Laokoon alone, without his sons. The Académie's historiographer was then André Félibien, who was asked to produce a record of the first cycle of lectures. Speaking of van Opstal's lecture, Félibien wrote: "If the figure exhibited in the Académie had been like the original, it would have afforded matter for a more extensive and most useful and pleasurable discussion; but since from so small a copy one has only a feeble idea of the beauties of the original, one could see only the most evident things, and a more extensive examination of all of the three figures that comprise this handsome group was adjourned to some later day."[18]

Analyses of classical sculptures, unlike those of paintings, were not conducted in the presence of the original but in front of casts or marble copies.[19] But it should be noted that these copies were not considered either reproductions or counterfeits. They were not seen as lacking that essential quality possessed, in our eyes, by the original alone: uniqueness. They were described and analyzed as if they were originals. Counterfeit classical objects existed — we know that many Renaissance artists took a mischievous pleasure in making them — but a copy of an antique sculpture was not considered a fake. It was an object whose reality and authenticity (what one might call its ontological status) was equal to that of its model, the original. Copies of classical works therefore have a thoroughly paradoxical identity: they are presented as autonomous but not independent works, individualized and yet generic. Copies of any given work exist in their own right, in relation to each other and finally in relation to one and the same original. And this last relationship is not exclusively referential. Each of the copies of the *Farnese Herakles* or the *Medici Venus* somehow *is* the *Farnese Herakles* or the *Medici Venus* itself. Known to be copies, they were nevertheless admired as if they were the originals. No such attitude could have prevailed relative to copies of paintings. The difference is not a historical peculiarity; it depends on a strange property inherent in the work of sculpture, that of presenting itself as a plural object, able to exist in different versions and different materials (plaster, marble, or bronze) while remaining self-identical, that is, while conserving the artistic and aesthetic value attached to the idea of a work. In painting, this value is attributed to the one and only original. Unlike painting, sculpture is not an art of the unique but of the multiple instance: an art of the replica (fig. 3).[20] This difference is strictly artistic in kind. It derives from the material conditions of the sculptor's activity and in large measure determines a sculpture's mode of existence on the level of both history and theory. The fact that a sculpture could be reproduced in some sense indefinitely made it possible for ancient art to be distributed throughout Europe in the form of casts and bronze or marble replicas. And these exercised, as everyone knows, a considerable influence over European art and taste from the seventeenth century on.[21] But this property is also partially responsible for the theoretical ostracism that sculpture has long suffered, one that has continued despite — or perhaps because of — the undeniable historical success it has enjoyed. The reproducibility of sculpture makes it difficult to define. Its identity remains obscure. What object does one refer to when speaking of a sculpture? For several reasons, the inadequacy of the criteria by which one habitually distinguishes original from copy and ranks them hierarchically is particularly glaring in the case of ancient sculpture. First of all, most of the works long considered original have turned out to be copies of lost originals. Second, many of the copies made in the seventeenth century were made from casts and not from originals or what were then believed to be the originals. The casts often came to function as originals, being copied by sculptors whose copies were then copied by students. Thus most of the copies of ancient works made for the *châteaux* of Versailles and Marly were produced in the studios of Versailles or Paris from casts that had been made in Italy by the students of the French academy in Rome and thence sent to the storehouse of royal antiquities. Some of the sculptors making these copies had never been to Rome and had therefore never seen the originals. The coup de grâce for any attempt to distinguish between copies and originals and between different sorts of copies (from the original, from the cast, or from other copies) is the fact that a copy might be considered superior to the original. This occurred with certain copies executed from originals in Rome by Pierre Legros II but also with a number of copies made in France from casts by Antoine Coysevox, such as the *Nymph with Shell* (fig. 4) or the *Crouching Venus,* both very different from the works on which they were modeled. Coysevox's free copies were admired both as copies and as original works. Though everyone knew that he was the maker of his *Crouching Venus,* he signed it in Greek with the name "Phidias."[22]

The fact that copies could be admired as original creations exemplifies the way in which seventeenth-century artists conceived of the practice of imitation. Imitation by a sculptor or painter was not the same as imitation by a copyist, whose only ambition was to produce as exact a replica as possible of the model. The true artist was never what the seventeenth century termed a "servile" copyist. An artist's imitation was not an act of submission but a gesture of appropriation, giving rise to an original work that bore the mark of its author and demonstrated the strength and inventiveness of his talent. Any classical artist, painter or sculptor, could take for his own La Fontaine's boast: "My imitation is no slavery."[23]

But the ability to imitate as an artist (rather than as a copyist) required long

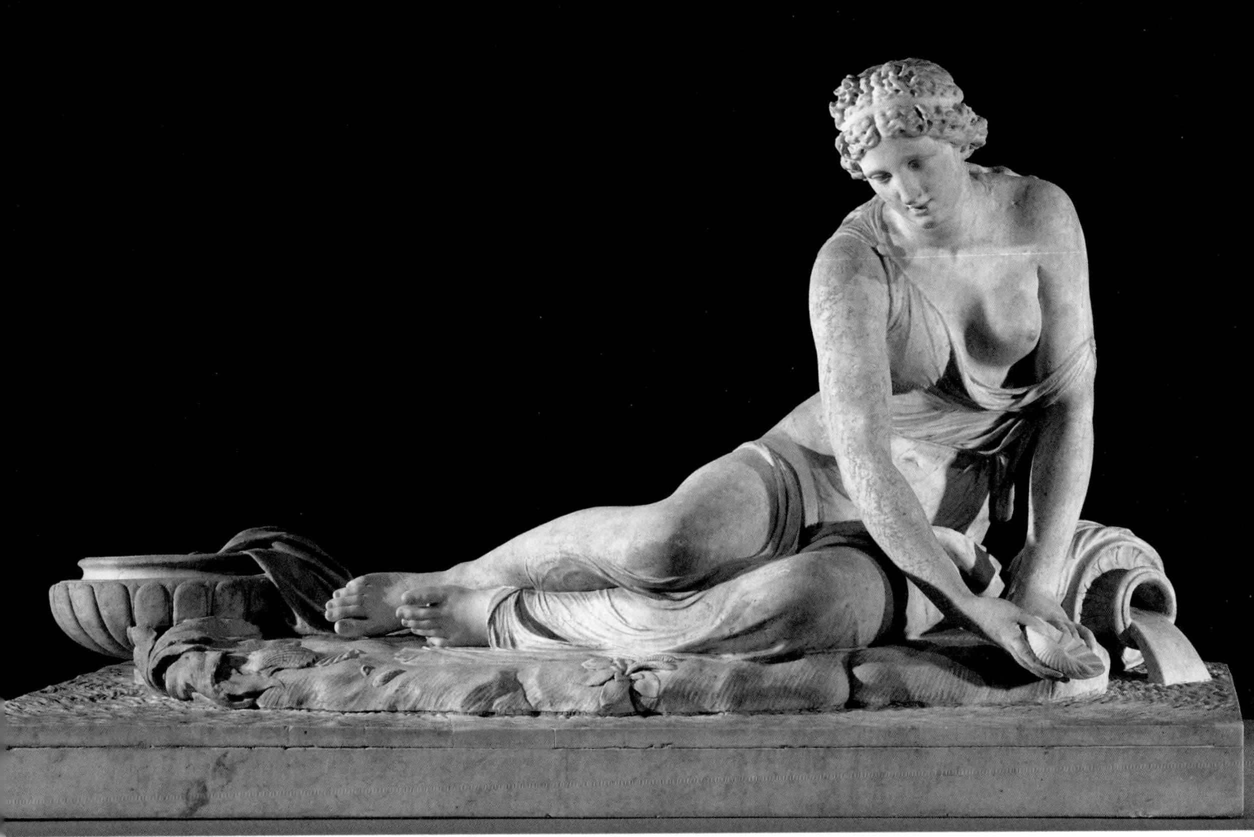

Fig. 4. **Antoine Coysevox (French, 1640–1720)**
Nymph with Shell, 1683–85, marble, 104 × 189 × 82 cm (41 × 74⅜ × 32¼ in.)
Paris, Musée du Louvre

study of the ancient model and long practice at copying it. This explains why the Académie placed so great an emphasis on the pedagogic value of studying the antique, bestowing on it an essential role in the training—theoretical and practical—of its students. And in this regard, too, the list of lectures given at the Académie between 1667 and 1679 is highly significant. We have already seen that, of the lectures devoted to the analysis of a particular work, there were many more on paintings than on sculptures. But for lectures on general topics, the ratio is reversed. Obviously, general questions also arose when Academicians were focusing on an individual work. The plan concerning the ordering of lectures adopted on 26 March 1667 required the Academician in the course of his analysis to raise one or two "questions" relating to a "difficulty" faced by practitioners of the art so that they could show how the problem was resolved in the work under analysis. Each work was therefore considered the more or less successful resolution

ARTISTIC DISPUTES AND PEDAGOGICAL DEBATES

of one or more problems faced by the artist, such as how to represent history, express passions, or distribute light and shade. But there were also lectures dealing directly with these topics.[24] Some dealt with difficulties specific to painting, such as shadow and color, others with problems specific to sculpture, such as the use of perspective in bas-relief. But most dealt with issues common to both arts: line, imitation, expression, proportions, the representation of the human body, and so forth. Now these lectures about particular topics rather than particular works were for the most part based on sculpture. When problems were dealt with that concerned painters and sculptors in equal measure, the art of reference was almost always sculpture. It might prima facie seem somewhat surprising that this preference was accorded in an Académie dominated, as we have seen, by painting. In fact it testifies to the importance of pedagogic goals in the thinking of the Academicians. Unlike the Italian academies of the Renaissance, the Académie was not simply a coterie of artists who gathered to talk about art. It was a school, an institution whose function was to train painters and sculptors. So we cannot fully comprehend the way in which art theory developed in these lectures without bearing in mind the requirement to teach and the demands implied by this condition.

Twelve teachers fulfilled this requirement. The teaching of drawing was fundamental, and students learned to draw primarily in the life class. The model was always male[25] and was often placed on a plinth in a pose imitated from sculpture. A new model was provided every fortnight and once a month a group was posed. In addition to the teachers of drawing and perspective, there were anatomy teachers, who were for the most part surgeons. Anatomy lessons were conducted using anatomical plates and engraved drawings after Vesalius, but students must also have had access to anatomical models. Our picture of anatomy lessons in the Académie of the seventeenth century—as gleaned from the surviving drawings, objects, and sculptures—is probably very incomplete. Michel Anguier's lecture of 3 September 1672, "Une méthode particulière qu'il faut tenir pour faire une figure anatomique de sculpture, et comme il convient de s'en servir pour la facilité du dessein" (A particular method to be observed in making an anatomical figure in sculpture, and how it should be used for easier drawing), raises a number of questions about the use not only of anatomical models but even of corpses.[26] Anguier suggests starting with a natural anatomy (a "natural body, flayed"), casting it in plaster, placing the "shapes cast" in accord with the natural musculature on a "natural skeleton" (already placed in a certain pose), and making a wax cast of the resulting figure. A living model is then placed in the same pose as the skeleton (that is, the position intended for the wax anatomical figure) in order to correct the failings of the cast, since "muscles that are dead and cold cannot act as if they were living and filled with natural warmth."[27] Anguier's method is so complicated and "particular" and so difficult to understand that one may reasonably suppose it was never put into practice. But it does nevertheless indicate that an Academician could envisage bringing corpses and skeletons into the Académie. However, the study of anatomy and thus of the nude was primarily conducted before sculptures such as the *Laokoon*, the *Borghese Gladiator*, or the *Farnese Herakles;* these were the models for students learning to distinguish the parts of the body and the movements of the muscles (fig. 5). Anguier's lecture on the *Laokoon*, given 2 August 1670, offers a fine illustration of the way in which the study of anatomy could become indistinguishable from the study of ancient sculpture. He begins with a question. The three sculptors of the *Laokoon*—Agesander, Polydorus, and Athenodorus—represented their figures in the nude. "Why nude?" he asks.[28] To answer, he first invokes the authority of the ancient philosophers: "The learned philosophers knew that every accurate investigation of the secrets of nature raised one of the veils concealing the Creator's face, since through knowledge of His creatures they attained knowledge of the Creator."

This first argument already contains within it a justification for the procedure adopted by Anguier in his analysis of the *Laokoon*, a group that had, from the moment of its discovery in 1506, been considered a masterpiece of the imitation of nature and a model of expression. His argument also bears the mark of ideas developed in many treatises of anatomy since the early seventeenth century. The thinking of Anguier's "learned philosophers" had been adopted by many learned anatomists of the first half of the century. They too claimed to fulfill the demands of both philosophy and theology in conducting anatomical research and practicing dissection. From the very dawn of the seventeenth century, doctors had attempted to demonstrate that anatomical study of the human body was a means of attaining knowledge both of oneself and of God. Dissection not only complied with the philosophical injunction to "know thyself" but also served to enhance our knowledge of God, since reflections of the presence of the creator could be examined in the body of his creature. Thus, in his *Histoire anatomique* (1610), the great anatomist Du Laurens, professor at the Université de Montpellier and doctor to Henry IV, entitled his fifth chapter "Combien est utile l'anatomie pour la connaissance de soi-même" (How anatomy serves self-knowledge) and his sixth "Combien sert l'anatomie pour connaître Dieu" (How anatomy serves our knowledge of God). But since the anatomists had borrowed their arguments from philosophy, Anguier preferred to invoke the ancient philosophers without intermediary in order to legitimate his own thought. Their authority presented a twofold advantage: it was indisputable and it could be invoked in favor of sculpture. The Greek sculptors had, after all, sat at the knees of those ancient sages who considered man an admirable reflection of the divine.

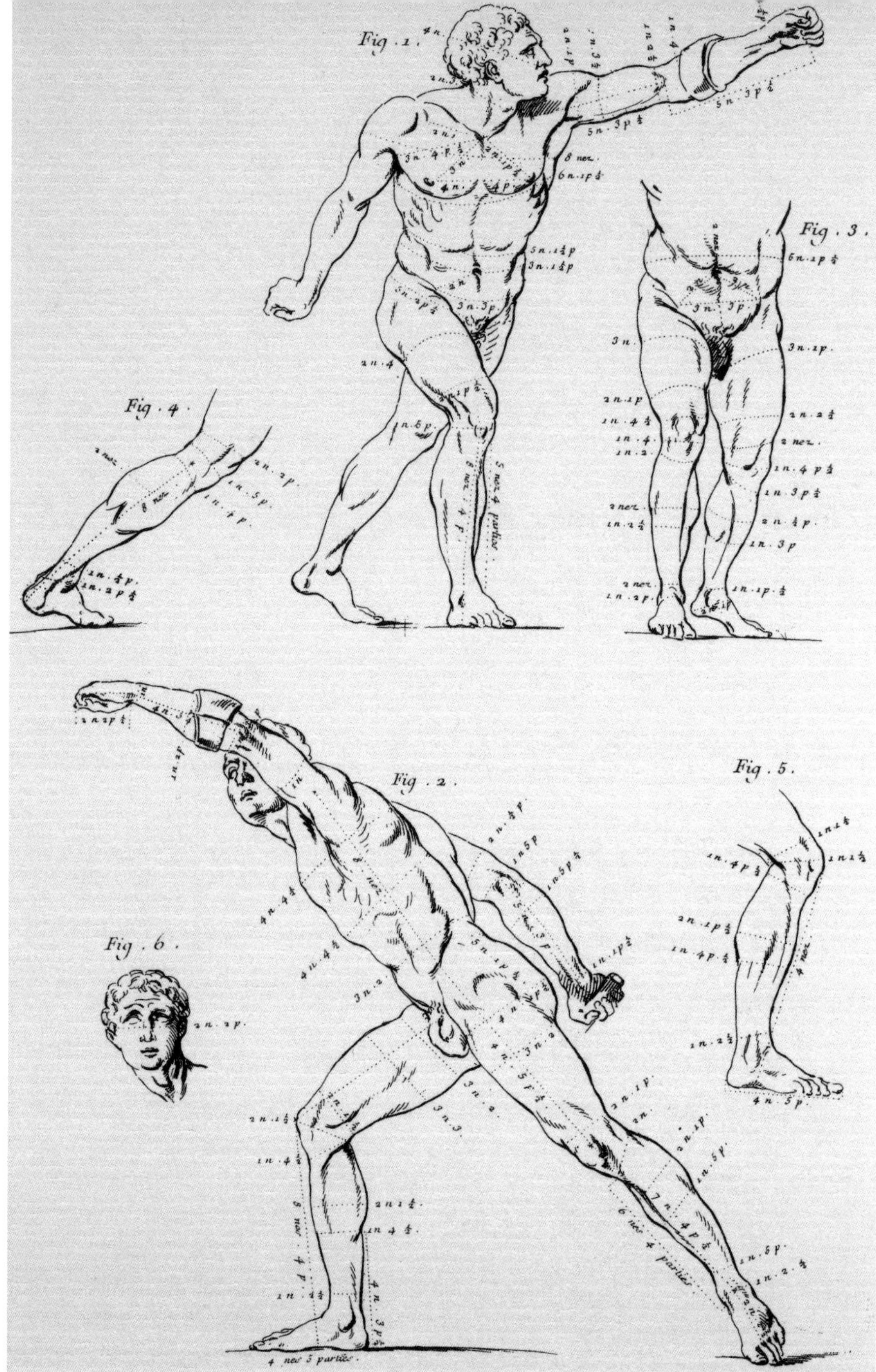

Fig. 5. **Benoit Louis Prevost (French, 1747–ca. 1804), after Jean Baptiste Corneille (French, 1649–95)**
Proportions of the *Borghese Gladiator*
From Denis Diderot, *Encyclopédie; ou, Dictionnaire raisonné des sciences, des arts et des métiers*
(Stuttgart-Bad Cannstatt: Friedrich Frommann, 1966), vol. 24, pl. 37
Los Angeles, Getty Research Institute

In the same way, the able Greek sculptors brought up in this learned school followed the path of beauty in stripping their figures of the veil of clothing and anything else that might cover the most beautiful and accomplished of all creatures. The Greeks called man a microcosm filled with divinity; the sages of Egypt called him an adorable and admirable animal. Pythagoras called him the measure of all things, Plato the marvel of marvels, and Zoroaster the statue and masterpiece in which nature's boldest effort appears. All these beautiful qualities impelled them to make nude figures not only of immortals but of mortals too.[29]

But this first response to the question "Why nude?" is essentially rhetorical. The notion of nudity as a means for the artist to manifest the greatness of the creator by revealing the admirable beauty and perfection of his creature does not long detain Anguier. The conventional references to Egyptian wisdom or the divine Plato are there only to afford a theological and metaphysical sanction for the mechanistic explanation of the emotions given a few lines later. In the real answer to the question "Why nude?" the body is no longer considered an object of wonder but an object of knowledge. The nudity is justified from a purely scientific point of view, on no other ground than its contribution to our knowledge of the mechanisms of the human body:

Such nudity is revealing of temperament: we see in the faces and throughout the body sadness, fear, anger, or joy; audacity, shame, and majesty likewise appear, shame in the cheeks and majesty in the chin, while pride makes itself known in the eyebrows. These passions come from the heart but manifest themselves in all of these parts. That is why the learned Greeks normally made their figures without clothing, so that by the agitation and movement of the muscles and veins the emotions and the passions of the soul could be discovered.[30]

In the first part of his analysis Anguier revisited the commonplaces and traditional references used to justify the rise of medical research, but this second part is clearly of Cartesian inspiration. And he opens himself to the accusation of incoherence in thus juxtaposing two somewhat contradictory points of view. The thesis of the mechanical body that underpins his Cartesian analysis was, after all, developed precisely in order to confound the theological argument so often made in early medical thought. Rigorous logic is clearly not Anguier's forte. But he is not arguing as a philosopher or scholar; he speaks as a sculptor, that is, an artist. He aspires to effectiveness rather than coherence and makes use of anything that can serve his art. His methodology is therefore very inclusive, and he is happy to place side by side a number of often contradictory explanatory models. He does this in his lecture of 9 November 1769 on the *Farnese Herakles,* which combines modern anatomical science with the very ancient theory of the humors and temperaments. The result is a kind of composite thinking, characteristic of a theoretical process whose goals are invariably practical, that is, artistic.[31] Indeed, his explanation of the *Laokoon* probably owes more to Le Brun than to Descartes. It follows fairly closely the analysis made by Le Brun in 1668 in his lectures on expression, which were in large part inspired by Descartes's *Traité des passions.* Le Brun borrowed extensively from the *Traité:* the distinction between action and passion, the division of passions into simple and composite, the order and number of the simple passions (six, as in Descartes: wonder, love, hate, desire, joy, and sadness), the role of the pineal gland, the functioning of the animal spirits, and so on.[32] Le Brun's explicit references to Descartes and the highly analytical style of his lectures cannot, however, conceal the fact that his doctrine too is somewhat composite. It bears the mark of various influences, notably that of *Les caractères des passions* by Marin Cureau de la Chambre, doctor to Chancellor Pierre Séguier. But Le Brun's primary inspiration is not to be found in treatises philosophical or medical but in the paintings of Poussin. Le Brun has in common with Anguier that he thinks as an artist; he constantly has his own and other artists' works in mind, using them to illustrate and justify his reflections. His references are artistic before they are textual and can only be comprehended and explained by the works that exemplify them. Thus, when Le Brun first attempted a sustained analysis of expression founded on the study of muscles, his subject was Poussin's *Israelites Gathering Manna in the Desert* and notably the aged man on the left of the painting, who sees a woman giving suck to her mother (pl. 1):

> He showed that this man does indeed represent a person in a state of astonishment and startled wonder; we see that his arms are drawn back and pressed against his side because, when one is greatly surprised, all the limbs generally draw back one against another, especially when the object that surprises us impresses on our mind only an image that makes us wonder at what is happening, while the action causes no fear or dread that might trouble our senses and give them reason to seek help and defend themselves against the thing that threatens them.... This is not the case with the other parts of his body. The spirits abandon them and therefore they remain still: his mouth is closed, as if he were afraid that some part of his thoughts might escape and because he cannot find words to express the beauty of the action. And, since this impedes the passage of breath, the stomach-parts are raised higher than usual, as appears from certain uncovered muscles.[33]

Le Brun may be his inspiration, but Anguier goes much further in his anatomical description of the figures of the *Laokoon.* Borrowing his terminology from François Tortebat's treatise on anatomy, Anguier as it were dissects every part of the body, including the veins and nerves, specifying the bones and muscles as he goes:

> We can see that he is crying out with all his might thanks to the contraction of the respiratory muscles and his open mouth, swollen throat, raised chest, inward-drawn epigastrium, the navel tucked in and the hips retracted....So it is true that all these muscles tremble and shiver. The groin down to the injured part is the most excited and tremulous and is therefore the most difficult to imitate because it is as if one saw it being moved by the many touches, which are so natural and so extraordinary that it is truly incomparable. The thigh on the same side stretches out and away from the injured part....Now, to recognize this trembling and palpitation of the muscles, we need to go into the sources of dread, which proceed from the brain. The brain is the foster-father and substance of the nerves, from which they take their birth and their spirits. For nerves alone give spirit and feeling to the muscles: they animate the muscles, not only through their larger parts but also through their little shoots, which extend through all the membranes and tunics of the muscles, and even through the flesh of the muscles of all parts of the body. This admirable figure clearly shows that the palpitation of the muscles is distinct from the trembling of fever, in which muscles raised by the nerves immediately relapse under their own weight. On the contrary, the greatest strength of the nerves is below the muscles, which violently pull on the membranes with a great judder at each redoubling of the pain. This is what is indicated by all the touches of the muscles and all the tenderness expressive of pain.[34]

Like Le Brun's, Anguier's analysis faithfully respects Descartes's definition of the human body in terms of figure and movement—his description of the bones pertains to the study of figure, and his description of the muscles to the study of movement.[35] For Anguier, the study of muscles is, in a sense, even more important than that of bones, since movement is what distinguishes a live from a dead body. Movement, he tells us, comes from the brain and is propagated through the nerves by the action of what he, following Descartes, calls the "animal spirits" (*esprits animaux*). Hence the need to know the cause of the stimulus that produces tension or relaxation in the muscles. Now, not all movements of the human body are explained by physical, that is, mechanical causes. As Descartes showed, they can also be caused by the will, by thoughts, and by certain "imaginations" or "perceptions" formed in the soul and which the philosopher for this reason calls the passions of the soul. Unlike the purely mechanical body of the animal, the human body can be moved by the action of the soul. The main difficulty for the artist is therefore to imitate what Anguier calls the "very nature" of the human body, the fact that it is expressive rather than simply mechanical. Pain must bend the statue's leg, terror open its mouth, and despair impel the raising

    ARTISTIC DISPUTES AND PEDAGOGICAL DEBATES

of its arm. This is the impression that the sculptor should seek. The marble figure must seem literally animated from within, like the *Laokoon.* In short, Anguier admires ancient sculptures so intensely because, in his view, they imitate the natural expression of the passions incomparably well: "They do not merely represent the external figure of the body but allow one in the marble to see the passions of the soul as it were burst forth and move the intestines and the guts."[36]

Antique sculptors thus imitated nature so perfectly—were able to give it such a "naïve" and "natural" representation (in seventeenth-century terms)—that it was impossible to see their figures as artificial ones. Pushing the logic of his argument to its extreme in his lecture "L'union de l'art avec la nature," Anguier quite simply says that these figures "can be termed natural."[37]

The Art and Manner of the Moderns

What do we have by Apelles today? Nothing.
— Denis Diderot[38]

Among the questions raised by Anguier's lecture on the *Laokoon,* one was much discussed in the Académie. It concerned the priority to be observed when teaching draftsmanship. Students learned to draw from the antique and from life and Anguier's arguments tend to suggest that imitation of ancient works should precede imitation of the model. But should they? The question had been debated a few years earlier during Gian Lorenzo Bernini's brief sojourn in France. When visiting the Académie, Bernini had repeatedly insisted that students should be made to draw from the antique and not from life so that they might acquire the "grand manner"; French painters too often displayed a weak and mean-spirited style, he said, which this reform might prevent. Paul Fréart de Chantelou's *Journal de voyage du Cavalier Bernin en France* offers a record of Bernini's sentiments on the first occasion when he spoke out on this subject, on 5 September 1665:

> Standing in the middle of the hall, surrounded by all the Academicians, he said that in his opinion the Académie should have casts of all the beautiful ancient statues, bas-reliefs, and busts for the instruction of young people and that they should be made to draw after the ancient manner, so that their notion of beauty should first be formed in this way; that this was of use to them throughout their lives; that it was ruination to set them from the outset to draw from nature, which was almost always weak and mean; if their imagination was filled with nothing else, they would be able to produce nothing beautiful and great but what could be found in nature.[39]

He returned to the subject a week later, on 13 September, this time explicitly criticizing the manner of French painters.

> He again said that the weakness of French painters was that they had a small-scale, tedious, petty manner; that to correct this, one must study the antique, above all the *Belvedere Torso,* and the Lombard painters.... He said again that, in the Académie, one should study antiquity, drawing on a large scale to acquire a grander manner, since the large always contained more detail than the small and the medium.... [One should] always draw with great exactitude, that is, finish drawings in every detail, because by doing so one acquired the habit and knack of making finished and complete drawings.[40]

Two years later, on 2 July 1667, van Opstal's lecture on the *Laokoon* reignited the debate begun by Bernini's remarks. According to Félibien, who summarized the lectures of 1667 for publication, the views expressed by the Academicians after the lecture were consonant with Bernini's:

> Since there is nothing in this statue that is not shaped with admirable art, everyone agreed that it should be the true study of painters and sculptors. But they should not simply have it before their eyes as a model for drawing.... These powerful expressions cannot be learned merely by drawing from life; one cannot place the model in a state in which the passions are active in him, and it is anyway difficult to copy the passions even from a person on whom they are really acting, because the passions of the soul change so quickly. It is therefore very important for workers [artists] to study the causes of these passions and, in order to see how their effects can be represented with dignity, it is, we may say, to these beautiful pieces from antiquity that they should have recourse, since one sees in them expressions that would be difficult to draw from nature.... There was no one present who did not agree that on this model one can learn to correct the defects normally found in the natural, for in this piece everything appears in a state of perfection and such as it seems that nature would make all its works, if there were no obstacles to prevent it imparting a perfect form to them.[41]

Reading Bernini's criticism of the French manner and Félibien's account of the discussion, one might easily infer that drawing was being taught exclusively from life at the Académie. How else can we explain the Academicians' insistence that students should draw from the antique in order to correct the defects of nature? But what is at stake in the debate is not whether one should *also* draw from ancient works — this was unanimously accepted — but whether one should *first* draw from antiquity, that is, whether Bernini's advice should be followed. The question concerned the painters first and foremost, since Bernini had criticized the French style of painting. This naturally elicited considerable interest in the Académie since the painters enjoyed, as we have seen, a dominant position in that institution. During the discussion that followed van Opstal's lecture, the arguments in favor of antiquity primarily concerned the expression of passions. The Academicians recognized that it was very difficult, if not indeed impossible, to study these in a natural model insofar as the model was not really feeling them but miming the signs of emotion; his expressions never had the power of the real thing because they were not the effect of a passion but merely an imitation of its effects. On the other hand, the expressions of people subject to strong emotions such as fear or anger and expressing them by natural signs (as distinct from the artificial signs of the model) were too instantaneous and fleeting; they succeeded one another too quickly for the artist, especially the novice, to record them. It would seem, then, that the Academicians agreed with Bernini in thinking that one should study from the antique but for slightly different reasons. Bernini favored imitating ancient works for the sake of style, and more particularly the grand manner, whereas the Academicians mainly emphasized the requirement to imitate nature and truth. The value that they attributed to the imitation of the antique rested on a notion of imitation notably different from that of either Bernini or the Italians in general. As we saw in Anguier's lectures, that value was essentially based on the idea that art is a form of knowledge and that arts such as painting and sculpture, which represent the appearance of things, impart knowledge about the nature of the things that they represent. This means that the artist cannot be content to imitate nature according to the idea of beauty but must also take truth into account; indeed, the idea of beauty must itself be imitated from nature and truth. Boileau's famous line—"Only truth is beautiful. Only the true can be loved"[42]—perfectly expresses the reluctance in French theory of imitation to dissociate beauty from truth. So it was not primarily for stylistic reasons—for the purpose of acquiring the grand manner—that the Academicians thought it necessary to imitate ancient pieces; it was in order to understand how to imitate nature in all its truth, that is, in its true beauty; for such was the nature that the ancient sculptors had so perfectly imitated. In an argument of perfect circularity, the Academicians derived the preeminence of antiquity from a definition of art as the imitation of nature and constructed their idea of nature on the basis of ancient art. This circularity is particularly evident in Le Brun's response to Champaigne, who had dared to criticize Poussin's painting *Rebecca at the Well,* saying that Poussin had copied excessively from the antique:

> But while M. de Champaigne was saying these things, M. Le Brun interrupted him and, speaking in favor of M. Poussin, said that knowledgeable men working toward the same discoveries and having a single goal could come to the same conclusion and resemble one another without either of them deserving the title of imitators or plagiarists. And there-

fore one must distinguish between competitors and copyists.... M. Poussin, having studied and discovered the true effects of nature by emulating the able artists of antiquity, had made a good choice of them and put them to good use; he could not fail to agree with their ideas. For if these distinctions were not made, one would do the great artists of antiquity the injustice of accusing them of copying one another, since, having taken nature and the truth for models, they could do no other than observe the same proportions and the same principles in their figures. In fact, the Greeks had great advantages over us. Their country normally produced better-built persons than our own, thus supplying them with more beautiful models; they wore garments that neither at all hindered the body nor spoiled the form of its apparent parts; even these garments only half-covered their bodies, which made it easier for their painters and sculptors to imitate the beauties of the body. To make things easier again, they constantly had before their eyes young slaves who were almost nude, not to mention their robust and well-built athletes, the frequent spectacle of whom gave these excellent artists ample matter for study and practice.[43]

Criticizing Poussin for copying from antiquity is, in Le Brun's view, as unjust as accusing ancient sculptors of copying one another on the grounds that their figures obeyed the same rules and respected the same proportions. If any resemblances were observable in these works, they derived from the model taken by all ancient sculptors: nature and truth. Their works resembled one another not because of mutual imitation but because they all imitated the same thing. And this was the reason why Poussin's figures too resembled ancient figures. Like the ancient sculptors, Poussin sought to imitate nature and truth and understood that, to this end, he had to imitate ancient sculpture and take it as his model. Greek artists, Le Brun adds, enjoyed the huge advantage of having more beautiful models available to them in greater number and of living surrounded by half-nude slaves. In this way they could imitate nature and truth directly on natural models, imitate nature as it were after nature, by studying the magnificent bodies that they constantly had before them. It is a common fallacy to suppose that Winckelmann was the first scholar to explain the perfection of ancient sculpture by the greater beauty of Greek bodies. This idea is already present in Le Brun. But it pertains in his work to an analysis notably different from the one developed by Winckelmann in the eighteenth century. The views about antiquity developed at the Académie belong, as we have seen, to a tradition of reflection about the teaching of art. In this tradition, the intertwining of pedagogic and theoretical objectives is all but inextricable. When debating whether imitation should first be taught from nature or from the antique, they were led to reflect on other issues, such as the status of mimesis and the definition of what one might call the French "manner"—that very manner that Bernini had described as weak and mean.

In the first semester of 1670, the Académie devoted a number of lectures to problems directly related to the teaching of painting. This series on pedagogy began on 4 January 1670 with a lecture (unfortunately lost) by Le Brun entitled "La manière de dessiner" (The way to draw). It continued with lectures by Noël Coypel (1 February 1670, "Le discernement à faire du génie des étudiants" [Discerning the aptitudes of students]), Jean-Baptiste de Champaigne (1 March 1670, on Poussin's *The Plague of Ashdod*), Boullogne (12 April 1670, on Titian's *Madonna and Child with Saint Catherine*), and Sébastien Bourdon (5 July 1670, "Les proportions de la figure humaine d'après l'antique" [The proportions of the human figure according to antiquity]). The discussions to which these lectures gave rise can be reconstituted thanks to Testelin, who summarized them in his *Sentiments des plus habiles peintres du temps* (Views of the ablest painters of our time).[44] By Testelin's account, the Academicians were rather divided on the subject, which puts him at odds with Félibien's version (written in 1667) of the debate that followed van Opstal's lecture on the *Laokoon.* For the most part, the Academicians agreed on the need to begin by imitation from the antique. But a certain number of them simultaneously defended the view that had earned Bernini's damning words in the first place; they continued to believe that "the principal study of drawing should be from life."[45] Still, according to Testelin, their opposition to the principles of teaching so trenchantly and dogmatically asseverated by Bernini came to a head during a debate about the diversity of manners adopted by students in imitating the model. Some, it was said, "imitated the natural in the simplicity of its form, while others embellished it by strengthening the outline, a procedure called 'forcing [*charger*] the outline' for the sake of 'grand taste.'"[46] Which "manner" should the students adopt? The Academicians could not agree. Those whom Testelin calls the "naturalists," among whom were Le Brun and Champaigne, stood out against the partisans of the "grand manner," notably Boullogne and Bourdon, who returned to Bernini's arguments:

> Those who opined in favor of these ornamental emphases [*charges d'agrément*] put forward as evidence the beauty of ancient figures, the great drawings of Michelangelo and the Carracci brothers and the other great painters of antiquity, arguing that one must from the outset fill one's mind with grand ideas in order to conform to these beautiful exemplars and make a habit of these grand and beautiful manners. They said that confining oneself to imitating weak and sickly nature, such as one commonly finds them doing, is more likely to lead students astray and cause them to adopt a small and weak manner. The opposite view, called "naturalist" because its holders think that the natural should always be exactly imitated in every respect, would restrict the draftsman to imitating objects simply and precisely as they are. Their reasons in regard to the students were to train them to a habit of accuracy and precision and, for the most advanced, to a naïve and fitting expression of all kinds of subjects.[47]

This must have been a long and lively discussion. The conclusion spared the pride of both parties by deciding in favor of neither: "It was agreed that the study of beautiful ancient figures was very necessary at the outset and even more advantageous than the study of nature. But it was affirmed that in either case one must labor to imitate the object exactly, if one was to gain from it the desired benefit, and that one should accustom both eye and hand to accuracy and precision, this being the foundation of the practice of painting."[48]

The student must therefore begin by drawing after the antique but must strive to give his imitation the accuracy and precision of a drawing from life. The pedagogic dispute thus concludes with a sort of compromise that seems to leave everyone in agreement: better start with the antique without, however, neglecting life study, for if the artist must imitate nature he must also imitate the natural.

Whereas the painters for the most part had varying shades of opinion — like Le Brun, who was a naturalist in tendency but defended the imitation of the antique, as we have seen him do in relation to Poussin's *Rebecca at the Well* — the opinion of a sculptor such as Anguier was much more univocal. One should, he believed, prefer the imitation of nature — and therefore of the antique — to imitation of the natural. His lecture of 9 July 1673 on bas-relief is exemplary in this regard. For the prize competition, the Académie's students had been requested to sculpt a bas-relief representing the passage of the Rhine by King Louis XIV and his army. Anguier criticized them for presenting this story "according to the recession [*dégradation*] and ordinary rule of perspective,"[49] that is, by diminishing the figures in proportion to their distance from the picture plane: "Following the order imposed by ordinary recession if a broad stretch of landscape is to remain visible, the main figures posed in the foreground must be small and very detached from the background, while those that are distant diminish in proportion and those that are beyond the river are so small and distant that they cannot be given the forms of men."[50]

In their attempt to create effects reliant on perspective, the students had done no more than multiply the number of ineffectual figures, confuse the scene that they represented, and make the story difficult to understand. Arranging figures according to the laws of perspective was not suitable, Anguier said, for bas-relief. The failure of ancient sculptors to observe those laws in bas-reliefs should not be attributed to ignorance. They were quite right to represent background figures as "strongly" and sometimes more strongly than those in the foreground:

This order in bas-relief, though natural, is quite unrelated to the bas-reliefs of the ancient sculptors, whose figures always serve a purpose and are never so far off that they are lost in the distance. They quite rightly kept their figures, foreground and background, as big as they could, so that they were fully visible and served to acquaint the spectator with the entire subject of the story using a small number of figures at the right distance to be seen.[51]

One must therefore, says Anguier, encourage the students to concentrate exclusively on the study of ancient bas-reliefs, in which "the order of nature is observed with exactitude," and discourage them from imitating the necessarily defective "natural order" found in works "made in the modern style" (figs. 6, 7). According to Anguier, then, the "modern style" consisted of perspective effects and imitation of the natural and this, in turn, meant doing as the painters do. Through this distinction between imitation of nature (and therefore of the antique) and imitation of the natural (and therefore of painting), Anguier was in fact raising a fundamental question and one from which important developments arose: the question of the specificity of the arts. He was trying to define a mode of imitation proper to sculpture and therefore different from that used in painting. And it is not surprising that this question arose in relation to bas-relief. How could depth be represented in what Regnaudin, giving a further lecture on bas-reliefs one month after Anguier's, described as "a flat work of limited projection"?[52] The sculptor of bas-relief faces a difficulty well known to the painters, which they had learned to solve through the use of perspective. They knew how to represent depth in the medium of "flat painting" (as the seventeenth century continued to term the art). Should sculptors be rebuked for attempting such perspectival effects in bas-relief? On this point, Regnaudin differed from Anguier. For him, the introduction of perspective in bas-relief not only illustrated the superiority of the moderns over the ancients; it illustrated the superiority of modern bas-relief over other forms of sculpture and even over painting itself: "Bas-relief combines painting and sculpture, taking what is most beautiful from either art. It combines the sculptor's geometrical drawing [displayed] in the figures in the foreground with the perspective drawing of the painter in the background figures."[53]

Regnaudin's argument was anathema to Anguier, who saw in this borrowing from painting a loss of identity for sculpture. It marked a heteronomy that endangered the greatness of the sculptural art, which was exemplified in the many illustrious examples that had come down from antiquity. The beauty of a bas-relief should derive from the resources of statuary and not borrow from the practices of other arts. Anguier does not share Regnaudin's "modern" point of view but his analysis nevertheless depends on an argument that can be considered modern, that is, the argument from specificity. For the next two centuries, the enemies of the ancient model appealed to this argument in order to defend a point of view diametrically opposed to Anguier's. Consequently there is something paradoxical about Anguier's defense of the ancient model against the "modern" method, since it is conducted in the name of a demand characteristic of modern thought.

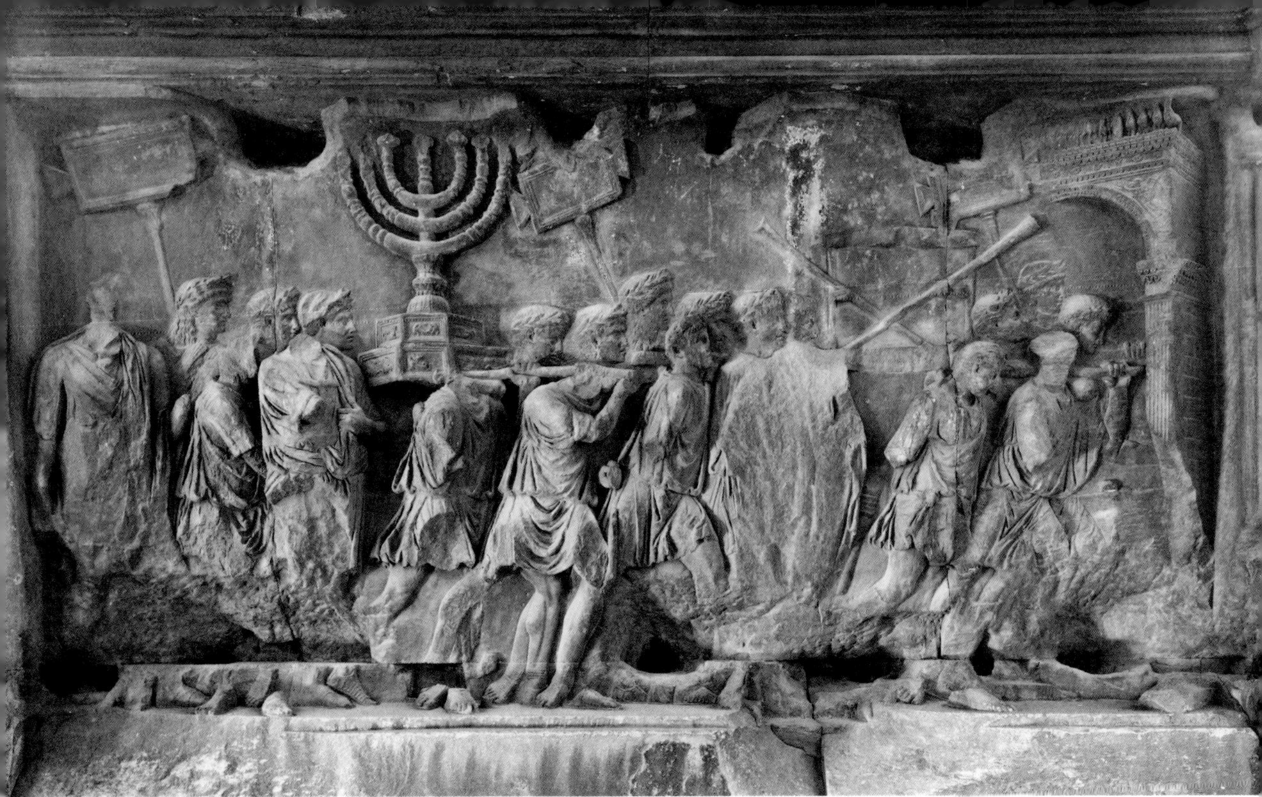

Fig. 6. *The Victorious Army of Titus with the Spoils from Jerusalem*
Ca. A.D. 90, marble, 204 × 380 cm (80¼ × 149½ in.)
Rome, Arch of Titus

And it was also in the name of specificity that de Piles opposed the theories presented in the Académie by partisans of line such as Anguier. But, unlike the other artists and art theorists, who expressed the requirement for specificity in diffuse and often confused fashion, de Piles appealed to it explicitly as the basis of his theoretical and critical enterprise. From his very first publications and throughout his *querelle* with the Poussinists he constantly invoked this argument, which returns under various guises in each of his works. His defense of color is thus nothing more or less than a defense and celebration of painting itself in all its difference, in the one respect that distinguished it from all other arts and from sculpture in particular. And it was again to defend the specificity of painting that he decided, late in his life, to return to the problem of teaching. The debate initiated by Bernini must by then have seemed a thing of the past. But the terms in which de Piles posed the problem were new. Dismissing the two contending theses already in the field, the naturalist and the antinaturalist, he attacked a component of academic training so fundamental that its status had always seemed unassailable: drawing.

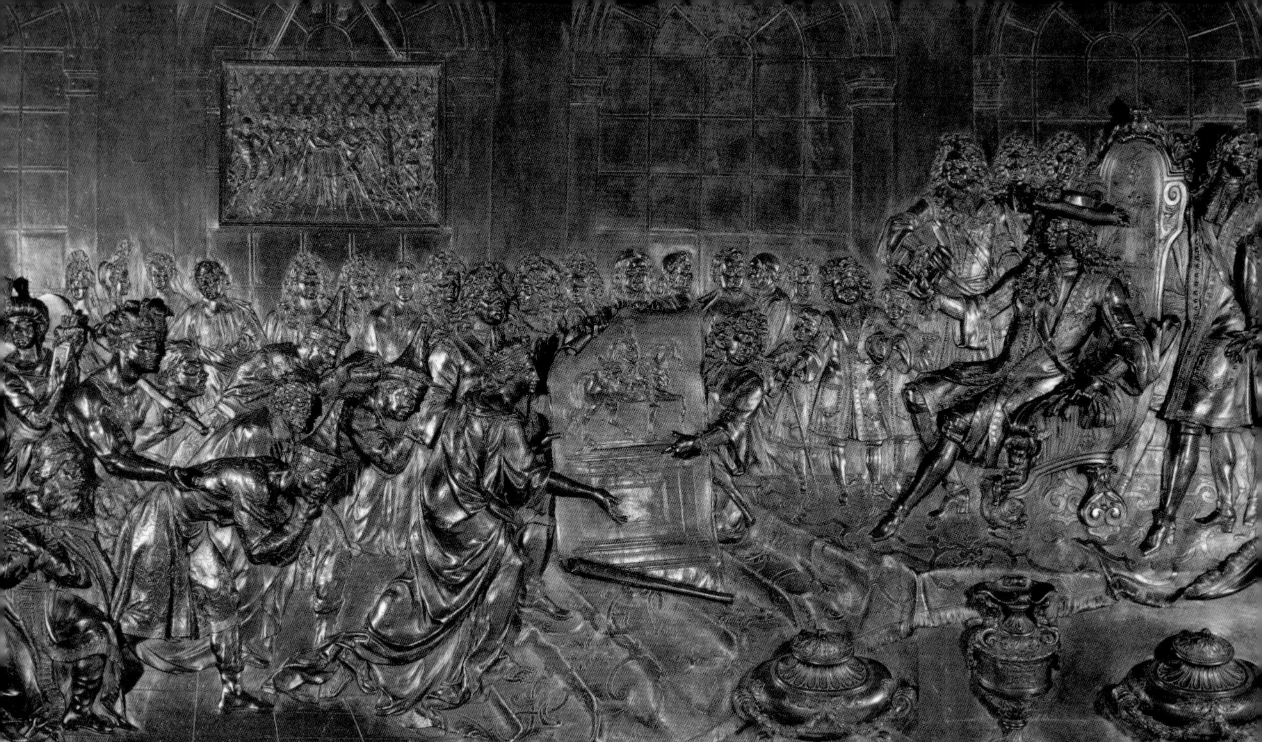

These were the years of glory for de Piles. His election to the Académie in 1699 confirmed the triumph of the ideas for which he had campaigned over several decades. Not only were they no longer shocking, they had become the Académie's prevailing orthodoxy. By the turn of the century, the colorist doctrine had effectively been adopted by the Académie, and de Piles could now intervene directly and as an insider in discussions about the function of the institution in general and about pedagogical questions in particular. On 4 September 1706, he gave a lecture, "L'ordre qu'on doit tenir dans l'étude de la peinture" (The order to be observed in the study of painting), proposing a thoroughgoing reform of the way in which painting was taught.[54] It involved the application of ideas that he had tirelessly defended for almost fifty years. His goal was to define how painting could be taught in accord with its nature, that is, to prescribe the conditions enabling a student to progress in the knowledge and practice of what was specific to his art. What form of teaching would train a painter to become a true painter? In the seventeenth century, imitation was considered the foundation on which any process of training must necessarily repose. The question of pedagogy could therefore be reduced to a more general and theoretical question: what mode of imitation was specific to painting? To that extent, de Piles's lecture is analogous to Anguier's, which raised precisely the same question in relation to sculpture. It is, in some measure, painting's reply to sculpture: a converse symmetrical response. Whereas Anguier refused to make the art of sculpture depend on that of painting, de Piles sought to define pictorial imitation without reference to sculpture. Whereas Anguier condemned sculptors whose works were made "in the modern way," that is, like paintings, de Piles criticized painters who worked "in stone," that is, "in the ancient manner," like sculptors.

De Piles's program comprised two parts. The first, which constituted a sort of general propaedeutic, was common to painter and sculptor. The second concerned only painters. The first part of the training rested entirely on the teaching of drawing. The student first learned to draw after ancient sculptures. Then came the study of geometry, anatomy (the true foundation of drawing, in de Piles's view), and proportions. Study of anatomy and proportions was conducted with the use of classical statuary. For proportions, de Piles also advised imitating Raphael, whose painting was, he said, very close to the antique—not necessarily a compliment coming from de Piles. When these stages had been completed, study of the model could begin:

> Let us suppose that a student has completed the studies of which I have just spoken, putting into them the time and concentration that they demand. They should be considered as steps that raise the mind to knowledge of the natural, such as it is and such as it ought to be.... This then is the place where study of the model should be placed, to which should be added that of contrast and balance, which together constitute that of posture.[55]

But since imitation of the model required the student to be able to give his figure roundness and relief and therefore to learn to arrange light and shade, this was also the moment at which the student must acquire the "understanding of light and shade called chiaroscuro."[56] By placing the study of chiaroscuro at this point, de Piles opened a breach in the first part of the student's training through which the flood tide of painting could enter, gradually occupying the entire terrain. For chiaroscuro was, in his eyes, one of the two elements that distinguished painting from sculpture, the other being color. Moreover, the definition of chiaroscuro given here by de Piles applies only to the art of painting, the study of which has not yet begun: "This understanding demands particular attention, and one must be the more strongly habituated to it because chiaroscuro is one of the main foundations of painting, because its effect attracts the viewer, because it underpins the composition of the picture, and because without it, all the care taken over particular objects would be a waste of effort."[57]

But no sooner has de Piles opened this breach than he hastens to close it. His intention was not, at this stage, to set painting apart from sculpture but to ensure an equitable reciprocity between the two arts. Future painters had always studied sculpture; now it was the turn of the future sculptor to study one of the essential components of the art of painting. And since, in this first part, sculpture and painting were to share what we now call a core curriculum, de Piles at this juncture dealt with the teaching of chiaroscuro independently of color. The acquisition of this "understanding of light and shade" was therefore to be conducted primarily through engravings and prints, that is, through the only values common to the painter and sculptor: black and white. The student was to learn to distribute light and shade with the pencil only and not yet with the brush.

This ends the first part of the painter's training, a part common to both painter and sculptor. The sculptor had learned to imitate outlines on a flat surface by drawing like a painter and the painter to imitate the relief of bodies in space, molding them like a sculptor: "Till now painting and sculpture have gone hand in hand because I suppose that the sculptor has trained himself to draw on paper just as I here desire that the painter, for his own benefit, should learn to mold. Now they must go their own ways if each is successfully to reach his goal, that of imitating nature by different means."[58]

A passage from the *Cours de peinture,* in which de Piles returns to this idea, contains a very illuminating remark about this difference of means, and more particularly the reasons behind it: "The goal of the painter and sculptor alike is indeed imitation but they reach it by different paths: the sculptor through solid matter and imitating the real quantity of objects, and the painter by imitating with colors the apparent quantity and quality of everything visible, so that he is obliged not only to please the eye but to deceive it with everything that he represents."[59]

This contrast between the "real quantity" imitated by the sculptor and the "apparent quantity and quality" imitated by the painter contains within it the seed of the distinction that de Piles proposed establishing between the two parts of the training. The second part, reserved for the painters, would teach how sight could be deceived by imitations of the appearance of objects. This is why it no longer involved the practice of drawing, which teaches one to imitate the real structure of objects, but the science of color, which relates exclusively to appearances, that is, to the domain of perceptible qualities. "The order that I have suggested till now relates only to the study of drawing, and what remains for me to say is principally concerned with color."[60]

And the method recommended by de Piles for learning the science of color is quite simply to copy the paintings of the great colorists: "The first attention that is required for a young student's [use of] color is simply to begin by copying whatever he thinks best colored, freshest, and most freely painted among the works of the great masters, among whom Titian, Rubens, and van Dyck occupy the first rank."[61]

Having learned to draw by copying sculpture, the student learns to paint by imitating painting. And he moves from imitating painting to imitating nature:

> Since color is admirable only insofar as it perfectly imitates nature, the young student, having acquired some familiarity with the practice of able persons, must also copy nature itself, examining it and comparing it with the works of the great masters that he has copied for himself. This practice will accustom his taste to the notion of truth and his eyes to perceiving it without impediment.[62]

Beneath the apparent continuity of this progression from drawing to color and from sculpture to painting is concealed a schism between the two parts of the training, a discontinuity that de Piles had planned from the outset. The conditions for it were carefully prepared in the first part of his program, in his reflections about chiaroscuro. It will be remembered that the study of chiaroscuro began with the imitation of the living model, that is, at the precise moment when the student began to draw from nature and no longer exclusively from the antique, and that it consisted of copying drawings and engravings by the great masters of painting. Drawing from the model thus coincided with a change of model in the other sense—a change of paradigm. When the student went on to study the live model, he began to turn away from sculpture and toward the work of painters.

The polysemy of the terms *nature* and *natural* in the language of the seventeenth century and the fact that they are often used without distinction by art theorists can cause confusion and cloud the interpretation of their works. We have already remarked on this, notably in relation to the discussion between Le Brun and de Champaigne concerning Poussin's *Rebecca at the Well*. The definition of painting as the imitation of nature was widely accepted in the Académie, and the Academicians all identified nature with truth. But they did not all ascribe the same sense to the word *nature*. It functioned as an authoritative tribunal but it could mean empirical reality or the essence of things, an ens rationis or an object of observation, nature real or ideal. As we have seen, it could be used with reference to "natural" or in opposition to it. And *natural* too has many different usages that affect its meaning. In addition to the fact that *natural* is employed now as a noun ("the natural"), now as an adjective, it can (like *nature*) refer to the object to be imitated, the manner in which it is imitated, and the effect of such imitation. It is said that the artist imitates the natural model, that he imitates the natural, and that his imitation is natural or produces a natural effect. This ambiguity—which allows the same word to signify the object, mode, and effect of imitation—is perfectly in accord with de Piles's theory, which makes color the means, principle, and goal of pictorial imitation. And the truth of that imitation (its adequacy to nature) is defined exclusively in terms of effect, that is, of the natural. Insofar as color consists of a perfect imitation of nature, the study of color maps onto the study of nature. So the student learns to imitate nature by imitating the pictures of the great masters; in this way he can acquire the knowledge of color that will make of him a true painter, meaning a painter able to give his imitation of nature the appearance of *le naturel.* But he must also practice imitating nature directly and not confine himself to copying paintings or he will run the risk of becoming what de Champaigne calls "a copyist of manner" (*copiste de manière*). A copyist of manner is one who imitates neither nature nor painting but a style of painting and naively believes that it is enough to imitate an artist to imitate the particular greatness of his art. On the one hand, one must learn to copy paintings to imitate nature; on the other, one must copy nature in order to know how, when copying paintings, to imitate painting, that is, to seek nature and truth in the imitation of art. Thus de Piles was not content simply to unite nature and art, as all his predecessors had done before him; he assimilated nature imitated by art to the natural imitation of art. The first consequence of this assimilation was, of course, to render superfluous all previous discussions concerning the imitation of nature and the preference that one should (or should not) accord the imitation of nature over natural imitation. But in the long run it also gave a new sense to the terms *nature* and *imitation* alike and therefore radically transformed the prevailing idea of art. Thanks to the identification of natural imitation with the imitation of nature, the word *nature* acquired a double connotation. The first is empirical and allowed imitation to be founded on observation. The second is pictorial since the natural, in de Piles's conception, was nothing other than an effect of art. And only painting could, by virtue of color and chiaroscuro, produce that effect.[63]

The two parts of de Piles's program, when presented in their intended order, seem much less heterogeneous than they in fact are. And this heterogeneity becomes apparent, as we have seen, with the last component of the first part, which deals with chiaroscuro. De Piles was, moreover, perfectly aware of this, since before he dealt with the study of color, which was reserved for painters, he observed that it was not necessary to follow his program in chronological order; a particularly talented student could start directly with the second part and study the first concurrently. This discontinuity clearly testifies to the transformation that the idea of nature underwent during the seventeenth century, a transformation whose effects were increasingly apparent in the practice of art. It is also evidence of a radically new conception of the historic role of painting, that is, of its place in history and more particularly in the history of art. By referring nature to painting and painting to nature, de Piles achieved two things at once.

In one and the same act, he broke the link attaching the artistic representation of nature to the ancient ideal and affirmed the autonomy of painting relative not only to sculpture but ipso facto to that same ancient ideal. He made painting something wholly alien to the ancient world. As he said about Rubens, the imitation of nature does not require one to believe that one is living among the ancient gods or in ancient Greece.

It is therefore no surprise that the copying of paintings—the imitation of painting—bulked so large in the second part of the painter's training. Imitating painting of necessity meant imitating the moderns. How could one copy the paintings of the ancients? All their works had been lost. The only paintings that a painter could see were modern ones. Among all the possible explanations for the historical alliance in Western culture between the defense of painting and that of modern art, one of the most obvious—blindingly obvious in its simplicity—is the disappearance of ancient painting.[64] Sculpture, one might almost say, was not so lucky. Apelles' *Calumny* and Timanthes' *The Sacrifice of Iphigenia* have no existence outside literature. A painter wishing to imitate ancient models could seek inspiration only in descriptions of paintings. Reference to ancient painting is exclusively textual and the fecundity of such references must be put down to the doctrine of *ut pictura poesis* (poetry resembles a painting). Its role and importance in the field of painting from the Renaissance forward testifies rather to the influence of literature on painting than to the hold of the past over the present.[65] In the case of sculpture, reference to the antique worked in a completely different way. Imitating ancient sculpture meant imitating things, not words. The artist could copy the *Laokoon, Farnese Herakles, Belvedere Torso, Borghese Gladiator,* or *Medici Venus.* All these works were there, before his eyes, in the form of casts, copies, or originals. It is altogether understandable that de Piles sought at all cost to dissociate the idea of nature from the model of antiquity. Identifying nature with the antique meant that painters who wanted to imitate nature had to imitate sculpture, since the only objects of ancient art to have survived into modern times were sculptures.

Consequently de Piles was not content to introduce a hierarchical separation between the teaching of drawing and that of color, that is, between study of the antique and life study. He conceived this divide on the basis of the opposition between sculpture and painting and gave it a sense that is no longer simply artistic but historical too. We might systematize his positions by saying that for him, sculpture is to painting what ancient is to modern. Of course, we should not interpret de Piles's theory in terms of the battle of the ancients and the moderns, though it undoubtedly pertains to that battle in some degree. De Piles's objective was very different from that of the moderns in general and Perrault in particular. De Piles's combat was waged on behalf of painting and nothing else. Perrault, by contrast, wished to defend the achievements of his century. Unlike de Piles, he sought to demonstrate the superiority not of one art over another but of the present over the past. This difference is clear in the passage of Perrault's *Parallèle des anciens et des modernes* that deals with sculpture: The *abbé* and the *chevalier,* both partisans of the moderns, acknowledge the greatness and beauty of ancient statuary and for once are in agreement with the *président,* the partisan of the ancients. There is only one point of difference; it concerns bas-relief and more especially an issue that we have already spoken of, the absence of perspective in ancient bas-relief. Thus the *abbé,* who may be thought to speak for Perrault, severely criticizes the arrangement and size of the figures on Trajan's Column: "In this column, the figures are almost all on the same line; and where there are any further back, they are as big and prominent as the ones in the foreground, with the result that they seem to have been placed on steps so that they can be seen one above the other."[66]

On this point, Perrault's opinion is the polar opposite of that defended by Anguier and closer to Regnaudin's point of view. He clearly prefers bas-reliefs "in the modern style" to ancient ones. If Perrault slides quickly over the subject of ancient statues in order to concentrate on bas-relief, his reasons are strategic or at least rhetorical. The real target of his criticism is not bas-reliefs. His gambit allows him to attack not ancient sculpture but ancient painting. Ancient bas-reliefs afforded a powerful argument in favor of the superiority of modern painting because they provided clear proof that the ancients were not acquainted with perspective. The *président* is perfectly aware of the *abbé's* intentions: "If modern sculpture is so far superior to that of the ancients in the respect that you suggest, today's painting must be greatly superior to that of the ancients, since sculpture learned all the secrets of recession and perspective from modern painting." This is precisely the *abbé's* point and he merely remarks, "Again I agree with you. You have drawn the right conclusion."

Whereas de Piles insists on the specifically modern character of painting relative to sculpture, Perrault is defending modern painting, that is, the superiority of modern over ancient painters. According to the *abbé,* modern painters undeniably paint better; they know about perspective, chiaroscuro, and the art of arranging groups: "the judicious assemblage of all figures intelligently placed with their colors shaded off according to the position they occupy in the plane."[67] These are all things that the ancient painters manifestly did not know. The *abbé's* evidence is the *Aldobrandini Wedding,* which he claims to have seen. Although these paintings are not of the time of Zeuxis or Apelles, he thinks they give a fairly accurate notion of ancient painting: "The colors are all of equal strength, nothing in the picture stands out, nothing recedes, and all the figures are more or less on the same line, so that it is much less a picture than a colored ancient bas-relief;

everything in it is dry and static, there is no unity, no connection and it lacks the softness of living bodies, the softness that distinguishes such bodies from the marble and bronze that may sometimes represent them."[68]

But the most important of Perrault's attacks on ancient painting are of course founded on Pliny's descriptions. Like his adversaries, Perrault has no direct experience to bring in as evidence. His image of ancient painting, like theirs, relies on the interpretation of texts. He has never laid eyes on an ancient painting.

It is easy to imagine the excitement generated among the scholars and art lovers of Europe when, a few decades later, the frescoes of Herculaneum came to light.[69] At last, some pieces of ancient painting were visible and judgments could be made on the evidence. Naturally, the first to celebrate were the partisans of the ancients. True, some were uncertain about these frescoes and thought, like Caylus, that the colors had deteriorated to such an extent that it was impossible to assess the paintings accurately. But everyone was convinced that they constituted a complete refutation of Perrault's arguments. Here was proof that the ancient painters were familiar with perspective and chiaroscuro and were no whit inferior to the greatest moderns. Marcello Venuti directed the excavations and went so far as to describe the *Theseus* as "the most beautiful thing in the world…more beautiful than the works of Raphael." The reaction of the moderns was swift. The attack was led by Nicolas Cochin II. He found the *Theseus* so admired by Venuti "of mediocre draftsmanship, lacking knowledge and finesse."[70] The ancient paintings were to his eye badly composed, their perspective was incorrect, and they were wholly lacking in the magic of color and chiaroscuro. His judgment was pitiless: the ancients were ignorant of everything that constituted the charm and merit of painting. For Cochin, the frescoes of Herculaneum finally and unarguably proved the crushing superiority of modern over ancient painters.

Notes

1. Johann Wolfgang von Goethe, "Die Antike gehört zur Natur," in *Maximen und Reflektionen,* in idem, *Sprüche in Prosa: Sämtliche, Maximen und Reflexionen,* ed. Harald Fricke (Frankfurt: Deutscher Klassiker Verlag, 1993), 19.1142.

2. This bas-relief was Prou's *morceau de reception* [translator's note: the piece that marked the artist's reception into the Académie] in 1682.

3. On the history of the lectures, see Bernard Teyssèdre, *Roger de Piles et les débats sur le coloris au siècle de Louis XIV* (Paris: Bibliothèque des arts, 1965); and Jacqueline Lichtenstein, *La couleur éloquente: Rhétorique et peinture à l'âge classique* (Paris: Flammarion, 1999).

4. Georges Guillet de Saint-Georges, lecture of 5 October 1686, in Jacqueline Lichtenstein and Christian Michel, eds., *Les conférences de l'Académie royale de peinture et de sculpture,* vol. 2, *De 1681 à 1699* (Paris: École nationale supérieure des beaux-arts, forthcoming).

5. Georges Guillet de Saint-Georges, lecture of 5 November 1689, in Jacqueline Lichtenstein and Christian Michel, eds., *Les conférences de l'Académie royale de peinture et de sculpture,* vol. 2, *De 1681 à 1699* (Paris: École nationale supérieure des beaux-arts, forthcoming).

6. Henri Testelin, *Sentiments des plus habiles peintres sur la pratique de la peinture et sculpture,* in Jacqueline Lichtenstein and Christian Michel, eds., *Les conférences de l'Académie royale de peinture et de sculpture,* vol. 1, *De 1667 à 1679: Les conférences au temps d'Henry Testelin* (Paris: École nationale supérieure des beaux-arts, 2007), bk. 2, 689–751.

7. Like the Italian *disegno* from which it derives, the French seventeenth-century *dessein* means design, project, purpose, pattern, and drawing. The orthographic—and therefore conceptual—distinction between *dessein* and *dessin* was not made until the eighteenth century. Translator's note: Depending on the context, the seventeenth-century word *dessein* is translated here as "design," "drawing," "draftsmanship," or "line."

8. Guillet, lecture of 5 November 1689 (note 5).

9. Guillet, lecture of 5 November 1689 (note 5).

10. Guillet, lecture of 5 November 1689 (note 5). Prou's work was, moreover, probably inspired by a Le Brun drawing.

11. Guillet, lecture of 5 November 1689 (note 5).

12. On the importance of detail and its capacity to disturb the sense of representation, see Daniel Arasse, *Le détail: Pour une histoire rapprochée de la peinture* (Paris: Flammarion, 1992).

13. Guillet, lecture of 5 November 1689 (note 5).

14. Georges Guillet de Saint-Georges, MS École nationale supérieure des beaux-arts 129.

15. In this, the Academicians were merely obeying the requirements stated in Article IX of the first statutes of the Académie, issued in 1648. See Anatole de Montaiglon, ed., *Procès-verbaux de l'Académie royale de peinture et de sculpture, 1648–1792* (Paris: J. Baur, 1875; reprint, Paris: F. de Nobele, 1972), 1:72.

16. Montaiglon, *Procès-verbaux* (note 15), 1:298.

17. The practice of reading aloud old lectures, which began in 1679, dictated our choice of end-date. The ratio remained relatively constant after that date, but the list of lectures is less significant.

18. Gerard van Opstal, "Sur la figure principale du groupe de *Laocoon,*" in Jacqueline Lichtenstein and Christian Michel, eds., *Les conférences de l'Académie royale de peinture et de sculpture,* vol. 1, *De 1667 à 1679: Les conférences au temps d'Henry Testelin* (Paris: École nationale supérieure des beaux-arts, 2007), bk. 1, 135. On 2 August 1670, Anguier lectured on the entire *Laokoon* group, having had a model of his own making transported to the Académie. In 1692, the king finally presented a cast of the *Laokoon* to the Académie.

19. In 1666, Colbert sent a cast of the *Farnese Herakles* to the Académie along with other ancient works. In 1671, he had "certain pieces of ancient bas-relief with the figures of Bacchus, Venus, young wrestlers, the

little faun, and Apollo removed from the king's storehouse of ancient works to remain at the Académie and serve for study there"; Montaiglon, *Procès-verbaux* (note 15), 1:366.

20. The fact that a sculpture can exist in many different forms without loss of identity raises an awkward question for anyone seeking to apply logical criteria to the arts. Goodman's distinction between authographic and allographic arts does not take sufficient account of the specificity of sculpture. From the point of view of an ontology of art — in the contemporary sense of an analysis of the states of things, relations, and predicates — sculpture differs not just from painting but from music and literature (which are considered allographic arts) too. Nor is it clear that painting is always an allographic art. See Nelson Goodman, *Languages of Art: An Approach to a Theory of Symbols* (Indianapolis: Bobbs-Merrill, 1968).

21. On this subject, see Francis Haskell and Nicholas Penny, *Taste and the Antique: The Lure of Classical Sculpture, 1500–1900* (New Haven: Yale Univ. Press, 1981); and Jean-Pierre Cuzin, Jean-René Gaborit, and Alain Pasquier, eds., *D'après l'antique*, exh. cat. (Paris: Réunion des musées nationaux, 2000).

22. "Coysevox, like Legros, won great admiration for his free copies, and the fact that the one artist worked from casts in France and the other from originals in Rome suggests that no clear distinction can be drawn between the two sets of copyists, just as no clear distinction can be drawn between the copies themselves and the original compositions often produced by the very same artists," write Haskell and Penny in *Taste and the Antique* (note 21), 41. The same point of view prevailed in the eighteenth century too. Thus Charles Antoine Pesselier wrote about Bouchardon's copy of the *Barberini Faun*: "It is a sleeping faun larger than life size, of which he made a model while in Rome after an ancient work in the Palazzo Barberini — an ancient work restored by Bernini. He took everything that was natural about this figure and made of it, by four or five

years' work, a perfectly beautiful original"; quoted in Aline Magnien, *La nature et l'antique, la chair et le contour: Essai sur la sculpture française du XVIIIe siècle* (Oxford: Voltaire Foundation, 2004), 74n113. The story of the copy of the *Laokoon* made by Bandinelli is no doubt the first example of this attitude toward copies of ancient pieces. Bandinelli made the copy at the request of Pope Clement VII, who had intended to give it to François I. But he found it so beautiful that he decided to keep it and send some original works to the French king in its stead.

23. Jean de La Fontaine, "Épître à Mgr l'Évêque de Soissons" (1687), in idem, *Oeuvres complètes* (Paris: Seuil, 1965), 493.

24. These lectures on general questions were initially rather few and far between (none in 1667, one in 1668 by Le Brun on expression, one in 1669 by Bourdon on daylight) but became more common after the 1670s.

25. Color was not taught by the Académie, which had no painting studio. Students practiced painting elsewhere in the studio of a master. Studios were first introduced at the Académie in 1863. The models remained exclusively male until the nineteenth century.

26. Michel-Andre Anguier, "Une méthode particulière qu'il faut tenir pour faire une figure anatomique de sculpture, et comme il convient de s'en servir pour la facilité du dessin," in Jacqueline Lichtenstein and Christian Michel, eds., *Les conférences de l'Académie royale de peinture et de sculpture*, vol. 1, *De 1667 à 1679: Les conférences au temps d'Henry Testelin* (Paris: École nationale supérieure des beaux-arts, 2007), bk. 2, 489–92.

27. Anguier, "Une méthode particulière" (note 26), 490.

28. The plan of the lecture, given on the first page of the manuscript text, is as follows: (1) Why nude, (2) Why seated, (3) Of expression, (4) About the cry, (5) Of the trembling of the muscles, (6) Of the beauty of the design through the handsome assemblage of muscles, (7) Of the children, (8) Of the arrangements and actions of the figures, (9) Of the function of iron armature, and (10) Of repairs;

Michel-Andre Anguier, lecture on the *Laokoon* (2 August 1670), in Jacqueline Lichtenstein and Christian Michel, eds., *Les conférences de l'Académie royale de peinture et de sculpture,* vol. 1, *De 1667 à 1679: Les conférences au temps d'Henry Testelin* (Paris: École nationale supérieure des beaux-arts, 2007), bk. 1, 379.

29. Anguier, lecture on the *Laokoon* (note 28), 379.

30. Anguier, lecture on the *Laokoon* (note 28), 379–80.

31. This way of thinking is not confined to the artist-theorists of the seventeenth century. It was adopted by many artists prior to the twentieth century and is characteristic of all forms of theory deriving from and intended for a particular practice, such as that of the artist. The definition of *bricolage* by Claude Lévi-Strauss would fit this form of artistic thought rather well. It could be described as eclectic, were it not that the term has, since the nineteenth century, acquired negative connotations in both philosophy and aesthetics.

32. Le Brun gave three lectures on general and particular expression: 7 April, and 6 and 10 October 1668. See Jennifer Montagu, *The Expression of the Passions: The Origin and Influence of Charles Le Brun's "Conférence sur l'expression générale et particulière"* (New Haven: Yale Univ. Press, 1994.)

33. Charles Le Brun, "Sur *Les Israélites recueillant la manne dans le désert* de Poussin" (5 November 1667), in Jacqueline Lichtenstein and Christian Michel, eds., *Les conférences de l'Académie royale de peinture et de sculpture,* vol. 1, *De 1667 à 1679: Les conférences au temps d'Henry Testelin* (Paris: École nationale supérieure des beaux-arts, 2007), bk. 1, 167.

34. Anguier, lecture on the *Laokoon* (note 28), 382–83.

35. The distinction between the study of bones and that of muscles is dealt with by the anatomy teachers. François Quatroult, a doctor of medicine, gave a lecture on 1 October 1670 entitled "Une idée succincte d'ostéologie" (A concise account of osteology), followed on 4 September 1671 by "Opérations de la nature humaine dans le mouvements de ses divereses parties" (Operations of human nature in the movements of its various parts). Jacques Antoine Friquet de Vauroze, another anatomy teacher, insisted in his turn on the usefulness of these two schools of medical science for the practice of art: "The anatomical doctrine of the human body, which is useful to the painter and the sculptor, has two parts. The first is called osteology and the second, that of the muscles, myology"; *Recueil sommaire des leçons académiques données aux élèves de l'Académie royale de peinture et de sculpture sous le rectorat de Monsieur Le Brun de l'année 1675 par le Sieur Friquet,* MS École nationale supérieure des beaux-arts 160.

36. Michel-Andre Anguier, "L'union de l'art avec la nature" (4 July and 1 August 1671), in Jacqueline Lichtenstein and Christian Michel, eds., *Les conférences de l'Académie royale de peinture et de sculpture,* vol. 1, *De 1667 à 1679: Les conférences au temps d'Henry Testelin* (Paris: École nationale supérieure des beaux-arts, 2007), bk. 1, 410–30.

37. Anguier, "L'union de l'art" (note 36), 418.

38. Denis Diderot, *Salon de 1765,* in idem, *Oeuvres complètes* (Paris: Club français du livre, 1970), 6:234.

39. Paul Fréart de Chantelou, *Journal de voyage du Cavalier Bernin en France* (Paris: Pandora, 1981), 157. Translated by Margery Corbett as *Diary of the Cavaliere Bernini's Visit to France,* ed. Anthony Blunt, annotated by George C. Bauer (Princeton: Princeton Univ. Press, 1985).

40. Chantelou, *Journal de voyage* (note 39), 182.

41. Van Opstal, "Sur la figure principale" (note 18), 130–31. When compared with Testelin's account, Félibien's summary seems less than exact. The Academicians were not, as he claims, unanimously in favor of Bernini's positions. See below, p. 38 and n. 44.

42. Nicolas Boileau-Despréaux, *Satires, Épîtres, Art poétique,* ed. Jean-Pierre Collinet (1701; Paris: Gallimard, 1985), epistle 9, line 43.

43. Debate following Champaigne's lecture of 7 January 1668, in Jacqueline Lichtenstein and Christian Michel, eds., *Les conférences de l'Académie royale de peinture et de sculp-*

ture, vol. 1, *De 1667 à 1679: Les conférences au temps d'Henry Testelin* (Paris: École nationale supérieure des beaux-arts, 2007), bk. 1, 196–204.

44. Testelin's work, *Sentiments des plus habiles peintres* (note 6), also allows us to reconstruct the tenor of Le Brun's lost lecture. It is a precious source of information about the debates that took place at the Académie.

45. Henri Testelin, "L'usage du trait et du dessin" (16 February 1675), in *Sentiments des plus habiles peintres,* in Jacqueline Lichtenstein and Christian Michel, eds., *Les conférences de l'Académie royale de peinture et de sculpture,* vol. 1, *De 1667 à 1679: Les conférences au temps d'Henry Testelin* (Paris: École nationale supérieure des beaux-arts, 2007), bk. 2, 703.

46. Testelin, "L'usage du trait" (note 45), 703.

47. Testelin, "L'usage du trait" (note 45), 703.

48. Testelin, "L'usage du trait" (note 45), 703–4.

49. Michel-Andre Anguier, "La maniére de Paris les bas reliefs" (9 July 1673), in Jacqueline Lichtenstein and Christian Michel, eds., *Les conférences de l'Académie royale de peinture et de sculpture,* vol. 1, *De 1667 à 1679: Les conférences au temps d'Henry Testelin* (Paris: École nationale supérieure des beaux-arts, 2007), bk. 2, 515–18.

50. Anguier, "La maniére de Paris" (note 49), 516.

51. Anguier, "La maniére de Paris" (note 49), 516.

52. Thomas Regnaudin, "Sur les bas reliefs" (5 August 1673), in Jacqueline Lichtenstein and Christian Michel, eds., *Les conférences de l'Académie royale de peinture et de sculpture,* vol. 1, *De 1667 à 1679: Les conférences au temps d'Henry Testelin* (Paris: École nationale supérieure des beaux-arts, 2007), bk. 2, 521.

53. Regnaudin, "Sur les bas reliefs" (note 52), 519–20. On the question of bas-relief in the seventeenth century, see Geneviève Bresc-Bautier, "'Ces bas-reliefs ne sont d'aucun usage en ce pays-ci': La fascination du bas-relief à l'antique et son rejet," in Olivier Bonfait, ed., *L'idéal classique: Les échanges artistiques entre Rome et Paris du temps de Bellori (1640–1700)* (Paris: Somogy, 2002), 299–316. The dispute about bas-relief was revived in the eighteenth century in more or less the same terms. In his *Réflexions sur la sculpture,* Falconet adopted a position close to that of Regnaudin and thus diametrically opposed to that of Anguier, whose lecture he quotes. Falconet writes: "Should anyone doubt that the laws of bas-relief are the same as those of painting, choose a painting by Poussin or Le Sueur; let an able sculptor make a model of it: you will see what a fine bas-relief it will make"; lecture given on 7 June 1760, in Etienne-Maurice Falconet, *Réflexions sur la sculpture: Lues à l'Académie royale de peinture et de sculpture, le 7 juin 1760* (Paris: Prault, 1761), 49. On the eighteenth-century debate, see Guilem Sherf, "De la malignité d'un microbe; l'antique et le bas-relief moderne, de Falconet à David d'Angers," *Revue de l'art,* no. 105 (1994), 19–32.

54. The lectures given by Roger de Piles at the Académie were collected in *Cours de peinture par principes* in 1708 (Paris: Gallimard, 1989).

55. De Piles, *Cours de peinture* (note 54), 197.

56. De Piles, *Cours de peinture* (note 54), 197.

57. De Piles, *Cours de peinture* (note 54), 197–98.

58. De Piles, *Cours de peinture* (note 54), 199.

59. De Piles, *Cours de peinture* (note 54), 154–55.

60. De Piles, *Cours de peinture* (note 54), 199.

61. De Piles, *Cours de peinture* (note 54), 201.

62. De Piles, *Cours de peinture* (note 54), 201.

63. The twofold connotation—empirical and pictorial—of the word *nature* is very clear in the way de Piles characterizes Philarque in his *Conversations sur la connaissance de la peinture et sur le jugement qu'on doit faire des tableaux* (Paris: Langlois, 1677; reprint, Geneva: Slatkine, 1970). Philarque is de Piles's spokesman in these dialogues. He is an old man who knew Rubens and has just arrived from England, where he has spent a number of years. This has taught him to "judge without prejudice." Accompanied by Caliste, who has lived in Rome, and Léonidas, who has just returned from a stay in Venice, he visits the gallery of the duc de Richelieu. There, before his dazzled young interlocutors, he launches into an extensive description of

the paintings of Rubens, analyzing Rubens's perfect imitation of nature. The fact that Philarque, the friend and champion of Rubens, has spent time in London is by no means insignificant: he has a different idea of nature. For an analysis of this text, see Jacqueline Lichtenstein, "De l'idée de la peinture à l'analyse du tableau," in "La naissance de la théorie de l'art en France, 1640–1720," special issue, *Revue d'esthétique* 31/32 (1997): 17–35.

64. As Caylus put it in the eighteenth century in his lecture "La vie de Sarrazin" (1 March 1749), in Jacqueline Lichtenstein and Christian Michel, eds., *Les conférences de l'Académie royale de peinture et de sculpture,* vol. 4 (Paris: École nationale supérieure des beaux-arts, forthcoming): "We daily admire the remains of the masterpieces of certain Greek sculptors, while we can only express our regret about the works of the most celebrated painters of antiquity."

65. Franciscus Junius's *De picture veterum libri tres* (1636) is exemplary of the purely textual functioning of reference to ancient painters. Rubens's letter thanking Junius for his book is particularly interesting in this respect. Having praised the importance and useful-ness of so complete a survey of the painting of the ancient world, Rubens expresses his regret that no one has yet thought to write a book about modern painters, that is, he says, a book founded not on the interpreta-tion of texts but on the study of pictures. See the letter of 1 August 1637 in Peter Paul Rubens, *Correspondance de Rubens,* trans. by Paul Colin (Brussels: Nouvelle société d'éditions, 1934), 1:144–46.

66. Charles Perrault, *Parallèle des anciens et des modernes* (Paris: Chez Jean Bapt. Coignard, 1692–97; reprint, Geneva: Slatkine, 1979), 63.

67. Perrault, *Parallèle* (note 66), 68.

68. Perrault, *Parallèle* (note 66), 71.

69. The excavations of Herculaneum were known in Italy from 1739 and from 1740 in England but elicited wide interest in France only after 1747. On this subject, see Christian Michel, "Les peintures d'Herculanum et la querelle des anciens et des modernes (1740–1760)," *Bulletin de la société d'histoire de l'art français* (1984), 105–17, which offers a most convincing explanation of this very surprising time-lag.

70. Charles-Nicolas Cochin (in collaboration with Jérôme Charles Bellicard), *Observa-tions sur les antiquités d'Herculanum, avec quelques réflexions sur la peinture et la sculpture des anciens . . . ,* 2nd ed. (Paris: Charles Antoine Jombert, 1755), 38. See also Christian Michel, *Charles-Nicolas Cochin et l'art des Lumières* (Rome: École française de Rome, 1993).

The Artist-Painter and the Philosopher-Sculptor

I should like to paint like a blind man who shapes a buttock with groping hands.
— Pablo Picasso

Noli me tangere

"Let us not circumscribe the sphere of our pleasures,"[1] wrote Diderot to his friend Falconet. Endlessly curious, Diderot practiced what he preached, writing with delight about a wide variety of subjects. Each pleasure was for him a locus of multiple exchanges, the result of a veritable interaction of all the senses, one sensation in a constellation of others and thus connected to a thousand other pleasures. How *can* the sphere of pleasure be circumscribed when pleasure is never circumscribed in any sphere but always overflows its own boundaries, opening onto other pleasures in the very movement by which it opens up to them? The idea that pleasure necessarily transgresses its own "order" (to use a term taken from Pascal) underpins not just Diderot's moral philosophy but his notion of aesthetic experience. This is clear from the way that he describes the pictures in his *Salons*. It is as if perception of the painting takes the spectator to an unstable and uncertain place, the point of intersection of many contradictory sensations. This is a strange place of ill-defined frontiers, subject to the ebb and flow of desire's constant vacillation between contact and distance. Thus in the *Salon de 1763*, he describes Chardin's *The Jar of Olives*:

> *This* is a painter; *this* is a colorist.... Because this porcelain vase is porcelain; because between these olives and the eye there is the water in which they float; because what else can one do but take these biscuits and eat them, cut open and press this Seville orange, open this wine and drink it, peel this fruit, push the knife into this pâté.... Oh Chardin, it is not white, red, and black that you grind onto your palette, but the very substance of things.[2]

The themes central to Diderot's aesthetic all find a place in this text: illusion, confusion between artistic and natural beauty, the idea of the divine painter, and—above all—the magic of color. The equation of color and painting in the first sentence is taken for granted: "*This* is a painter; *this* is a colorist." Diderot then sets about justifying the equation in his usual way, making analysis of the work synonymous with its effect on the spectator. And the effects are seemingly twofold. They affect subject and object alike. Both undergo strange transformations. Under the impact of a tactile sensation, the spectator's gaze is changed; he feels that he could, if he so wished, touch the objects represented on the canvas. But they disappear as he approaches only to reappear as he steps back: "Move in and everything blurs, flattens itself out, and disappears. Step back and everything re-creates and reproduces itself."[3]

Assailed by these contradictory sensations, perception oscillates between vision and touch, distance and proximity. And from this oscillation emerges a world of multiple and changing appearances, a reality that escapes definition and vanishes just when it seems one might grasp and dwell on it. A transformation of an almost cyclical kind runs like a current between sight and the visible, and its effect is to transform both perception and the thing perceived. It is a twofold metamorphosis; it is wrought by the object and returns to it like a retroactive effect altering its cause, since the transformation of the picture effected by the eye derives from the transformation of the eye effected by the picture. The emotion elicited in the viewer draws the body toward the object.[4] One wants to touch what one sees; the desire to touch draws one in closer, so that one can see more clearly; and these movements combined with the fluctuations of desire constantly modify one's perception of the painting.

The first transformation therefore concerns the sense of sight: "what else can one do but take these biscuits and eat them." In the *Salon de 1759,* Diderot was already describing two little Chardin pictures in similar terms: "Never anything but nature and truth: if you were thirsty, you would take the bottle by the neck; the peaches and grapes awaken appetite and one's hand goes out toward them."[5]

True painting—the painting of a colorist like Chardin—does not stimulate the sense of sight alone. It awakens appetite. What the gaze battens on, the hand reaches out for. The spectator would like to be able to take these fruits and taste them, seize the bottle and drink from it, approach the woman's body and caress it.[6] It is as if the pleasure of sight were, in this case, inseparable from the desire to touch. But the conditions of aesthetic experience compel this desire to remain itself and nothing else. Visual pleasure entails an impulse to touch that must never be fulfilled: the subject must keep his distance, content with wanting but never attempting to touch. Tactile pleasure would sate the desire to touch but annihilate the possibility and pleasure of contemplation.

Let us imagine a spectator who obeys the impulse to touch. As he approaches the image, he would—like Narcissus grasping at his reflection in the water—see it dissolve and lose shape and outline. "Move in and everything blurs, flattens itself out, and disappears." The spectator might, like Narcissus, be driven out of his wits, acting like those madmen who must at all costs touch a painting, sometimes tearing at the canvas in their headlong desire. If the spectator inhabited by this crazy impulse were to break through the space between himself and the representation and lay hands on the picture, what he touched would bear no relation to the object that had, till then, existed in his perception—the object to which his desire was reaching out. He touches no biscuit, bottle, or woman's body but a simple material surface from which all forms have vanished. He saw an image but touches paint.

To see is to want to touch. But the pleasure of seeing requires that this desire be contained. To see is to want to move closer. But the pleasure of seeing requires one to keep one's distance. Above all, do not touch. Or touch only delicately, tactfully, that is, with the fingertips of sight, without ever making contact.

It makes no sense to want to touch a painting. We know that these grapes do not exist, that this flesh is painted and therefore fake. We know that this pâté has no consistency. "What else can one do but take these biscuits and eat them?" Anything but. What I see is not a biscuit; I cannot therefore want it. Everything here is illusion, both the object and the desire that it is intended to elicit. Diderot knows this perfectly well, as his conditional shows: "If you were thirsty, you would take the bottle by the neck." But the spectator will not take the bottle. He is not thirsty and he is not fool enough to grasp at an inexistent bottle. He knows that there is no bottle and that, if he is thirsty, he thirsts for the image and not the thing. Only a madman grasps at a fake bottle. To believe in the pictorial illusion and consider the image as if it were the object itself is madness. That belief would imply another and more drastic one, namely, that all worlds are real. It supposes that one is incapable of envisaging the existence of a merely possible world—which might, after all, be one of the definitions of madness. A person who believes in the mirages of painting is thinking in a language from which the conditional tense is lacking. He does not say, "I would take this bottle if I were thirsty and if it were a true bottle" but "I take this bottle because it makes me thirsty."

The conditional is essential. It largely determines the significance of this paean of praise to the illusionistic power of painting. The problem of pictorial illusion is all too often incorrectly stated because the role of the conditional has been ignored. The conditional implies a distancing; it maintains the object seen in its place and the spectator in his. It is our guarantee of the distinction between the image and the real and speaks for a subject who is not taken in, who knows that the illusion of which he speaks does not exist but is merely a fiction in which he pretends to believe. Examples of the conditional abound in writings on painting, in particular where the subject is the beauty of color. We often find it in the works of de Piles, as when he celebrates one of Rubens's bacchanals: "The flesh of this female satyr and her children seems so truthful; it is easy to imagine that if I reached out I should feel the warmth of the blood."[7]

This way of exalting the powers of painting is a commonplace of colorist rhetoric and tirelessly repeated by French writers until the end of the nineteenth century. Balzac's novel *Le chef-d'oeuvre inconnu* (*The Unknown Masterpiece*) offers a perfect example of this descriptive model. Criticizing Porbus's picture, Frenhofer speaks in terms strangely reminiscent of de Piles or Diderot: "I could never believe this splendid body was animated by the breath of life. If I were to put my hand on that breast, firm and round as it is, it would feel as cold as marble!"[8]

The relations between image and illusion raise a genuine problem, one that requires an analysis of the means by which painting in particular contrives to produce a certain kind of effect. But it is not a genuine problem of knowledge and has nothing to do with issues of error, mendacity, or truth. The reason being that there never is any pictorial illusion, unless perhaps for the innocent, the credulous, or the mad. It is strictly for the birds. It is striking how often the cases of pictorial illusion handed down by tradition involve creatures thought to lack reason: children, servants, peasants, and above all animals. Too often we forget or pretend to forget that praise of pictorial illusion is a descriptive trope borrowed from the rhetoric of eulogy. The illusion is a literary and theoretical fiction. It corresponds to nothing real and is never described as a real experience, unless by those who wish to convince us of the dangers of painting and pretend to be unaware of the fact that we are perfectly able to distinguish fiction from reality. In painting, the illusion is itself a fiction. It is a pseudo-illusion that cannot deceive because it presents itself as such. As Cochin writes: "It is not a real illusion since it survives in paintings so small that their proportions reveal its falsity."[9]

The defect of certain philosophical analyses of the pictorial illusion is, on the one hand, ignoring the elementary laws of psychology and perception, while on the other considering the spectator naive and credulous to the point where he might easily succumb to the deceit of images and believe in their reality, if the temple guardians—the philosophers—were not there to alert him.[10] But the spectator is not as naive as the philosophers would like us to believe. He knows very well that these grapes, these shoes, this glass of wine, this woman's body, do not exist or rather exist only as images. He knows it all the better for sometimes regretting that this is so. After describing Greuze's *A Girl with a Dead Canary,* Diderot confesses: "My friend, are you not laughing out loud to hear this very serious character entertain himself by consoling a child in a painting for the loss of her bird—or indeed for anything else at all? But then again, look! How beautiful she is! How moving! I don't like to make people suffer, but all the same, I should not terribly mind being the cause of her affliction."[11]

"So much art to gull a bird?" is Perrault's ironic inquiry.[12] He is talking, of course, about Zeuxis, who was famous for painting grapes so realistic that birds were said to attempt to eat them. Can art fool children, as Plato claims? Reread the famous discussion in *Sophist* in which a child is taken in by a picture. You will see that the pictorial illusion that Plato so vigorously denounces requires a most improbable spectator, such as one rarely encounters even among children.[13] To convince us of an imaginary danger, Plato invents a no less imaginary child and asks us not merely to believe in but to identify with him. And unlike the innocent inventions of art, which aspire only to please us, contriving at worst to disconcert us, Plato's invention really does want to deceive us by presenting itself as truth. Philosophy would have us prefer the moral—or rather moralizing—fable of the abused spectator to the amiable but unconvincing fiction of the pictorial illusion. This kind of thinking has driven analysis of pictorial illusion into a philosophical aporia. To help it escape, we need only substitute for the image of the credulous spectator one that does him the justice he deserves as a reasoning subject. In short, we should apply what W. O. Quine calls "the principle of charity" and allow the spectator a minimum of intelligence, knowledge, and lucidity.[14] In exchange, we must clearly distinguish the fictions of art from those that ask to be believed: illusion, mendacity, and trickery.

No one has defended this obligation with greater ardor than Abbé Dubos, who takes up the question of pictorial illusion in his *Réflexions critiques sur la poésie et sur la peinture:* "There can be no illusion for a man in his right mind, unless he has previously had an illusion inflicted on his senses."[15]

Pursuing a tradition solidly anchored in French seventeenth-century thought, Dubos develops his arguments by comparison with the theater. Pictorial illusion, he says, exists no more than does the famous theatrical illusion, which is still discussed though no sane spectator has ever believed in it. We shed tears for the unhappy fate of Rodrigue and Chimène (in Corneille's *Le Cid*), but our sight is never so blurred that we forget that we are watching a representation:

The same applies in painting. The merit of Raphael's picture of Attila is not to seduce us into believing that we are truly confronted with the sight of Saints Peter and Paul flying through the air and threatening the barbarian king, who is surrounded by the troops he has brought to sack Rome. But in the said painting...the imitation is so lifelike that the impression made on the spectator is in great measure such as the event itself would have made.[16]

The impression is "in great measure" owed to the verisimilitude of the imitation, but the pleasure accompanying it is entirely due to our awareness of the fictive character of the representation by which the impression was created. Aesthetic feeling differs from the true feelings of pleasure or pain elicited by the spectacle of a real event. It is not produced by the representation of an object; its source is the effect on the spectator of the representation of his relationship to an object when he knows that this object is nothing more than a representation. The pleasure felt by a spectator before a work of art is in some sense reflexive. It is not the direct effect of the sensation caused by the picture because it includes the knowledge that this sensation is caused by a picture. The illusion can produce a sensible pleasure but can never be the source of the aesthetic pleasure; that pleasure necessarily implies a reflective perception, detached from the immediate perception given in the sensation. Aesthetic pleasure, Kant tells us in the *Kritik der Urteilskraft* (*Critique of Judgment*), is born of "reflection on the forms of things," that is, of a judgment interested not in the existence of the object but only in its representation.[17] And this is indeed how Dubos conceives of aesthetic feelings. If the pleasure that we take in the sight of images were dependent on the power of the pictorial illusion, the effect ought to disappear with its cause. In fact, he notes, pictures please us "although we know perfectly well that they are only a canvas on which colors have been artfully placed," that is, that they are pictures.[18]

In the eighteenth century, the principle of imitation remains sacrosanct but almost everyone attempts to show that imitation in painting has nothing in common with what is commonly understood as "illusion"; in other words, that the pictorial illusion, as Cochin puts it, is not a true illusion.[19] In the supplement to the *Encyclopédie,* under the heading "Illusion," Marmontel delivers a magnificent analysis of the paradoxical nature of this illusion-effect, which can be enjoyed only by those whom it does not deceive. Like theatrical illusion, the pictorial variant is only a "semi-illusion," he says, "a continuous error constantly intermingled with the reflection that corrects it; a way of being deceived and not taken in":

> In the arts of imitation, truth is nothing, verisimilitude is all; not only do we not require reality of these arts, we do not even require that their pretend reality be an exact resemblance. In tragedy, it has been well observed that the illusion is not complete.... For all the alarms of the imagination, our eyes tell us that we are still in Paris while the scene is set in Rome. And to prove that we never forget the actor behind the character that he represents, it is when we are most moved that we cry, "Ah, how well acted!"... Even if it were possible to create a complete illusion by perfect resemblance, art should avoid doing so, just as sculpture does, which does not color marble lest it become frightening. There are spectacles such that a moderate illusion is agreeable and complete illusion would be repel-

lent or painful.…Imagine a painted perspective so perfect that from a distance it really seemed to be a piece of architecture or a distant landscape; all the pleasure of art would be lost to you at that point and restored only when, coming closer, you realized that the painter had imposed on you.…We should not therefore believe that…the best painter of nature is the most faithful copyist: for if the imitation were a perfect resemblance, it would subsequently have to be altered in some particular in order to allow the soul the confused sense of its own error and the secret pleasure of perceiving the adroitness with which it had been deceived.[20]

We understand why even the most realistic imitation can never, as Dubos says, make the same impression on spectators as "the event would have made" but only one "in great measure" equivalent. Only an imitation genuinely giving the impression of reality could produce an impression identical to that produced by reality. But this imitation would not then be an object of aesthetic pleasure, since the spectator, thinking he was confronted with something real, would not know that he was reacting to a picture. As Quatremère de Quincy says, "Should the object of imitation ever be confused with its image, that very confusion, robbing us of our awareness of the imitation, would annihilate both the effect and the pleasure it produces."[21]

The impression productive of aesthetic feeling is, then, never identical with a true impression, that is, one caused by a real event. The image in the picture is merely the realistic imitation of an event and the aesthetic feeling is merely the realistic imitation of a feeling. Dubos points this out in pithy fashion: "The copy of the object should, as it were, excite in us a copy of the feeling that the object itself would have excited."[22]

The analyses of Dubos and Marmontel are thus consistent with the Kantian definition of aesthetic feeling but perhaps modify its meaning as they specify it in greater detail. For them, aesthetic feeling is the result of a twofold thought process, which gives rise to a twofold reflexivity. It supposes a subject conscious both of the mimetic nature of the representation and of the mimetic nature of the emotions that this representation provokes. Only to the extent that the spectator is aware of the paradoxical nature of the various emotions by which he is overcome at the sight of a painting or spectacle can he feel a pleasure deriving from aesthetic experience. And only then can he experience a true feeling, aesthetic pleasure—the only feeling that transcends the mimetic order prevailing in this universe of simulacra and representation. "If you were thirsty, you would take the bottle." So this is not a true desire any more than it is a true bottle. No, what the lover of painting wants is to see, and when he sees, to imagine that, if he were both thirsty and credulous, he could perhaps believe that the bottle is real and want to take hold of it—because it is so well painted.

But there are those in whom the sight of a bottle does indeed induce thirst, a thirst so great as to abolish both sight and knowledge: people who are driven mad by the sight of an object that does not exist. Why would anyone lose his head at the sight of a picture? What drives people so mad that they take a knife to a painting?[23] Under what illusion are they laboring? It is surely very different from that which filled Narcissus with love then pain. Our lunatic acts out of fury not despair. Narcissus struck at his own heart and body; attacking the picture, the madman attacks the image in its material existence. But a pictorial image is not like a shadow projected on the walls of a cave or the portrait of a face floating in the water. It is not a simple appearance transformed by rippling or by changes in perception. This image exists as a thing. It possesses all the qualities of a solid body: stability, opacity, and resistance. Its surface is impervious to either light or human gaze unless it has first been pierced by a fist or lacerated by the point of a knife. The image can blur or dissolve without the paint disappearing. Move too close and the eye can no longer distinguish the forms and contours. You no longer see the image, but you can still see the paint. In fact, you can see nothing else. Here it remains: an object of durable existence, a thing of insistent visibility regardless of any representation it may bear—like reality. This might indeed drive one to madness.

Narcissus died of despair when he found that his beloved was nothing more than a phantom invented by his own desire, when he realized that it was nothing more than an image: his own image. But perhaps he too would have been enraged if he had seen something else take the place of this evanescent image and fill the space left by its disappearance. If, instead of dissipating in the melancholy transparence of clear water, his desire had shattered against the opaque reality of a painting, how would he have reacted? Perhaps he would have sought to destroy not himself but the painting. Do the madmen who slash paintings really want to make off with the objects they see represented on the canvas? Perhaps they simply want to touch the image, the one and only object of their desire, to reassure themselves that it is real. And they discover that this image is "nothing more than a vapor breathed onto the canvas," as Diderot so wonderfully says about Chardin; nothing more than a "spume" that dissolves if one comes too close.[24] And where the image disappears, they find a picture: an "incomprehensible" thing, as Diderot also says, composed of "thick layers of color applied one over the next and whose effect transpires from the inside out."[25] They want to grasp an image and their desire runs into a wall, that "wall of paint" described by Balzac in *Le chef-d'oeuvre inconnu*. Some then commit irreparable acts. Bereft of an image whose secret the canvas so jealously preserves, they furiously belabor the painting.

Distinct in this respect from the madman, the lover of painting never confuses the image and the picture. The simulacra of objects represented on the canvas produce in him only a simulacrum of desire. Of course, he sometimes experiences a real desire to touch. But it is not the image that he wants to touch; it is the picture — not the false apple, the false grapes, the false bottle, but this veritable still life. Visual pleasure may even awake in the art lover a desire that, mad as it may be, is by no means the gesture of a madman: not to destroy but to decamp with the painting. Diderot makes no bones about admitting this desire. If he could become invisible to the spectators under whose gaze he and the paintings both find themselves, he would happily make off with certain canvases, spiriting them away to a place where he could enjoy them in secret, unseen by anyone. "How quickly I'd have them under my jacket if no one were looking," he says of two little Loutherbourg landscapes.[26] Seized by an urge to possess, he does not allow himself to perform this socially reprehensible act, but neither does he renounce his acquisitive impulse. He can make them his own and own the deed. This larceny is effected by description. If he cannot smuggle the painting out under his jacket, he can at least abscond with its image — not the image *in* but the image *of* the painting. And, in the intimacy of his study, having donned his famous dressing gown, sheltered from others' eyes, he can again give body to that image by re-creating it in words. Perhaps the art critic is ultimately no more than a failed or rather a repressed art thief. But he is in any case a most generous thief, one who passes his booty on to his friend so that the readers of Grimm's *Correspondance littéraire* can enjoy it in their turn: "I will describe the paintings for you and my description will be such that, with a little imagination and taste, we can realize them in space and arrange the objects more or less as we saw them in the canvas."[27]

It may be forbidden to steal the painting but the writer can nevertheless steal the art of the painter; he can become a painter himself in order to restore the image that has imprinted itself on his memory, inventing another picture, both similar and dissimilar since he paints it with his own hand, adding a touch here and there and perhaps even a whole section that he judges necessary for its completion. These corrective additions naturally comprise anything that can be "painted" only in words: first and foremost, words themselves, those that the author places in the mouths of the characters, but thoughts too, intentions, feelings, things that painting can express but never show. Above all the author can add temporality: the succession of events and their duration, which pictorial narration, forced to select a single instant, can never represent. As Correggio said, "Anch'io son pittor" (I too am a painter). And it is precisely in the *Salon de 1763,* where he confesses his desire to steal the two Loutherbourg paintings, that Diderot cites Correggio's famous remark. But here again he introduces that marker of distancing, the conditional tense:

If, to be an artist, one needed only have a vivid sense of the beauty of nature and art, bear a tender heart in one's breast, have been granted a soul that scuds before the merest breath, and have been born such that the sight or perusal of something beautiful is heady and transports and leaves one supremely happy, I should clasp you to me, I should throw my arms around the necks of Loutherbourg or Greuze and exclaim: My friends, "Son pittor anch'io."[28]

And if possession of these qualities were sufficient to make one a painter, Diderot could honestly claim that status. Alas, it does not. Other qualities are required. To be a painter, one must also be able to mix colors, handle a brush, and paint delicate brushstrokes. But if Diderot cannot paint pictures, he can make his descriptions so vivid to his readers that it is as if the paintings were before their very eyes. The author must therefore ask his readers to bestow on him the title he longs for. If he cannot say "Anch'io son pittor," he can persuade others to say of him: "Anche lei è pittor," he too is a painter.

"If you were thirsty, you would take the bottle by the neck," Diderot says about Chardin, and about Loutherbourg, "I should take the painting if no one were looking": two actions equally out of bounds for the lover of painting. He must not touch the image if he wants to go on looking at it, and he cannot touch the picture because he would be seen. He cannot take the bottle by the neck because there is no bottle to take, and he must not lay hands on the painting because hands would be laid on him. But, if we are to believe Diderot, the dream of these two forbidden gestures is inseparable from the desire to write. They are the secrets inscribed in the heart of visual pleasure.

The blind are unacquainted with this pleasure. For them, sight does not resemble touch. It is the other way round: touch is said to resemble sight. The lover of painting keeps his distance from both his desire and its object, touching what he sees without touching it. The madman is too close to both his desire and its object and cannot either touch what he sees or see what he touches. The blind man is midway between the two: he sees what he touches without seeing it, with the tips of his fingers. He sees with his hands and perceives with his skin.

It is well known that the eighteenth century developed a deep fascination with the blind and especially with those who had been deprived of sight from birth. Restoring sight to those born blind, the cataract operation fueled philosophical discussion about the relative importance of the innate and the acquired, the empirical origin of ideas, the relationship between reason and experience, and the differences between the various orders of sensation. Observation of the recently cured blind shed new light on Descartes's findings in his "Dioptrique" about the relations between sight and touch and confirmed his theory that "the blind see with their hands." The theoretical dialogue between the philosopher and the blind began with Descartes and continued throughout the eighteenth century, encountering a number of vicissitudes along the way. The most notable of these was no doubt Molyneux's blind man. In a letter to his friend Locke, Molyneux had asked him what would happen if a blind man who had learned to acquaint himself with objects by touch should recover his sight. Would he then be able to distinguish a globe from a cube without touching? Locke answered, as we know, in the negative. By including Molyneux's letter in the chapter about perception in the second edition of his *Essay Concerning Human Understanding,* he made "Molyneux's problem" famous and gave it an epistemological status that proved decisive for the whole of eighteenth-century thought.[29] Now it is interesting to note that the problem was set out immediately after an analysis of the way in which judgment modifies the information supplied by sensation and that this analysis ends with a reference to painting. The ideas that we receive via our senses, says Locke, are often altered by judgment without our being aware of the fact. When we look at a globe of uniform color, we do not see a convex form but a flat circular one, he says, before adding in conclusion, "as is evident in painting."[30] Thus painting is invoked to illustrate the gap between purely sensorial vision and perception, in which an act of judgment has always intervened. From the point of view of simple vision, a real globe is indeed no different from a painted globe. We see things not as they are in reality but as they are in painting; that is, flat. And it is here, after this reference to painting, that Molyneux's blind man is introduced into the second edition. We only see flat forms "as is evident in painting"[31] but the bodies that we see are in fact three-dimensional, as is evident to the blind man who knows them not by sight but by touch. Pictorial illusion is thus only a particular example of the rule that holds for vision in general. It tells us the truth about vision, namely that it invariably supplies us with a false and illusory image of reality. Leibniz introduced Molyneux's blind man in very similar fashion into his *Nouveaux essais sur l'entendement humain* (*New Essays on Human Understanding*), that is, after a reference to painting. Analyzing the mechanism of the pictorial illusion, Theophilus explains why we can be taken in by "a flat painting" and wrongly believe that what comes from an image is derived from a body. Philalethes then proposes that Theophilus should consider Molyneux's problem. Rejecting Locke's position, Leibniz answers in the affirmative. He claims that the newly cured blind man should be capable of identifying the cube and the globe simply by visual inspection and without touching them, as long as he knows that one of the two bodies is a cube and the other a globe. He merely has to use his reason, combined with the memories left by the sensations of touch:

> If there were not that way of discerning shapes, a blind man could not learn the rudiments of geometry by touch, nor could someone else learn them by sight without touch.

> However, we find that men born blind are capable of learning geometry, and indeed
> always have some rudiments of a natural geometry; and we find that geometry is mostly
> learned by sight alone without employing touch, as could and indeed *must* be done by a
> paralytic or by anyone else to whom touch is virtually denied. These two geometries, the
> blind man's and the paralytic's, must come together, and agree, and indeed ultimately rest
> on the same ideas, even though they have no images in common.[32]

Following the path whose logic thus leads us from sight to touch, we find ourselves confronted with a bizarre painting, which Salvador Dalí might have entitled *The Meeting of the Blind Man and the Paralytic on the Tabula Rasa of Analytic Dissection.* But no painter will ever represent this surrealistic encounter because it can take place only in the abstract universe of philosophical discourse. Though the blind man and the paralytic can have the "same ideas" they can have "no images in common," as Leibniz says. They can coincide in geometrical space but their minds can never meet in the space of the painting.[33] How could a person born blind discern the forms and figures on a picture?

Diderot takes up the subject of those born blind in his *Lettre sur les aveugles* (*Letter on the Blind*). But unlike Locke and Leibniz, he is immediately interested in its aesthetic implications. Speaking of Saunderson, a famous blind man, Diderot writes: "Saunderson's sight was in his skin; he had so exquisitely sensitive an epidermis that if a draughtsman had sketched a friend's portrait on his hand, he would undoubtedly—given a little practice—have recognized it. Feeling the succession of sensations made by the pencil, he would have declared: 'It's Mr. So & So.'"

Diderot concludes: "So there is such a thing as painting for the blind; their own skins would be the canvas."[34] The very abrupt concluding sentence evokes the strange image of a blind man's body transformed into a picture by a painter's hand. On Diderot's account, the painter wishing to paint for a blind man should paint forms directly on the blind man's body, using skin as his support, tracing contours in the swellings of muscle and the soft expanses of flesh. If the Shroud of Turin embodies the metaphysical ideal of a true image, that is, an image integral with its original, this notion of painting for the blind is the expression of a completely different dream, one that could have arisen only in the eighteenth century and in the mind of an art critic: the dream of an image integral with the body of the spectator. A person blind from birth could never say "anch'io son pittore," I too am a painter. But he could say "anch'io son pittura," I too am a painting. Here is one thing that neither Locke's nor Leibniz's blind man would ever have dreamed of saying.

Whatever the differences between our three blind men—those of Locke, Leibniz, and Diderot—they are all invested with the same theoretical function:

to help us understand what it means to see. This is no doubt why the arguments made about them in each case include a reference to painting, though each philosopher refers to it, as we have seen, in a very different fashion. There is a paradox here; painting is the only art that a blind person can never appreciate, still less practice, since it is an art made exclusively for the organs of sight.

But is it not more than a little strange, when one thinks about it, that the philosophers, and particularly the philosophers of the Enlightenment, should systematically have asked those who could not see or, better still, had never been able to see, to enlighten them about the mechanism of vision? Diderot takes this paradox a step further; he is suspicious of the witness of a blind man such as Molyneux's, that is, of a man formerly blind. Given the choice between a formerly blind man whose vision has been restored and a self-blinding philosopher, Diderot unhesitatingly opts for the latter: "I should have less confidence in the replies of a person seeing for the first time than in the discoveries of a philosopher who had long meditated on this subject in the dark; or, to adopt a poetic diction, who had plucked out his own eyes the more easily to discover how vision works."[35]

Pluck out your eyes to discover what vision is. Cease to see the better to know. Blind yourself the better to see. Is philosophical knowledge therefore a "blind thinking"? Or, at the very least, thought for the blind? Or should we define it as the thinking of men who aspire to blindness in order to construct a kingdom where philosophers might at last be kings? Since Plato, the language of knowledge has borrowed its most common metaphors from the lexis of vision. To know is to see: to see with a vision that goes beyond the visible, to see with the eyes not of the body but of the soul. But this "intuition," this intellectual vision metaphorically designating the process of true knowledge, is itself no more than a metaphor. And that metaphor conceals another, the metaphor of touch. Is understanding not always (first and foremost) a question of grasping? Is it not the philosopher's dream to come so close to the truth that he can seize it, to reduce the distance separating him from Being to the point where he can put out his hand and touch the concept and the truth? The eyes of the body always put some distance between themselves and their object, distancing themselves from it the better to relate to it. Those of the soul desire on the contrary to come as close as possible to their object, till they are one with it. What one calls true knowledge is in fact analogous to touching. It is conceived on the model of vision but the vision that is its model is that of those born blind, which is touch. Has it not been a commonplace since classical antiquity that one must be blind to philosophize well, close one's eyes in order not to be distracted in one's meditations, seek the obscure in order to finally experience the unadulterated pleasure of contact with truth? Is not thought like the owl of Minerva that wakes only with the waning of the day? Unless it is the very activity of thinking that inevitably brings darkness at the blaze of noon. As Diderot writes, "At midday in the street, for one who thinks deeply, it is night, deepest night."[36]

Midday: the hour of the shortest shadow, when objects are most brightly lit and reality is most clearly illuminated. For those who think "deeply," midday is always darkest midnight, because so-called profound thought is not interested in the things illuminated by the sun; it scorns bodies and despises images and reflections. Profound thought is interested not in the visible but in vision. It turns away from things to look only at the eye, like the lover in the engraving after Goltzius (see frontispiece), too fascinated by his mistress's eye to see his own image reflected in the mirror. It is not the visible but vision — the eye — that philosophical thought would like to put its finger on. And how can one touch an eye without blinding it or closing its lid, thus preventing it from seeing? To see with the mind and to see with the hands are fundamentally one and the same thing: in either case, seeing is touching rather than seeing. This is why, as Diderot tells his correspondent, the philosophers seeking to define vision naturally compare it to touch: "Madame, open Descartes's *Dioptrique* and there you will find the phenomena of vision related to those of touch and optical plates full of male figures busy seeing with poles. Descartes and all those who came after him have been unable to give us any clearer ideas about vision; and the great philosopher had in this respect no greater advantage over our blind fellow than do the common people, who also have eyes."[37]

On the path to enlightenment, says Diderot elsewhere, the philosopher advances "blindfold" and "steps gropingly forward."[38] The reincarnation of Oedipus or some new Tiresias, he makes his way with the aid of a stick: "For what was this Tiresias who had read the secrets of the gods and possessed the gift of predicting the future, unless a blind philosopher whose memory comes down to us through fable?"[39]

All philosophers aspire to the status of those born blind. Recounting how the *aveugle de Puiseaux,* a man blind from birth, expressed his notion of a mirror, Diderot adds: "Had Descartes been born blind, he would, I believe, have prided himself on such a definition."[40]

And this blind-from-birth Descartes would no doubt have found it much easier to solve the problem of the union of body and soul: "If ever a philosopher deaf and blind from birth makes a man on the pattern of Descartes's, I can assure you, Madame, that he will place the soul in the fingertips."[41]

Not content to have put the philosopher's eyes out, Diderot now has him born deaf too. He thus deprives him of the two senses that put the subject in contact with external reality but do not abolish the distance that separates him from it. In his twofold infirmity, the philosopher is abandoned to his own devices. Entirely autarchic, a mere bachelor apparatus, the monadic body of the philosopher now lacks any doors and windows. Diderot has definitively stopped up all the openings through which images and sounds, colors and noises might enter.

Everyone knows that silence and solitude are necessary for the work of thinking. Montaigne and Pascal have given beautiful expression to the fact that a mere nothing, the sound of a weathercock or the buzzing of a fly, is sufficient to distract us from the most profound meditations and prevent us from reasoning.[42] But how can we strain the imagination so far as to hypothesize not merely a deaf and blind philosopher but one born with these two conditions? Does not Diderot say, just two pages later, of those born deaf, dumb, and blind: "They grow but remain feebleminded"? If this is true, then his philosopher, assuming he could ever exist, would be the most unfortunate of men, sealed into his imbecility. True, he would still have fingers with which to touch. But how could this sense assist him if we maintain our unlikely hypothesis of his becoming a philosopher? Remember that our invalid is supposed to be a Cartesian, that is, someone for whom bodies are merely geometric and abstract figures, flexible and changeable realities known only through the mind's observations. Our philosopher, born blind and deaf, would not therefore be at all handicapped in his quest for truth if he were one-handed or paralytic as well. He would still have a mouth with which to eat and a nose with which to smell; he could still enjoy the taste of food (if anyone was good enough to put food in his mouth) and smell the scent of perfumes. But it is difficult to see what cognitive function could be fulfilled by the faculties of taste and smell. Too deeply immersed in the world of the physical, these two senses scarcely lend themselves to metaphorical use, the sole route by which sensation can attain the domain of truth. One can "see" an idea, "touch on" a theoretical difficulty, "hear out" a problem, but one never "scents" an argument and one rarely "tastes" a concept, unless one adopts a purely aesthetic position in relation to truth, that is, judges it simply according to taste—which simply means denying the existence of truth. An idea can raise a hubbub; it can have brilliance and even solidity but it can never have a smell or taste. The vision of the blind philosopher must therefore cast what light it can upon a world entirely lacking in sensible qualities. If the blind philosopher makes a man on the pattern of Descartes's, he will surely give him a merely vegetative soul.

But if every philosopher is in some way blind, the form of painting for the blind suggested by Diderot could equally be a painting for philosophers. With a little practice, he says, Saunderson would be able to identify a friend whose portrait was traced on his hand. Thus, with a little more practice, a blind man would be able to recognize, even love a drawing, and appreciate the rightness of an outline, the precision of a line. But how could he enjoy the place of light and shadow and the beauties of chiaroscuro, or take pleasure in the radiance of color?

In the *Essay Concerning Human Understanding*, Locke distinguishes simple ideas according to their provenance: some enter the mind through a single sense, others through several, others by reflection, and, in the last category, some enter by a mixture of both sensation and thought. And to illustrate the first category, Locke naturally gives the example of the ideas of light and color, which can enter only through the faculty of sight.[43] A person born blind could therefore learn to draw, but, as Diderot observes, he could never learn to use color, having no "memory of anything but sensations captured through touch."[44]

If one asked a blind man to give a ruling in the debate about line and color, he would indisputably rule against the Rubenists and in favor of the Poussinists, that is, the partisans of line. And the idea that drawing pertains to touch was one that Diderot surely borrowed from de Piles, who deduced from it consequences that could not help but interest the author of the *Lettre sur les aveugles*. De Piles's argument for assigning line to sculpture rather than painting was based, we have seen, on the relation he discerned between drawing and touch. And he naturally concluded from this that, unlike painting, sculpture was compatible with blindness. One could sculpt in the dark. One could reproduce contour, mass, texture, and volume without seeing them. All one had to do was follow the forms with one's fingers, feeling the hollows and projections with one's hand, like the blind sculptor who claimed to have "eyes in his fingertips." De Piles reports this man's observations at some length: "I feel my original, examine its dimensions, convexities, and cavities, and try to keep them in my head. Then I begin working with the wax and by comparing the one and the other, placing a hand now here, now there, I finish the work as best I can."[45] Which is the conclusion Diderot reaches after telling us Saunderson's story: "And so we see that a blind people could have its sculptors" (pls. 2–8).[46]

But if we follow Diderot's logic, this first conclusion brings a second in its wake. If every philosopher is in some sense blind, what goes for the blind must go for philosophers. A people of philosophers could therefore have its sculptors too. Unlike the god of theologians, who often takes on the aspect of *Deus pictor*, the god of philosophers is generally a sculptor-god. The *Lettre sur les aveugles* could, in this light, be read as a little treatise on sculpture or more precisely on the relationship between sculpture and philosophy, a new version of the *paragone* describing the close links between the methods of the sculptor and the procedures of philosophy.

This was certainly the perspective in which Herder read it. His analysis of sculpture follows a direct line of descent from Diderot's *Lettre sur les aveugles,* on which he draws extensively.[47] One might say that Herder confines himself to drawing all the aesthetic consequences of Diderot's arguments, which he explicitly accepts. The difference between them, as we shall see, is that Herder welcomed them gladly. His *Plastik* (*Sculpture*) is indeed a philosophical homage to sculpture; he establishes it as the philosophical art. Taking a new line on the *paragone*, Herder develops a completely new comparison between painting and sculpture, founded on exclusively philosophical criteria. It consists of placing each of the two arts at opposite ends of the scale of truth and contrasting them on the basis of their respective truth-values. Whereas painting is, he says, only "depiction, *imagination, representation*"[48]—in other words, mere imagination and dream—"sculpture is *truth*."[49] This distinction between painting and sculpture derives from a purely speculative move by Herder. It cannot be thought to conclude the debate about the *paragone* begun in the Renaissance. *Plastik* is not the work of an art historian or art theorist or even an art lover. Still less is it the work of a connoisseur. It is the work of a philosopher. Its author is a complete stranger to the world of art and his artistic references are those supplied by the literature. Herder knows Falconet's *Réflexions sur la sculpture* and Hogarth's theory of the serpentine line but his principal sources are Lessing and Winckelmann. Inspired by the analysis of the *Laokoon*,[50] Herder wishes to distinguish between painting and sculpture in the same way that Lessing had distinguished literature from the visual arts. Herder's book therefore represents the first systematic effort to apply to the visual arts the idea of a frontier developed by Lessing in relation to *ut pictura poesis*.[51] But Lessing had defined this frontier in terms of the limits imposed by the very nature of the two kinds of representation. He had founded it on what might be called objective properties inherent in artistic forms, that is, whether they pertain to the arts of time or space. Herder took a further—a philosophical—step by seeking the origin of those borders in the subject of the spectator. He is not greatly concerned to examine differences of the objective kind between painting and sculpture. Rather, he wishes to determine what he calls the "subjective boundary stone."[52] This is defined as the difference between vision and touch: "sight gives us *dreams,* touch gives us *truth*."[53] In this sense, *Plastik* is a reflection on touch rather than sculpture. Returning to the questions Diderot had raised about persons born blind, Herder develops his arguments about the haptic sense and its cognitive function on an unprecedented scale. His analysis rests on an argument identical to the one used by Locke and Leibniz about Molyneux's problem, that is, that vision, unlike touch, only ever gives us a false and illusory idea about reality because it reduces bodies to surfaces. Without the contribution of touch, says Herder, sight affords us "only a panel of light and color, and thus only the flattest and emptiest pleasure."[54] Only touch, he says, allows us to know bodies in their substantial reality: their corporeal nature. Those born blind have a signal advantage relative to those who can see, an advantage already noted by Diderot, that they are never distracted from their thoughts and can, as it were, touch truth directly with their fingers: "A blind person who uses his sense of touch to explore the world around him is free of distractions and is able to develop concepts of the properties of bodies that are far more complete than those acquired by the sighted, who must glide across on a beam of light."[55]

If, to become a philosopher, one had to choose between two infirmities, touch without sight or sight without touch, Herder would not hesitate: one should choose the first. The soul's activity is, he says, "a form of *touching* that feels in the dark,"[56] that is, a touching without seeing. To add to our curious gallery of portraits born of the philosophical imagination, which already features the blind, the deaf, the dumb, and the paralytic, Herder produces the strange new figure of the man who can do nothing but see. This hypothetical figure has innumerable eyes with which to see but no hands with which to touch: "An ophthalmite with a thousand eyes but without a hand to touch would remain his entire life in Plato's cave and would never have any concept of the properties of a physical body."[57]

Now it is clear why painting is a dream and sculpture the truth. In sculpture, "everything is to the highest degree *substantial, true* and *determinate*."[58] Weighed on the scales of concept and truth, the activity of the sculptor and even the blind sculptor (above all the blind sculptor) is infinitely superior to that of the most talented painter: "A blind sculptor, even a sculptor who was born blind, would make a wretched painter. But in sculpture he is not at any disadvantage and would probably even surpass a sighted peer."[59]

Sculpture is clearly an art for philosophers, who can appreciate it without leaving the shadowy inner world in which they constantly find themselves. This is something that they cannot do with painting. "Holy night, mother of gods and men, come over us," Herder writes.[60]

The philosophers' praise of sculpture is peculiar, and it is not clear that the sculptor's art has much to gain by it. This philosophical paean is in fact nothing other than a hymn to the night (pls. 9, 10).

Stone and Flesh

The gaze without pupils, the unreflecting mirror of things.
— Maurice Merleau-Ponty[61]

In the *Salon de 1763,* the section devoted to sculptural works is prefaced by a sentence in which Diderot, with superlative cheek, warns his readers: "Long as I have been on the painters, with the sculptors I shall be short."[62]

He was no less brief in the *Salon de 1765,* concluding his description of the sculpture with a few words addressed to Grimm: "Thus you are delivered from the sculptures and so am I. You see, my friend, how a hundred works of sculpture can be dismissed with less effort than five or six pictures."[63]

The brevity of the description in the *Salon de 1765* contrasts with the length of the text that introduces it, in which Diderot sets out in great detail his ideas about sculpture. If he is short with the sculptors, he is much more expansive concerning the reasons why sculpture induces such brevity. He admits from the outset that for the most part he finds it difficult to judge the qualities of a sculpted figure. He has confidence in his taste when it comes to judging pictures but none when it comes to sculpture. Faced with a statue, he often prefers to rely on the artist's judgment. "There is scarcely a single art-lover who can distinguish a very beautiful thing in sculpture from something commonplace.... I should dare to buy a picture on the basis of my own taste and judgment; for a statue, I'd take the artist's advice."[64]

The need to have recourse to someone else's opinion testifies, in his view, to the limitations of sculpture rather than those of his own judgment or taste. Should taste not be enough for the art lover? Surely he should be able to judge a work without recourse to other criteria, such as the expertise of the connoisseur or the technical competence of the artist. "Judging is one thing and making is another."[65] Diderot gives several reasons why his judgment about sculpture is less than certain. The first and, no doubt, most important is that the art of the sculptor seems to him infinitely less magical than that of the painter. The latter must, for every new picture, contrive new methods of making something out of nothing:

> Here is the block of marble; within it is the figure that must be extracted. Here is the canvas, it is flat, this is the surface on which you must create; the image must emerge, press forward, stand out, so that I can move around it, if not I then my eye; it must come alive.... The sculptor who can draw and has expression and facility with the chisel has everything; with these, he can set about making a nude and succeed. Painting requires more again.... Sculpture is made for the blind and those who see; painting is destined for the eye alone. But sculpture undoubtedly has fewer objects and subjects than painting. One can paint what one wants. Sculpture—severe, grave, and chaste—must choose. It sometimes plays around the sides of an urn or vase, even in the grandest and most moving compositions; in bas-reliefs one sees children frolicking on the sides of a basin soon to receive human blood; but even in playful mode, sculpture retains a sort of dignity and is serious even when it jests.... It cannot abide the clownish, burlesques, or the jocular. It finds even the comical unbearable for the most part. No laughter in marble. In the sensual it retains a mysterious studied quality, something rare and exquisite telling me that its work is long, laborious, and refractory. You can take up the paintbrush and place on canvas a frivolous idea created in an instant and effaced in a breath. Not so with the chisel. Investing the artist's thought in a hard, recalcitrant, everlasting material, it must perforce

make a choice original and extraordinary. The pencil is more libertine than the brush and the brush than the chisel.…Sculpture cannot abide mediocre technique or a commonplace idea. A slight failure of line—beneath notice in a painting—is unpardonable in a statue. But this only goes to show that, if there is less for sculpture to do, one more strictly requires one's due of it.[66]

In this new version of the *paragone,* the same idea returns under a multitude of guises: sculpture is much more remote from nature and truth than painting because it cannot hope to seize the accidental, the instantaneous; it cannot express the ephemeral, the fleeting, or the random. In short, it cannot represent those imperceptible moments and evanescent impressions that are the very movement of life. That, says Diderot, is why a statue is more difficult to judge than a painting: "Painting reminds me in a hundred different ways of what I have seen; not so sculpture."[67]

To judge a painting, he tells us, we need no more than the eyes nature has bestowed upon us. But how can they help us judge a figure of stone—an object whose weighty, cold immobility is so much at odds with the fragile qualities of the perceived world and with the fundamentally unstable nature of our perceptions? What sculptor could ever represent the way in which emotion finds expression in a face? It is a difficult enough task for the painters: "What torture for them in the face of a man, this fabric in constant movement, which changes, relaxes, colors, and fades according to the infinite multitude of alternations in that veering featherweight thing we call the soul."[68]

Critical of his portrait by van Loo, Diderot expands on this theme:

Over the course of a single day I had a hundred different physiognomies that varied as things affected me. I was serene, sad, dreamy, tender, violent, passionate, or enthusiastic. But I was never as you see me there.…I have a mask that deceives the artist; perhaps because too many things are blended together; perhaps the impressions of the soul form so rapid a succession, with each in turn depicted on my face, that the eye of the painter finds me never the same from one moment to the next. So his task becomes much more difficult than he thought.[69]

Few painters have captured those impalpable nuances reflecting the fleeting states of the soul: the barely visible furrowing of the forehead, the imperceptible blush of a cheek, the tiny trembling of the nostrils or at the corner of the lips. Fewer still can render the infinite delicacy of skin tone, giving us to feel the blood pulsing beneath the skin as it imparts a color so subtle that the colors of the palette seem impotent to create it. You have to be a great colorist to convey what Diderot calls "the feeling of flesh" like Chardin, who "makes flesh whenever he chooses."[70] Lagrenée, about whom Diderot is not always very kind, manages it in certain of his figures, such as Hersé and Mercury: "Oh beautiful flesh, beautiful feet, handsome arms, fine hands, beautiful skin; the life and tones of the blood transpire; beneath this delicate, sensitive covering I follow the imperceptible blue-tinged course of the veins and arteries.... The flesh of art rivals that of nature."[71]

For Diderot, representing human flesh is certainly the greatest challenge nature has ever thrown down before art. This is why sculpture is, in his eyes, so much less capable of likeness than painting: "The material it uses is so cold, so refractory, so impenetrable; above all, the principal difficulty with its imitation lies in the secret of softening this cold, hard material in order to make soft, sweet flesh of it."[72]

Diderot's entire aesthetic rests on the imitation of nature. But his conception of mimesis is rather different from that which prevails in the classical tradition and which can still be found in most of the art theorists of the eighteenth century. For Diderot, a true imitation of nature does not just mean imitating the wealth and diversity of the visible world; it does not at all mean imitating the beauty of an ideal nature; it means capturing the movement that brings nature alive and constitutes its principle—imitating nature as a living process, as *natura naturans* and not *natura naturata*.[73] That is when art truly rivals nature and the artist becomes the equal of the gods. This conception of the ideal of artistic mimesis does not overthrow the traditional hierarchy of the arts. In respect to the *paragone* or *ut pictura poesis,* Diderot's position is barely distinguishable from the tradition prevailing in art theory since the Renaissance. But while the hierarchy of the arts remains the same, it rests on a different notion of imitation. The relative position of each art is decided on the basis of its capacity to imitate the movement and rhythm of nature through its own means. For Diderot, painting is superior to sculpture and, in the last analysis (whatever he says or implies), literature is superior to painting. And the superiority of either derives from a mimetic ideal whose criterion is not nature as a repertory of forms but nature as a mechanism of transformation.

Yet Diderot is not wholly indifferent to sculpture. Certain of his descriptions of sculpture express feelings as exalted as those inspired in him by the paintings of Vernet or Chardin. But this enthusiasm does not affect his system of evaluation, which is surprisingly constant. The criteria he brings to bear on sculpture are invariably pictorial. This is true even when he praises sculpture. The rhetoric is the same: he eulogizes the artist for giving marble the appearance of flesh. Thus, in the *Salon de 1763,* he describes Falconet's *Pygmalion and Galatea* (fig. 8):

How soft the flesh! No, it cannot be marble. Put a finger on it; the hardness of the material is gone, it will give beneath your touch.... One knee on the ground, the other raised, his

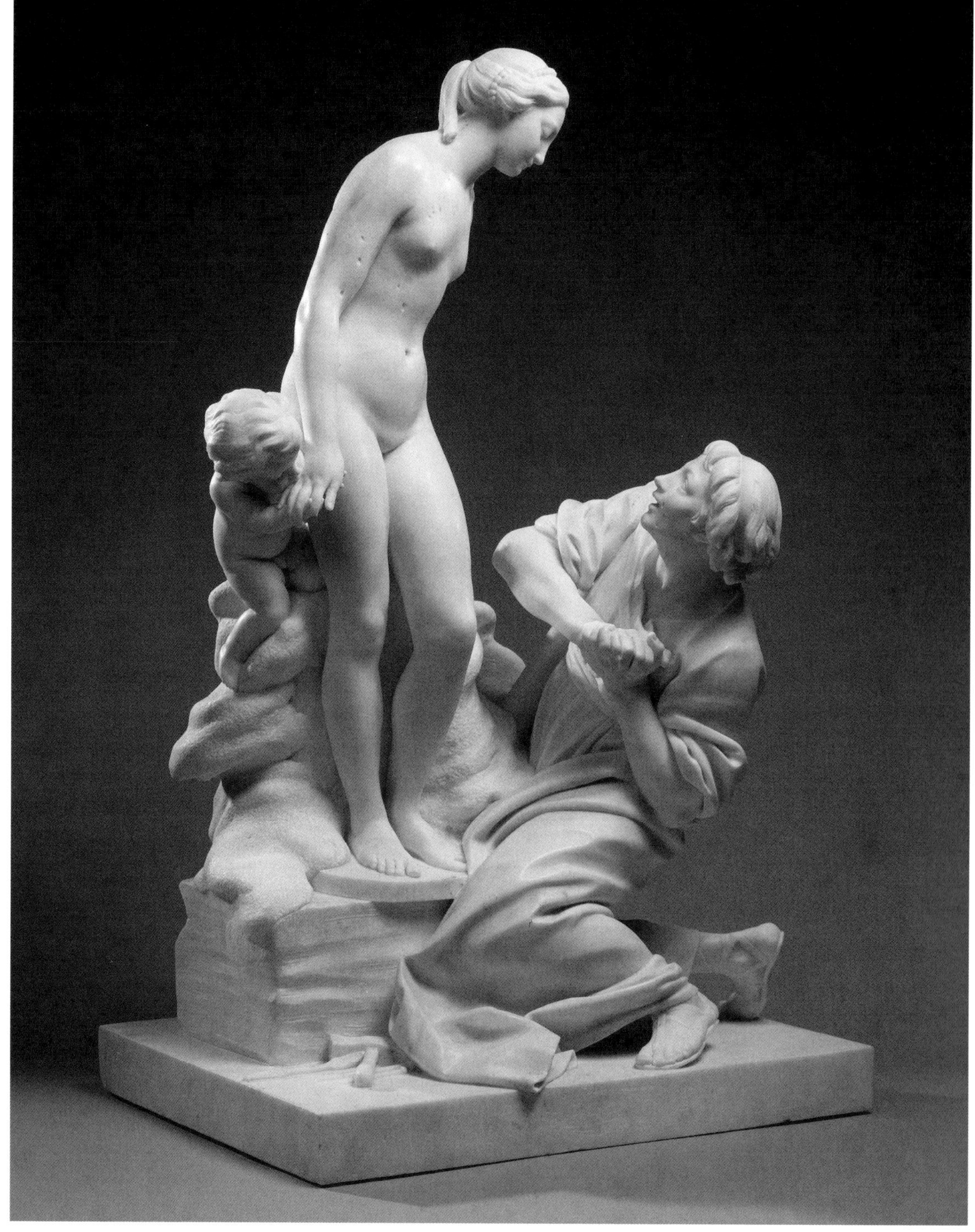

Fig. 8. Etienne-Maurice Falconet (French, 1716–91)
Pygmalion and Galatea, 1761, marble, 83.5 × 48.2 × 26.1 cm (32⅞ × 19 × 10¼ in.)
Paris, Musée du Louvre

hands clasped firmly together, Pygmalion gazes up at his creation....Oh, Falconet, how did you do it? In a single piece of white stone, surprise, joy, and love are blended together. Rival of the gods! They may have brought the statue to life, but you have renewed the miracle and done the same for its sculptor.[74]

Diderot in his turn reproduces this miracle by the power of a description that brings to life both the statue and the statuary's art. Nature, art, and myth are stirred together in vertiginous fashion; the reader becomes the last link in the uninterrupted chain by which the successive artists have transmitted the miracle. Now the reader, too, can bring it alive in his turn. Falconet has renewed the miraculous transformation of stone into flesh; the effect of Pygmalion's kisses is rehearsed by the statue beneath Diderot's astonished gaze. The miracle is transmitted a first and then a second time through artistic creation, finally bearing fruit in the pleasure of the aesthetic experience. And to help us grasp this miracle, to help us, as it were, reach out a hand and touch it, the author asks the reader to repeat the gesture made by the sculptor-lover and to take Pygmalion's place: "Put a finger on it; the hardness of the material is gone, it will give beneath your touch." But this too is a fictive gesture, like those one might wish to make at the sight of an apple or a pâté painted by Chardin. The spectator can no more caress Galatea than he can grasp the bottles or the grapes. The imperative here is a marvelous rhetorical device whose purpose is to bring about the desire for the act rather than the act itself.

The metamorphosis performed upon Galatea by the spectator's eye is precisely the substitution of painting for sculpture: no, it is not marble, it is flesh. Falconet is a great sculptor because he possesses the magical power attributed by Molière to Mignard or by de Piles to Rubens: beneath our very eyes he makes dead things live and gives stone the appearance of flesh. Such then is, for Diderot, the meaning of Ovid's story. The myth of Pygmalion recounts not only the metamorphosis of love but that of the arts: the transformation of sculpture into painting. And is Cupid not of all the gods the one best able to soften a heart of stone, transforming stone into flesh? He too is a painter.

Falconet is a great sculptor because his work makes one forget sculpture and think of painting. He too is a painter. As is Houdon, especially in his statue of the maréchal de Tourville, of which Diderot observes: "This figure has movement; the chosen moment is sublime; this is not sculpture, it is painting; it is a fine van Dyck" (fig. 9).[75]

Clearly, Diderot sometimes likes sculpture. He likes it when it gives the illusion of flesh and movement, that is, when it produces an effect like those of a colorist painting.

Now, in the eyes of his contemporaries, the art of rendering flesh is precisely

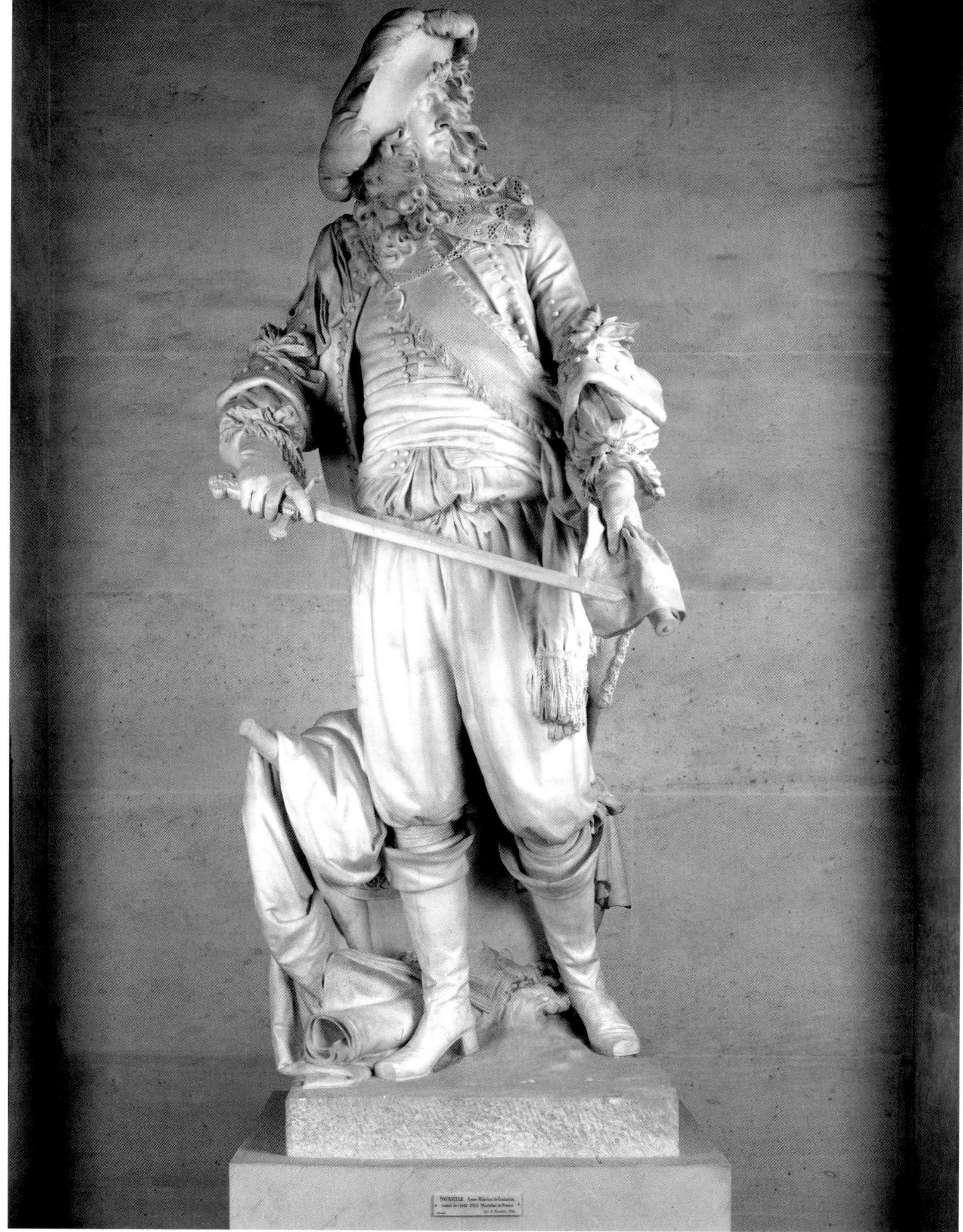

Fig. 9. Jean-Antoine Houdon (French, 1748–1828)
Anne-Hilarion de Costentin, comte de Tourville, maréchal de France, 1781,
marble, height: 223 cm (87¾ in.)
Versailles, Châteaux de Versailles et du Trianon

what constitutes the originality of modern sculpture and its superiority over that of the ancients. As Falconet writes about Puget, this aspect of sculpture was neglected by the Greek artists but has "been brought in our own day to a higher degree of perfection. In what Greek sculpture do we find the impression of skin, of the softness of the flesh and the fluidity of the blood, so excellently rendered as in the works of this celebrated modern sculptor?" (figs. 10, 11).[76]

The distinction between line and color, which for de Piles defined the difference between sculpture and painting, now establishes a frontier within the sculptural art between the art of the moderns and that of the ancients. The transfer of this distinction bears witness to a change in taste pinpointed by Charles-Antoine Jombert: "The taste that distinguishes modern sculptures from those of the Greeks is…analogous to those creatures whose greatest charm is their plumpness. Today, this taste—or, to call it by its veritable name, this seductive manner of treating the art—is to sculpture what color is to painting."[77]

Reference to plumpness (*embonpoint*) cannot help but evoke the ripe flesh of Rubens's women. De Piles could hardly have dreamed of so complete a triumph: by the eighteenth century, even the sculptors have become Rubenists. The softness (*morbidezza*) so much admired by the Italians in Titian, the soft flesh that dazzled de Piles in paintings by Rubens, is now celebrated in sculpture too. When Dézallier d'Argenville describes a work by Puget, he does so in a vocabulary borrowed lock, stock, and barrel from the traditional rhetoric of the colorists: "He gave life to marble and made it tender; the hardest stones grew soft beneath his chisel, receiving the flexibility that so beautifully characterizes flesh and can be sensed even through drapery."[78]

In this respect, Diderot's taste is perfectly at one with that of his time. Like many of his contemporaries, he seeks in sculpture the imitation of flesh, truth, and nature: precisely what constitutes the beauty and perfection of painting. He likes sculpture when he finds in it what he likes in painting. But that does not mean, in his eyes, that the sculptor should take up the painter's methods, for example, by using color. Sculpture should not imitate painting but painting's effects, while remaining, as Falconet puts it, within its "prescribed bounds," that is, it should never try to abolish the difference between it and painting. Besides, even if it wanted to, it could not. Stone cannot be made to resemble flesh simply by adding color. Sculpture is not painting. In sculpture, color loses its properties and cannot produce coloristic effects: "What would painting's truest and most beautiful colors be like on a statue? The effect would be bad, I think.…The true alongside the fake makes a repellent contrast and the truth of color could never match the truth of the thing. The thing is the statue: alone, isolated, solid, and poised to move. It's like Roslin's beautiful zigzag embroidery on wooden hands, his beautiful, truthful satin on a mannequin."[79]

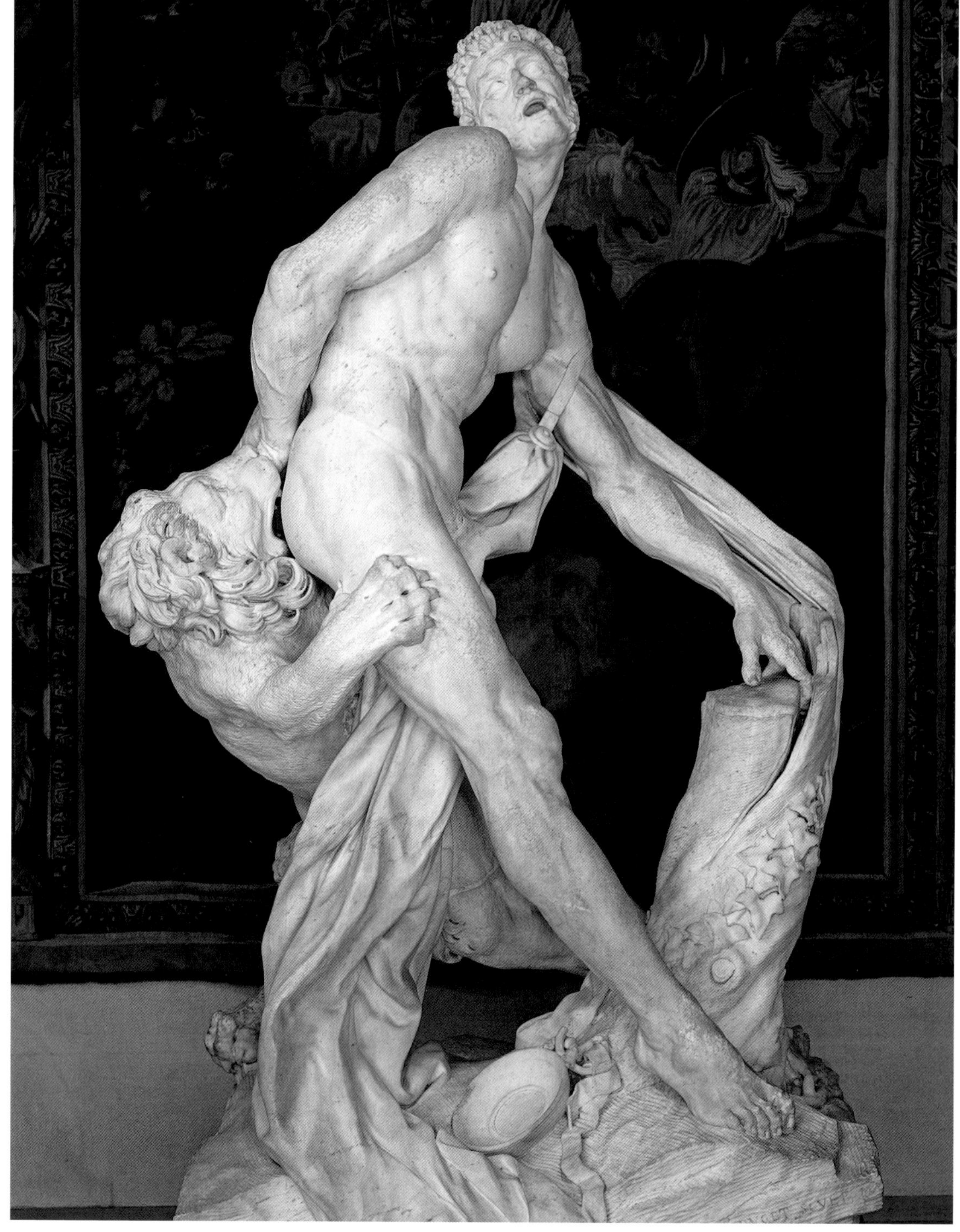

Fig. 10. **Pierre Puget (French, 1620–94)**
Milon of Croton, 1682, marble, 270 × 140 cm (106¼ × 55⅛ in.)
Paris, Musée du Louvre

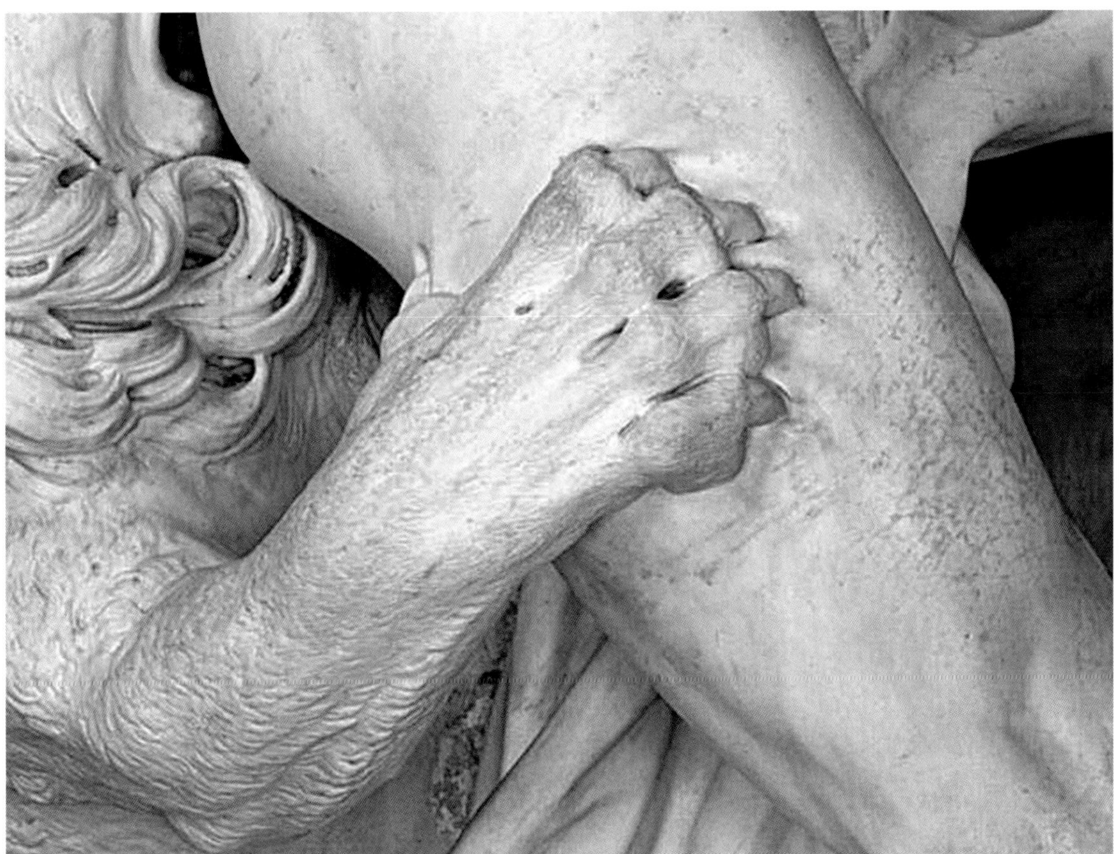

On this point, Falconet's view is slightly less trenchant than that of his friend Diderot. Falconet also condemns color in sculptures but admits that it can produce interesting effects if well used and harmoniously distributed. Sadly, these conditions are not often met:

True, certain very able sculptors have enlisted the aid of color, a recourse much exploited in painting. Rome and Paris can both supply examples. No doubt materials of varied colors could, if intelligently used, produce picturesque effects. Inharmoniously distributed, however, such collocations render sculpture disagreeable and even shocking. The brilliance of gilding and the brusque contrast between the discordant colors of different marbles will dazzle the eye of the people, who always bow before the flashy and the meretricious. But a man of taste will be disgusted.[80]

    THE ARTIST-PAINTER AND THE PHILOSOPHER-SCULPTOR

The fact is that Falconet is a sculptor and Diderot a critic. Falconet speaks of art as an artist unwilling a priori to exclude experiment. And he is principally anxious to avoid the risk run at this time by any argument against color, that of seeming to defend the antique model. So while he rejects the use of color in sculpture as repugnant to taste, he also manifests a degree of indulgence for what he considers an innovation introduced by the moderns and particularly by the Italians, who did not hesitate to use colored marble.[81] Whatever his reservations, he feels he must defend the superiority of the moderns over the ancients and therefore not condemn a practice favored by the Italians.[82] The more absolute position held by Diderot is in that respect more difficult to justify and holds certain rhetorical dangers for someone who praises modern artists.

The idea that color is at odds with the essential nature of sculpture is one that Diderot shares with the partisans of ideal beauty. Following Winckelmann, they were working out a new definition of art based on the study of ancient sculpture. By taking classical Greek statuary as the most pure and accomplished expression of beauty, Winckelmann's theory prepared the ground for a return of the primacy of line. It was then thought that Greek statues had always been as they are now, that is, devoid of color. The polychrome statues known at the time were generally rejected as the "invention of tasteless priests" and "a custom practiced only during the barbarian epochs of antiquity."[83] The belief that ideal beauty excluded color and derived essentially from line was therefore founded on an inaccurate vision of ancient art. This mistaken image of Greek sculpture came to justify a certain conception of art, of which it was at once the model and the illustration. Through a historical error, the alliance between beauty and line, questioned by Italian and subsequently by French colorists, was again forming around sculpture. The alliance took place under the auspices of German thought, which, in these new forms, resumed the ancestral combat between stone and flesh. Dislodged from its hegemonic position by de Piles, line was to enjoy a second coming. The aesthetic that brought this about served a particular metaphysics of art and showed a clear preference for sculpture.

Diderot had read Winckelmann, and the little treatise on sculpture in the *Salon de 1765* cited above was directly inspired by his views.[84] But though he took over most of Winckelmann's definition of sculpture, he drew radically different aesthetic conclusions. All the reasons put forward by Winckelmann for the superiority of sculpture became in Diderot's hands arguments further demonstrating the superiority of painting. Far from disputing the analysis of Winckelmann and other self-proclaimed admirers of ideal beauty, Diderot drew on it to justify aesthetic conclusions that led in the opposite direction. Indeed, Diderot's arguments stand at the head of a current of opinion that was to prove exceedingly influential in the nineteenth century. The reasons put forward by the partisans of ideal beauty in an effort to demonstrate the superiority of sculpture seemed to Diderot proof of its limitations. In the *Salon de 1765* he performed a tour de force, rejecting the Winckelmannian aesthetic without ever contesting the definition of sculpture on which it rested. Like Winckelmann, Diderot thought that "sculptors are more attached to the antique than painters." He willingly concedes that sculpture is "severe, grave, and chaste . . . serious even when it jests" and that it requires "a more stubborn and profound enthusiasm." He further admits that sculpture, unlike painting, which can allow a certain facility, "cannot abide a commonplace idea" or "mediocre execution." And though "chaste sculpture . . . shows the nudity of the sexes more often and more frankly" than painting, this is no doubt because "its mores, more primitive and innocent morals than those of painting, are also better, and because it thinks less of the present moment than of times to come."[85] Yes, all this is true. But precisely these qualities — severity, chastity, nudity, innocence, and eternity — are philosophical rather than aesthetic qualities. They are moral virtues related to the laws of nature rather than to the criteria of representation. They answer the requirements and purposes of reason and truth rather than those of art.[86]

We see, then, that Diderot does not for a moment contemplate undoing the link established by Winckelmann between sculpture and the expression of an ideal. For him, too, sculpture aspires to the universal and timeless in both its forms and materials. Here we remember that durability had been one of the reasons invoked by certain Italian artists in favor of sculpture. Unlike painting, they said, sculpture resisted the depredations of time. Those who defended the superiority of painting had, of course, contested the legitimacy of this argument. They claimed that this property belonged to neither art nor artist; it was to the credit not of sculpture but of the material from which sculpture was made. Diderot's originality consists in considering the properties of the material itself as an element essential to the definition of the art. Unlike Lessing, who established major distinctions on the basis of a purely representational criterion — deducing the specificity of each art from the limits of representation, making poetry an art of time and painting an art of space — Diderot distinguishes sculpture from painting by taking account of what Greenberg would, two centuries later, call the limits imposed by the nature of the medium.[87] Diderot does not speak, as Hegel was to do, of a perfect equation between material form and representative content. But we cannot help but be struck by the correspondences that Diderot consistently establishes between the nature of the material used in each of the two arts and the nature of the representations that they are able to create. In the delicacy of color, the rapidity of the brushstroke, Diderot recognizes the qualities that he also attributes to living nature and that make of it not merely an object to be painted but an object for painting as such. In his view, only painting can adequately represent nature, rendering its fragility, movement, and sensuality and, in short, imitating it in all its truth. Sculpture, on the other hand, belongs to a different system of analogies. How could life take root in the cold solidity of marble or stone? He is quite explicit about this in the *Salon de 1765:* "I believe that it is after all less capable of likeness than painting. The material that it uses is so cold, refractory, and impenetrable."[88]

The materials of sculpture require suitable content, a content that has the same qualities of permanence and stability. Ideals or great principles might afford precisely this. They are objects to be sculpted not painted. Painting favors ephemeral realities; its light, color-laden strokes are made to seize the instant or represent the accidental. Sculpture creates a grave and solemn universe in which forms exist as substances: permanent, unchangeable, and immune to the depredations of time. As Diderot puts it in the *Salon de 1765,* the chisel is undeniably less libertine than the paintbrush: "No laughter in marble."[89]

Yes, sculpture and duration are close kin. But this is precisely why Diderot refuses to see sculpture as the highest form of visual art. It is the expression of a metaphysical dream of beauty and belongs to the philosophical universe of thought. And it shows this by an absence of color, by the whiteness and pure nudity of its forms. The exemplary anti-cosmetic art by its very nature, sculpture in Winckelmann's definition (and therefore in Diderot's too) perfectly accords with the Platonic definition of art. It embodies the Platonic idea of art, that is, in the terms of the *Gorgias,* of a beauty that rests not on the mendacious artifice of cosmetics but on the proportions proper to a body shaped by gymnastic exercise. But this idea of art and beauty is profoundly alien to Diderot's artistic ideal. His colorist aesthetic necessarily implies the triumph of painting.

We find confirmation of this in what he says about sculpture in his more specifically philosophical writings. Inferior to painting in his system of the fine arts, sculpture nevertheless plays an essential role in his theory of knowledge. It is, indeed, his favorite metaphor for the analytic methods by which knowledge is attained. We cannot be surprised by this when we know that touch, as he wrote in his *Lettre sur les sourds et muets* (*Letter on the Deaf and Dumb*), is "the most profound and philosophical sense."[90]

Since classical antiquity, philosophy has often borrowed the vocabulary of sculpture to describe the dynamic aspect of cognitive activity. Thus Plato frequently uses verbs such as *mold* and *fashion* to refer to the education of the body and indeed of the soul. No less familiar is the model of the statuary in Aristotle, who illustrates his theory of the four causes with the example of the sculptor.[91] But it is of course in the eighteenth century that this metaphor becomes widespread in philosophical discourse. Buffon was the first to imagine a statue when describing the awakening and progress of man. The image was picked up again a few years later by Condillac.[92] Under the heading "Encyclopédie" in his *Encyclopédie,* Diderot compares his project for a universal, analytic dictionary of human knowledge to a colossal statue. This metaphor, often found in Diderot's works, is therefore in itself somewhat banal, especially in the eighteenth century. His originality consists in expanding it and inscribing it into an analysis whose coherence is, despite its apparent contradictions, remarkable. The *Discours sur la poésie dramatique* offers a particularly striking example. Toward the end of the *Discours,* Diderot himself enters the scene in the guise of a character named Ariste, whom he portrays thus: "He had been dubbed 'the philosopher' because, born without ambition, he had an honest soul whose gentleness and peacefulness had never been eroded by envy. He was, besides, grave of manner, severe in his style of life, and austere and simple in his speech. He lacked nothing of the ancient philosopher but his cloak, for he was poor and content to be so."[93]

Grave, austere, simple, and impoverished, this philosopher has all the qualities that Diderot elsewhere ascribes to sculpture. We should not, therefore, be surprised if he talks like a sculptor:

> I see at once that, since the ideal man that I seek is a composite like me, the ancient sculptors, by settling on the proportions that they thought most beautiful, have already made a part of my model.... Yes. Let us take a statue and bring it to life.... But this ideal general model is impossible to make unless the gods lend me their intelligence and promise me their eternity.... But why...should I too not imitate the sculptors? They made a model suitable to their condition, and I have mine.... Here are the observations, which, multiplied without end, train the statuary and teach him to change, strengthen, weaken, deface, and reduce his ideal model from the state of nature to any state he likes.[94]

Echoing this portrait of the philosopher-sculptor comes a matching portrait of his friend Falconet, the sculptor-philosopher: "He is boorish and polite, affable and brusque, tender and harsh;...he kneads clay and marble and reads and meditates; he is gentle and caustic, serious and jocular; he is a philosopher, believes in nothing, and knows why."[95]

Every property of the sculptor's activity can, it seems, serve as a paradigm of reason. Like sculpture, reason molds and shapes a reality to which it seeks to give a solid and permanent form. And it works in the same way: it reduces, removes, and eliminates, cutting away everything that is superfluous. It will be remembered that the artists of the Renaissance distinguished between the arts on the basis of their proceeding, like sculpture, through the removal of matter, *per via di levare* or, like painting, by its addition, *per via di porre.* Analytic reason undoubtedly proceeds like sculpture, *per via di levare.* This perhaps explains the privileged status sculpture clearly enjoys in philosophical minds.[96] Moreover, reason too has no need of light; it is its own light and can, like the sculptor, go about its work in the dark. "A statue," says Herder, "does not have its own light: it exists constantly in light."[97] Painting, by contrast, constantly needs light because it is "destined for the eye alone," as Diderot so often says.

And this difference between sculpture and painting is plainly manifested in sculpture. Sculpture foregrounds it. The way in which it represents the eye clearly shows that sculpture cannot represent the gaze. Philostratus the elder had already observed that sculpture is incapable of "registering the brilliance of the eyes."[98] For Diderot, sculpture—that art for the blind—cannot ever produce what one might call the impression of a glance: "Excavate the orbit of the eyes and fill them with enamel or colored stone, then see how you like it. You can see from the majority of their busts that they preferred to leave the globe even and solid rather than tracing in the iris and marking out the pupil. They had rather one imagined the sitter blind than show a punctured eye."[99]

Though Diderot's observations here refer exclusively to antique sculpture, they raise a question that directly concerned modern sculpture. Unlike most ancient sculptors, who preferred to leave "the globe even and solid," many modern artists—including some of the most illustrious—often preferred to mark the iris and hollow out the pupil.[100] Is it better to hollow out the eye or leave it smooth (figs. 12–19)? The question was extensively debated during the eighteenth century.[101] The anonymous author of *Lettre sur la peinture* approves of hollowing out the eye, arguing that the sculptor can in this way render the expression of passion: "If passions find expression in the eyes, the pupil plays the principal role.... This is why Michelangelo, Algardi, Bernini, Puget, and Sarrazin, and, in their wake, several excellent modern artists have elected in certain works to express them by using the chisel to cut out its form; this produces a shadow that renders their effect rather well."[102]

Whereas expression in painting is rendered by color, in sculpture it is an effect of shadow—the slight shadow created by a hollow: a particular effect of light that is produced by the darkness of the cavity. But the author of the *Lettre* also acknowledges that this solution is unsatisfactory from the point of view of truth and is at best the lesser of two evils: "It is true that the surface of the eye is naturally smooth and that there are no hollows to mark out the pupils, without which sculpture cannot render them. One can imitate nature only very imperfectly by this means. But this defect ultimately seems a better recourse than making figures that resemble the blind."[103]

Caylus argues for exactly the opposite position, condemning in the name of truth the procedure used by sculptors to palliate the lack of color. Hollowed-out eyes do not exist in nature: "Since sculpture cannot color things, since it can render only salient parts in order to create shadows and imitate the forms afforded

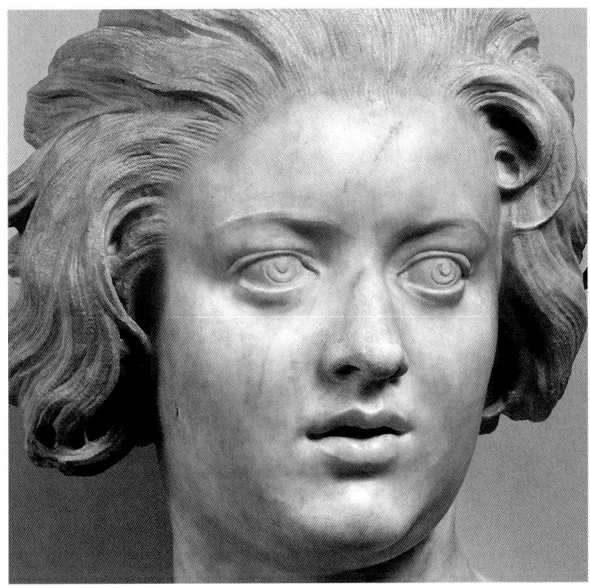

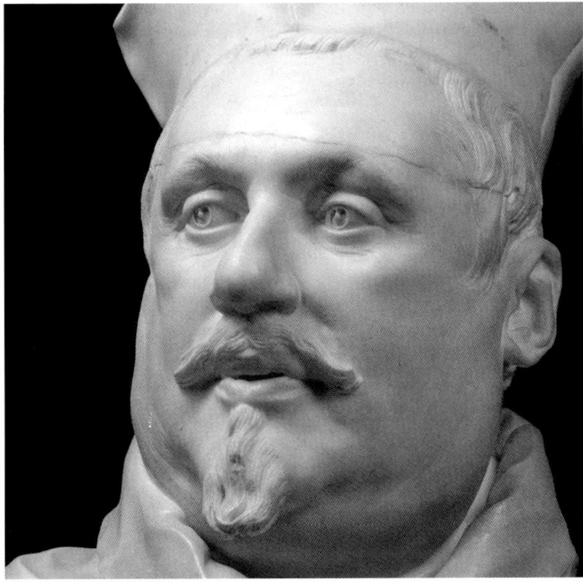

        THE ARTIST-PAINTER AND THE PHILOSOPHER-SCULPTOR

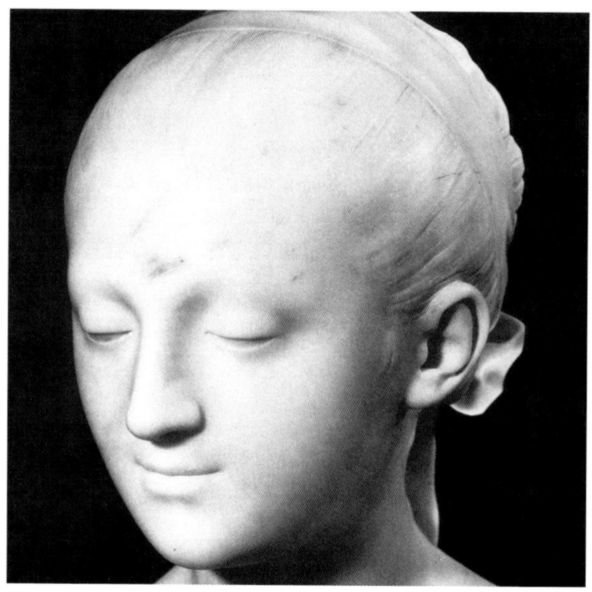

Fig. 14. Jean-Antoine Houdon (French, 1748–1828)
Little Lise (detail), 1775, marble, height (with base): 47 cm (18½ in.)
St. Petersburg, State Hermitage Museum

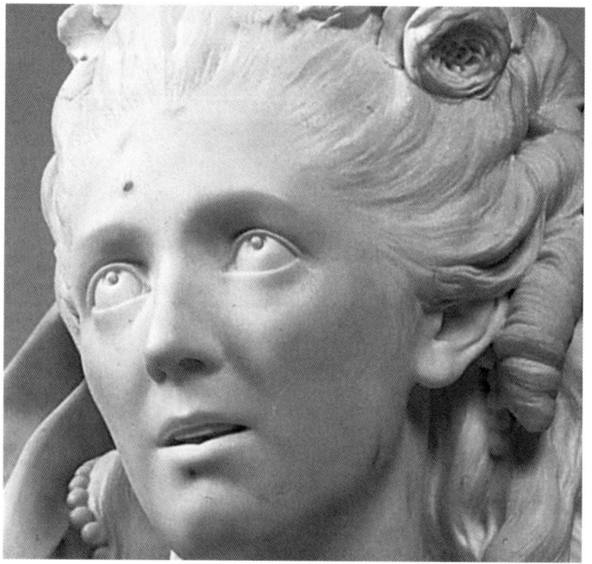

Fig. 15. Jean-Antoine Houdon (French, 1748–1828)
Sophie Arnould (Paris, 1740–Paris, 1802), Singer (detail), 1775, marble,
81 × 51 × 29.5 cm (31⅞ × 20 × 11⅝ in.)
Paris, Musée du Louvre

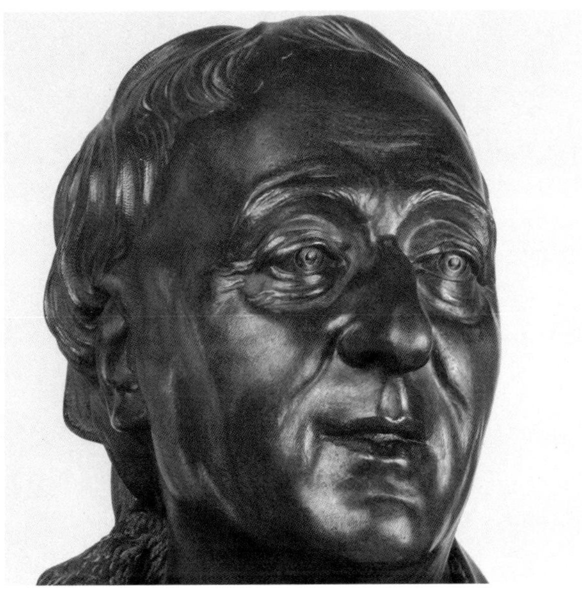

Fig. 16. Jean-Baptiste Pigalle (French, 1714–85)
Denis Diderot (Langres, 1713–Paris, 1784), Writer (detail), 1777, bronze,
52.2 × 34.5 × 25.5 cm (20½ × 13½ × 10 in.)
Paris, Musée du Louvre

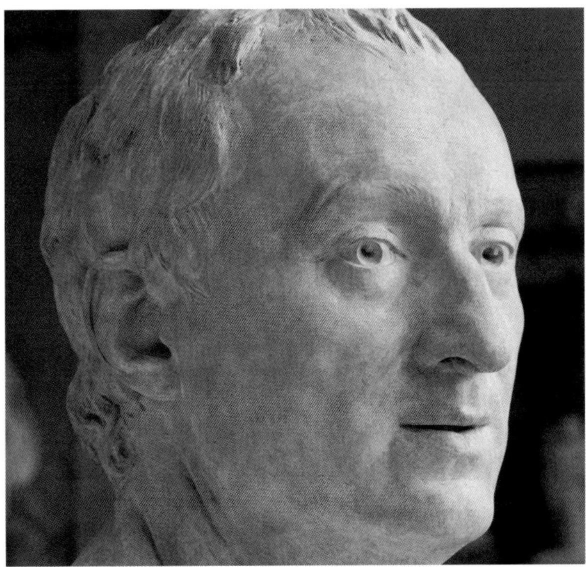

Fig. 17. Jean-Antoine Houdon (French, 1748–1828)
Denis Diderot (Langres, 1713–Paris, 1784), Writer, (detail), 1771, terra-cotta,
without base: 46 × 26.9 × 22.2 cm (18⅛ × 10⅝ × 8¾ in.)
Paris, Musée du Louvre

     THE ARTIST-PAINTER AND THE PHILOSOPHER-SCULPTOR

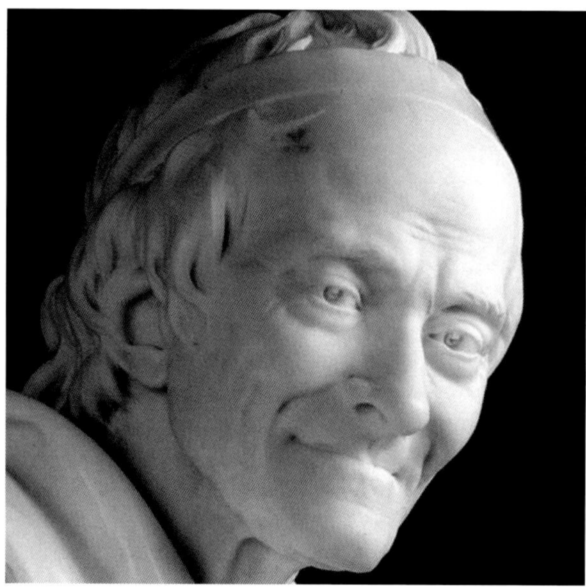

Fig. 18. Jean-Antoine Houdon (French, 1748–1828)
Voltaire (detail), 1781, marble, height: 138 cm (54⅜ in.)
St. Petersburg, State Hermitage Museum

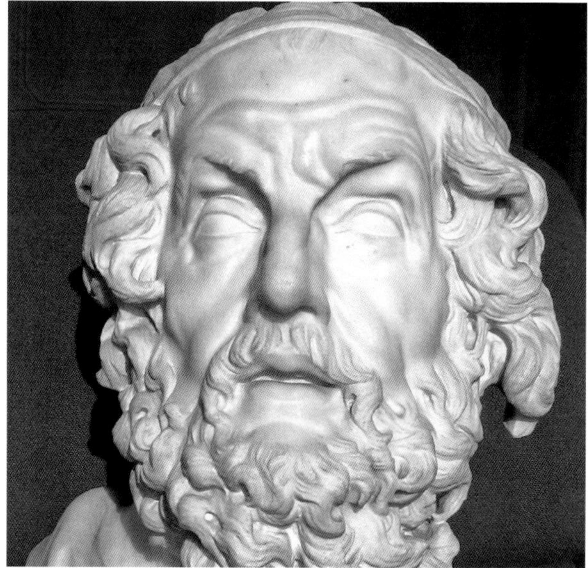

Fig. 19. Pierre Puget (French, 1620–1694)
Homer (detail), ca. 1693, marble, height: 46.5 cm (18¼ in.)
Lyon, Académie des sciences, belles-lettres et arts

by the objects that it chooses to represent; and since the pupils, if they are to be perceptible, must be so by dint of color, the sculptor should not attempt to indicate them by characteristics that they themselves do not possess."[104]

If pupils cannot be made perceptible without color, sculptors must once and for all give up the idea that they can make them as visible as painters can. In imitating the expression of the eye, nothing can replace color nor make up for its absence. The sculptor cannot use his chisel *per via di levare* to produce the effect that the painter magically obtains *per via di porre,* with one further touch of the brush. Diderot in fact summarizes the debate to perfection. The sculptor has no other choice than to let the spectator "imagine the sitter blind" or "show a punctured eye." Smooth or hollow, sculpture's eyes can never represent the gaze. They can only show the absence of that gaze.

The sense of the conditional tense, to which we drew attention earlier, has now become clearer. How can a statue lend itself to the literary invention of glances exchanged—to the fictive reciprocity by which a spectator in his turn imagines himself the object of someone else's gaze and thus a subject existing under the eye of another (pls. 11, 12)? Diderot can invent such a fiction relative to a painting because the painter, unlike the ancient sculptor, "traces in the iris" and "marks out the pupil." And he does so, unlike the modern sculptor, by imitating nature and truth. The painter does not confine himself to drawing the form of the eye; he gives this eye a gaze by delicately placing in its center or corner a spot of color, a little touch that can cause the spectator to hesitate by allowing him to imagine (not to believe, but to pretend to believe) that the eye of the figure that he contemplates is not only seen but seeing.[105] And it is no doubt this little dash of paint—a fleck of pure visibility at the heart of vision—that allows Diderot's imagination to run riot, to the point where he invents a dialogue among the characters that he sees represented on the canvas, lends them words, questions, answers, hesitations, and sighs, as he does in his description of *Girl with a Dead Canary.* The novels that he invents when describing a picture are the mark of an extremely subtle rhetorical strategy, which belongs in the long tradition of *ut pictura poesis;* it allows the writer to ensure the triumph of literature over painting by substituting his own account of the picture for the image itself. But these fictions also constitute the finest homage that the author can make to painting, since they all have their source in the extraordinary power that the silent figures exert over him. The figures seem to him so vivid that he might almost expect to hear them speak and cannot help speaking to them himself. He does not even need to see the eye in order to imagine the gaze. A lowered eyelid, a face hidden behind a hand, the curve of a back, the movement of a neck, a gesture, a pose, a shadow: painting has innumerable ways of suggesting the gaze and indicating its direction. Whether they are turned toward him or away from him, whether their eyes rest on or ignore him, Diderot bestows a gaze on all the characters whom he sees depicted on canvas. But in the invariably visible eyes of sculpture, he can see no such gaze. Painted figures may make it clear that they are not looking at him; by contrast, sculpted figures, even when they are looking at him, invariably show that they do not see him. This is no doubt why Diderot is so "short" with the sculptors. These white statues that stare at him with their blind eyes, opaque or hollowed out, tell him that they have nothing to say, that they are indifferent to his existence and impervious to his gaze. And if he is "expansive with the paint- ers," that is first and foremost because he perceives in the pictures of all these colorist painters something like the promise of a glance inviting him to speak and engage them in conversation.[106]

Philosophers and poets long remained in thrall to the eerie blind gaze of sculpture. "What a glance [in] these pupil-less eyes!" writes Baudelaire about sculpture in his *Salon de 1859*.[107] Discussing sculpture in his *Philosophie de l'art,* Taine notes: "the eyes lack pupils."[108] But it is in Hegel that one finds the most remarkable description of a sculpted figure; it "not merely lacks what is properly the color of painting but also the glance of the eye." Consequently when the spec- tator "looks at these shapes, soul cannot meet soul nor eye eye."[109]

In the shadow described in the *Lettre sur la peinture,* the shadow formed by the absence of the pupil, the nineteenth century saw nothing so much as a reflected image of the absence of color. It is as if in the vacant, opaque eyes of sculpture the very hollow of the eye outlined in negative the locus of color and therefore of painting.

Notes

1. Denis Diderot to Etienne-Maurice Falconet, 29 December 1766, in Denis Diderot, *Oeuvres complètes,* ed. Roger Lewinter (Paris: Club français du livre, 1970), 7:711.

2. Denis Diderot, *Salon de 1763,* in idem, *Arts et lettres (1739–1766),* ed. Jean Varloot, vol. 13 of idem, *Oeuvres complètes* (Paris: Hermann, 1980), 379–80.

3. Diderot, *Salon de 1763* (note 2), 380.

4. This conception of emotion is faithful to the sense that Cicero gives to *movere* as a movement of the soul entailing a movement of the body.

5. Denis Diderot, *Salon de 1759,* in idem, *Arts et lettres (1739–1766),* ed. Jean Varloot, vol. 13 of idem, *Oeuvres complètes* (Paris: Hermann, 1980), 76.

6. If painting is a woman, as the iconographic and poetic traditions suggest, the spectator's gaze is always taken to be masculine. The spectator envisaged and constructed in discourse on painting is never a woman. But, contrary to what is claimed by a certain widely diffused feminist tradition, this is not simply because these texts were written by men.

7. Roger de Piles, *Conversations sur la connaissance de la peinture et le jugement qu'on doit faire des tableaux* (Paris: Langlois, 1677; reprint, Geneva: Slatkine, 1970), 145–46.

8. Honoré de Balzac, *The Unknown Masterpiece,* trans. Richard Howard (New York: New York Review of Books, 2001), 11–12.

9. Charles-Nicolas Cochin, "De l'illusion dans la peinture," in idem, *Oeuvres diverses de M. Cochin...; ou, Recueil de quelques pièces concernant les arts* (Paris: Charles Antoine Jombert, 1771), 3:223.

10. The empiricist philosophers are almost alone in avoiding this error. Berkeley, Hume, and Russell helped me to understand the problem of pictorial illusion, as did Dubos and Diderot. The solutions to this problem proposed by Gombrich and Gibson are illuminating but by no means definitive.

11. Denis Diderot, *Salon de 1765,* in idem, *Salon de 1765: Essais sur la peinture,* ed. Else Marie Bukdahl, Annette Lorenceau, and Gita May, vol. 14 of idem, *Oeuvres complètes* (Paris: Hermann, 1984), 182.

12. Charles Perrault, *Parallèle des anciens et des moderne* (Paris: Chez Jean Bapt. Coignard, 1692–97; reprint, Geneva: Slatkine, 1979), 201.

13. See Plato, *Sophist,* 234b–d; and Plato, *Republic,* 10.598c.

14. Affording the spectator the benefit of the doubt does not simply mean ceasing to consider him a priori as ignorant and credulous; it also means supposing that the minimal conditions required for the perception of a work of art are met. This implies beginning with the hypothesis that he is, as Eddy M. Zemach puts it, a normal spectator, placed in "standard conditions of observation." This is clearly not what Plato postulates in *Sophist,* nor Kant in his third *Kritik.* On this question, see Eddy M. Zemach, *Real Beauty* (University Park, Pa.: Pennsylvania State Univ. Press, 1997); and Kendall L. Walton, *Mimesis as Make Believe: On the Foundations of the Representational Arts* (Cambridge, Mass.: Harvard Univ. Press, 1993).

15. Jean-Baptiste Dubos, *Réflexions critiques sur la poésie et sur la peinture* (1710; Paris: École nationale supérieure des beaux-arts, 1993), pt. 1, sec. 43, p. 145.

16. Dubos, *Réflexions* (note 15), 146.

17. Immanuel Kant, *Kritik der Urteilskraft,* in Ernst Cassierer et al., eds., *Immanuel Kants Werke* (Berlin: Bruno Cassierer, 1922), 5:261.

18. Dubos, *Réflexions* (note 15), 146.

19. The quest to distinguish imitation from illusion is continuous with the entire tradition of thought about artistic mimesis developed since the Renaissance. Art theory has always sought to differentiate the form of imitation realized in art from resemblance and illusion, in this espousing the Aristotelian conception of mimesis. The distinction between imitation and resemblance is not merely consubstantial with the theory of mimesis; it is also the factor defining the difference between Platonic and Aristotelian mimesis.

20. Jean-François Marmontel, "Illusion," in the *Supplément à "l'Encyclopédie";* republished in idem, *Éléments de littérature,* vols. 5–10 of idem, *Oeuvres complètes* (Paris: Née de La Rochelle, 1787), 8:138.

21. Antoine-Chrysostôme Quatremère de Quincy, *De l'imitation* (Paris: Trettel & Würtz, 1823; reprint, Brussels: Archives d'architecture moderne, 1980), 80.

22. Dubos, *Réflexions* (note 15), 10. In this same section, Dubos also explicitly states: "The passions aroused in us by these imitations are merely superficial" (p. 9).

23. Of course, the analysis developed here relates exclusively to pictorial illusion. It cannot be applied to those who destroy pictures for political or religious reasons, who are infinitely more numerous and considerably more dangerous than the madmen of whom I speak. Political and religious madness rests on other beliefs and other forms of illusion.

24. Diderot, *Salon de 1763* (note 2), 380.

25. Diderot, *Salon de 1763* (note 2), 380.

26. Diderot, *Salon de 1763* (note 2), 386.

27. Diderot, *Salon de 1765* (note 11), 26.

28. Diderot, *Salon de 1763* (note 2), 385.

29. The importance of the role played by "Molyneux's problem" in seventeenth-century thought was underlined by many contemporaries. Thus Jean-Bernard Mérian wrote: "This problem occupies a prominent place in modern philosophy. The most celebrated men of our century, men like Locke and Leibniz, have researched it. It has sown the seed of important discoveries, which have in their turn effected considerable changes in our knowledge of the human mind and above all in the theory of sensations"; Jean-Bernard Mérian, *Nouveaux mémoires de l'Académie royale des sciences et belles-lettres* (Berlin: Chrétien Fréderic Voss, 1772), 258. See Francine Markovits, "Diderot, Mérian et l'aveugle," postface to Jean-Bernard Mérian, *Sur le problème de Molyneux* (Paris: Flammarion, 1984), 193–282. See also Joelle Proust, ed., *Perception et intermodalité: Approches actuelles de la question de Molyneux* (Paris: Presses universitaires de France, 1997).

30. John Locke, *Essay Concerning Human Understanding*, ed. John W. Yolton (London: J. M. Dent, 1961), 1:114.

31. Locke, *Essay Concerning Human Understanding* (note 30), 1:114.

32. Gottfried Wilhelm Leibniz, *New Essays on Human Understanding,* trans. and ed. Peter Remnant and Jonathan Bennett (Cambridge: Cambridge Univ. Press, 1996), 137 (emphasis added).

33. For this meeting of minds to be possible, pictorial space would have to be homogeneous with geometric space. And it will be remembered that their heterogeneity, which makes it impossible to submit pictorial mimesis to the criteria of geometry, was one of the arguments used by Plato in *The Laws* (667–68) to condemn painting.

34. Denis Diderot, *Lettre sur les aveugles,* 2nd ed. (Paris: E. Droz, 1963), 38.

35. Diderot, *Lettre sur les aveugles* (note 34), 47.

36. Denis Diderot, *Élements de métaphysique,* in idem, *Le rêve de d'Alembert,* ed. Jean Varloot, vol. 17 of idem, *Oeuvres complètes* (Paris: Hermann, 1987), 467. Jacques Chouillet puts it beautifully: "While the century of 'enlightenment' dwells with understandable curiosity on the moment when the blind awaken to light, Diderot attempts to travel in the opposite direction: exploring with the blind the shadows of the inner world, groping at the infrastructures and itineraries of compensation, touching with his fingertips, if he can, the reality of the mind"; Jacques Chouillet, *La formation des idées esthétiques de Diderot, 1745–1763* (Paris: Armand Colin, 1973), 141.

37. Diderot, *Lettre sur les aveugles* (note 34), 6.

38. Denis Diderot, *Pensées sur l'interprétation de la nature,* in idem, *L'interprétation de la nature (1753–1765),* ed. Jean Varloot, vol. 9 of idem, *Oeuvres complètes* (Paris: Hermann, 1981), 43.

39. Diderot, *Lettre sur les aveugles* (note 34), 39.

40. Diderot, *Lettre sur les aveugles* (note 34), 4.

41. Diderot, *Lettre sur les aveugles* (note 34), 18.

42. "My mind is sensitive, and quick to take flight; when it is absorbed into itself, the slightest buzzing of a fly will torment it to death," says Michel de Montaigne in *Essays,* trans. J. M. Cohen (Harmondsworth, U.K.: Penguin, 1958), 365. Pascal says much the same: "The mind of this sovereign judge of the world is not so independent that it cannot be disturbed by the first nearby clatter. It does not need a cannon's roar to immobilize its thoughts, the noise of a weathercock or a pulley will

do. Do not be surprised if he cannot gather his thoughts at the moment — a fly is buzzing in his ear. That is enough to make him incapable of giving sound advice"; Blaise Pascal, *"Pensées" and Other Writings,* trans. Honor Levi (Oxford: Oxford Univ. Press, 1995), 21.

43. Locke, *Essay* (note 30), 1:92.

44. Diderot, *Lettre sur les aveugles* (note 34), 16.

45. Roger de Piles, *Cours de peinture par principes* (Paris: Gallimard, 1989), 161.

46. Diderot, *Lettre sur les aveugles* (note 34), 37.

47. Johann Gottfried Herder, *Sculpture: Some Observations on Shape and Form from Pygmalion's Creative Dream,* trans. and ed. Jason Gaiger (Chicago: Chicago Univ. Press, 2002).

48. Herder, *Sculpture* (note 47), 52.

49. Herder, *Sculpture* (note 47), 45.

50. See Gotthold Ephraim Lessing, *Laocoon: An Essay upon the Limits of Painting and Poetry: With Remarks Illustrative of Various Points in the History of Ancient Art,* trans. Ellen Frothingham (Boston: Little, Brown, 1910).

51. On this subject, see Alex Potts, *The Sculptural Imagination: Figurative, Modernist, Minimalist* (New Haven: Yale Univ. Press, 2000), 28–29; and Michael Podro, "Herder's *Plastik,*" in John Onians, ed., *Sight and Insight: Essays on Art and Culture in Honour of E. H. Gombrich at 85* (London: Phaidon, 1994), 341–53.

52. Herder, *Sculpture* (note 47), 43.

53. Herder, *Sculpture* (note 47), 38.

54. Herder, *Sculpture* (note 47), 63.

55. Herder, *Sculpture* (note 47), 37.

56. Herder, *Sculpture* (note 47), 41.

57. Herder, *Sculpture* (note 47), 36.

58. Herder, *Sculpture* (note 47), 98.

59. Herder, *Sculpture* (note 47), 64.

60. Herder, *Sculpture* (note 47), 82.

61. Maurice Merleau-Ponty, *The Visible and the Invisible,* ed. Claude Lefort, trans. Alphonso Lingis (Evanston: Northwestern Univ. Press, 1968), 143. Translator's note: Lingis translates: "As soon as we see other seers, we no longer have before us *only the look without a pupil, the plate glass of the things with that feeble reflection*" (emphasis added). The context here seems to require a more obvious reference to the unsilvered mirror (*glace sans tain*) of things.

62. Diderot, *Salon de 1763* (note 2), 408.

63. Diderot, *Salon de 1765* (note 11), 308–9. As Jean-René Gaborit observes, "In Diderot's art criticism, sculpture occupies only a rather modest place"; Jean-René Gaborit, *Diderot et l'art de Boucher à David: Les Salons, 1759–1781,* exh. cat. (Paris: Réunion des musées nationaux, 1984), 431.

64. Diderot, *Salon de 1765* (note 11), 279–80. It is noteworthy that Diderot says exactly the same thing about drawing: "Only the masters of the art are good judges of draftsmanship; everyone can judge color"; Denis Diderot, *Essais sur la peinture, pour faire suite au Salon de 1765,* in idem, *Salon de 1765: Essais sur la peinture,* ed. Else Marie Bukdahl, Annette Lorenceau, and Gita May, vol. 14 of idem, *Oeuvres complètes* (Paris: Hermann, 1984), 350.

65. Diderot, *Salon de 1765* (note 11), 279–80.

66. Diderot, *Salon de 1765* (note 11), 280–82.

67. Diderot, *Salon de 1765* (note 11), 280.

68. Diderot, *Essais sur la peinture* (note 64), 357.

69. Denis Diderot, *Salon de 1767,* in idem, *Salon de 1767, Salon de 1769,* ed. Else Marie Bukdahl, Michel Delon, and Annette Lorenceau, vol. 16 of idem, *Oeuvres complètes* (Paris: Hermann, 1990), 82–83. His critique of van Loo's painting is one of the most beautiful illustrations of the writer's desire to be painter: to be able to say "anch'io son pittor" (I too am a painter). Diderot compares van Loo's portrait to the one that he himself gradually draws as he develops his critique, steadily effacing the portrait he describes in order to replace it with a self-portrait, thereby proving that he is a better painter than his friend.

70. Diderot, *Essais sur la peinture* (note 64), 24.

71. This is Diderot's description of *Mercury, Herse, and Aglaura* in his *Salon de 1767* (note 69), 134.

72. Diderot, *Salon de 1765* (note 11), 282.

73. Diderot's conception of artistic imitation is not unconnected to the idea of *imitatio* developed by medieval theorists. At the same time, it anticipates a theme that would be close to the hearts of the romantic thinkers. And in many respects it also anticipates the distinction made by

numerous twentieth-century artists between imitation of the process and imitation of the object.

74. Diderot, *Salon de 1763* (note 2), 409–10.

75. Denis Diderot, *Salon de 1781*, in idem, *Héros et martyrs: Salons de 1769, 1771, 1775, 1781,* ed. Else Marie Bukdahl et al. (Paris: Hermann, 1995), 357.

76. Etienne-Maurice Falconet, *Réflexions sur la sculpture: Lues à l'Académie royale de peinture et de sculpture, le 7 juin 1760* (Paris: Prault, 1761), 32–33.

77. Charles-Antoine Jombert, *Méthode pour apprendre le dessin* (Paris: De l'Imprimerie de l'auteur, 1755; reprint, Geneva: Minkoff, 1973), 90.

78. Antoine-Nicolas Dézallier d'Argenville, *Vies des fameux sculpteurs depuis la Renaissance des arts avec la description de leurs ouvrages* (Paris: Debure, 1787; reprint, Geneva: Minkoff, 1972), 2:195–96.

79. Diderot, *Salon de 1765* (note 11), 285. Diderot's argument against color in sculpture is very different from Marmotel's (note 20). Marmontel's purpose is principally to ensure that a difference is maintained between the pseudo-illusion produced by pictures and veritable illusion. Marmontel criticizes color in sculpture because it produces what he calls "full illusion," which he deems revolting and painful. Diderot's condemnation rests on a view almost diametrically opposed: such color can never produce the effect of illusion. These two apparently contradictory arguments coexist until the nineteenth century in all the writers who denounce the use of color in sculpture. Sculptural illusionism is criticized as impossible on the one hand and frightening on the other; it is often condemned on both counts at once.

80. Falconet, *Réflexions* (note 76), 15–16.

81. Falconet here speaks only of colored marble and not of the artificial coloring of marble or stone, that is, painted sculpture. Discussion of color in sculpture does not include the issue of painted sculpture, which had to wait until the nineteenth century.

82. The same argument—adducing the innovations of Italian sculptors to defend the superiority of the moderns over the ancients—recurs in the passage about bas-relief, concerning which Falconet takes the same view as Regnaudin and Perrault (see chap. 1, n. 52): "We who have taken our painting well beyond that of the ancients in the understanding of chiaroscuro, shall we not dare to do the same in sculpture? Bernini, Legros, and Algardi have shown us that it is the role of genius to expand the excessively narrow compass traced by the ancients in their bas-reliefs"; lecture given on 7 June 1760, in Falconet, *Réflexions* (note 76), 39.

83. "These enamel eyes, gilded hair, and all these rich inventions of ancient statues seem to me the invention of tasteless priests," says Diderot in his *Pensées détachées sur la peinture,* in idem, *Héros et martyrs: Salons de 1769, 1771, 1775, 1781,* ed. Else Marie Bukdahl (Paris, Hermann, 1995), 428. His judgment echoes that of Caylus. See *Vies d'artistes du XVIIe siecle: Discours sur la peinture et la sculpture…* (Paris: Renouard, H. Laurens, 1910), 192: "This usage, practiced in the barbarian times of antiquity, was maintained throughout Europe till the renewal of the arts. One can still see in our villages statues of saints precisely daubed with various colors. The coarse senses of our peasants are struck by this combination and this is the only use that can be found for it." Rumors about the polychrome nature of Greek sculpture were already circulating in Winckelmann's time but it was not until the nineteenth century and the publication of Quatremère's *Le Jupiter olympien ou l'art de la sculpture antique considéré sous un nouveau point de vue* in 1814 that archaeological evidence for polychrome sculpture was taken into account in the teeth of the prevailing taste. On this subject, see the remarkable catalog of the exhibition held at the Van Gogh Museum in Amsterdam, July–November 1996: Andreas Blühm et al., *The Colour of Sculpture, 1840–1910,* exh. cat. (Zwolle: Waanders, 1996).

84. Winckelmann's *Geschichte der Kunst des Alterthums* (*History of Ancient Art*) of 1764 was translated into French in 1766. However, starting in autumn 1764, the *Journal* *encyclopédique* had published a detailed account of the work over five issues.

85. Diderot, *Salon de 1765* (note 11), 281–83.

86. In the same text about Winckelmann, Diderot goes on to say: "Ask this charming enthusiast by what means Glycon, Phidias, and the others contrived to make such beautiful and perfect works, and he will tell you: through the feeling of liberty, which elevates the mind and inspires great things; the rewards of the nation and public esteem; sight, study, and constant imitation of the beauties of nature, respect for posterity, the intoxicating sense of immortality, assiduous work, the happy influence of morals and genius.... And undoubtedly there is a not a single point in this reply that one would dare contest"; Diderot, *Salon de 1765* (note 11), 278.

87. In his magisterial work on painting, Étienne Gilson dwells at length on the fundamental role of material factors in the elaboration of artistic forms. Using arguments from Aristotle and Aquinas, Gilson again poses the questions specific to what he calls an "ontology of art," questions that bear on identity, substratum, the form-material relationship, properties, and so on. "The specificity of the work of art extends to the elements of which it is composed," he says. He returns again and again to what he calls, in Focillon's expression, the "formal vocation" of the material used by the artist. This "defines for [the artist] a field of possibilities, which, wide as it may be, is not infinite.... The formal vocation of materials implies that not every material can accept every form"; Étienne Gilson, *Peinture et réalité* (Paris: J. Vrin, 1958), 58, 63, 66.

88. Diderot, *Salon de 1765* (note 11), 282.

89. Diderot, *Salon de 1765* (note 11), 287.

90. Denis Diderot, "Lettre sur les sourds et muets," in idem, *Premières oeuvres 2*, ed. Norman Rudich and Jean Varloot (Paris: Éditions sociales, 1972), 99.

91. For Plato, see esp. *Phaedo,* 82d; *Timaeus,* 88c; *The Laws,* 789e; *Gorgias,* 483e; and *Republic,* 377b–c. For Aristotle, see *Physics,* 2.3.

92. "We imagined a statue whose interior organization was like our own and animated by a mind devoid of any kind of ideas. We further supposed that the all-marble exterior prevented the use of any of his senses, and granted ourselves the liberty to open them as we chose to the various impressions of which they are susceptible. We felt we should begin with the sense of smell, since it is, of all the senses, the one that seems to contribute least to the knowledge of the human mind"; Étienne Bonnot de Condillac, *Traité des sensations* (London: De Bure l'aîné, 1754), 5–6.

93. Denis Diderot, *Discours sur la poésie dramatique,* in idem, *Le drame bourgeois,* ed. Jacques Chouillet and Anne-Marie Chouillet, vol. 10 of Denis Diderot, *Oeuvres complètes* (Paris: Hermann, 1980), 422.

94. Diderot, *Discours* (note 93), 425. This text is reminiscent of a celebrated passage from Plotinus's first *Ennead:* "Withdraw into your-self and look. And if you do not find yourself beautiful yet, act as does the creator of a statue that is to be made beautiful: he cuts away here, he smoothes there, he makes this line lighter, this other purer, until a lovely face has grown upon his work. So do you also: cut away all that is excessive, straighten all that is crooked, bring light to all that is overcast, labour to make all one glow of beauty and never cease chiselling your statue, until there shall shine out on you from it the godlike splendour of virtue, until you shall see the perfect goodness surely established in the stainless shrine"; Plotinus, *The Enneads,* trans. Stephen MacKenna (London: Penguin, 1991), 54 (I.9).

95. Diderot, *Salon de 1765* (note 11), 289.

96. The history of philosophy from Plato to Ludwig Wittgenstein and on to the more recent "analytic" trends suggests that philosophical thought likes to proceed *per via di levare* (by reduction). But some philosophers think *per via di porre* (by addition). In this second category one should no doubt place Aristotle, most of the Scholastics, Hegel (of course), and a few others.

97. Herder, *Sculpture* (note 47), 62.

98. Philostratus, *Imagines,* bk. 1, prologue,

295k. In his analysis of the Greek *Kolossos,* Jean-Pierre Vernant underlines the importance of "the void of the eyes," which expresses "the play of absence within presence." For the Greeks, eyes are, he says, "the avenues and instruments of erotic seduction"; Jean-Pierre Vernant, *Figures, idoles, masques* (Paris: Juilliard, 1990), 26.

99. Diderot, *Salon de 1765* (note 11), 285.

100. On the various ways of hollowing out the eye and marking the pupil, see Marie Thérèse Baudry and Dominique Bozo, *La sculpture: Méthode et vocabulaire* (Paris: Imprimerie nationale, 1978).

101. On this subject, see Aline Magnien, "Callistrate et le discours sur la sculpture à l'âge moderne," in Philippe Hoff and Paul-Louis Rinuy, eds., *Antiquités imaginaires: La référence antique dans l'art moderne, de la Renaissance à nos jours* (Paris: Presses de l'École normale supérieure, 1996), 21–41.

102. *Lettre sur la peinture et* (Paris: n.p., 1748), cited in Aline Magnien, *La nature et l'antique, la chair et le contour: Essai sur la sculpture française du XVIIIe siècle* (Oxford: Voltaire Foundation, 2004), 317–18. I am indebted to Magnien's work in this field.

103. *Lettre sur la peinture et* (note 102), 317–18.

104. Anne Claude Philippe Caylus, *Recueil d'antiquités égyptiennes, étrusques, grecques, romaines et gauloises* (Paris: Desaint & Saillant, 1752), cited in Aline Magnien, *La nature et l'antique, la chair et le contour: Essai sur la sculpture française du XVIIIe siècle* (Oxford: Voltaire Foundation, 2004), 319.

105. Unlike sculpture, said Herder, "paintings are not blind; they look and speak"; Herder, *Sculpture* (note 47), 56. And Herder too ascribes this difference between painting and sculpture to color: "Some statues are given *eyeballs.* If this is to be tolerable, they must be merely *suggested;* the majority of statues, and the best, have none. . . . In the most beautiful ages statues did not require drapery or colors, eyeballs or silver; art stood naked like Venus, and this was all the adornment and riches it needed. As everyone recognizes, painting is a different matter. Painting is made for the eye and speaks directly to the eye: for color is simply the division of a ray of light, the language of vision"; Herder, *Sculpture* (note 47), 56.

106. This way of describing the relationship between the spectator and the picture in terms of conversation is very close to the ideas of de Piles, who frequently returns to the "conversational air" produced by painting. A picture must, he says, "call out to" the spectator, invite him to come closer and converse with it. However, in de Piles it is not clear what in painting speaks. Sometimes it is the figures, sometimes the characters represented, and sometimes the picture as a whole.

107. Charles Baudelaire, *Salon of 1859,* in idem, *Art in Paris 1845–1862: Salons and Other Exhibitions,* trans. and ed. Jonathan Mayne (London: Phaidon, 1965), 205.

108. Hippolyte Adolphe Taine, *Philosophie de l'art* (1881; Paris: Hachette 1909; reprint, Geneva: Slatkine, 1980), 24.

109. Georg Wilhelm Friedrich Hegel, *Aesthetics: Lectures on Fine Art,* trans. T. M. Knox (Oxford: Clarendon, 1988), 2:731, 1:521. As we know, for Hegel sculpture embodied the art of the classical ideal. And Hegel's analysis of this classical ideal is somewhat reminiscent of Diderot's: "When the classical ideal is at its true zenith, it is complete in itself, independent, reserved, unreceptive, a finished individual which rejects everything else"; Hegel, *Aesthetics* (this note), 1:532.

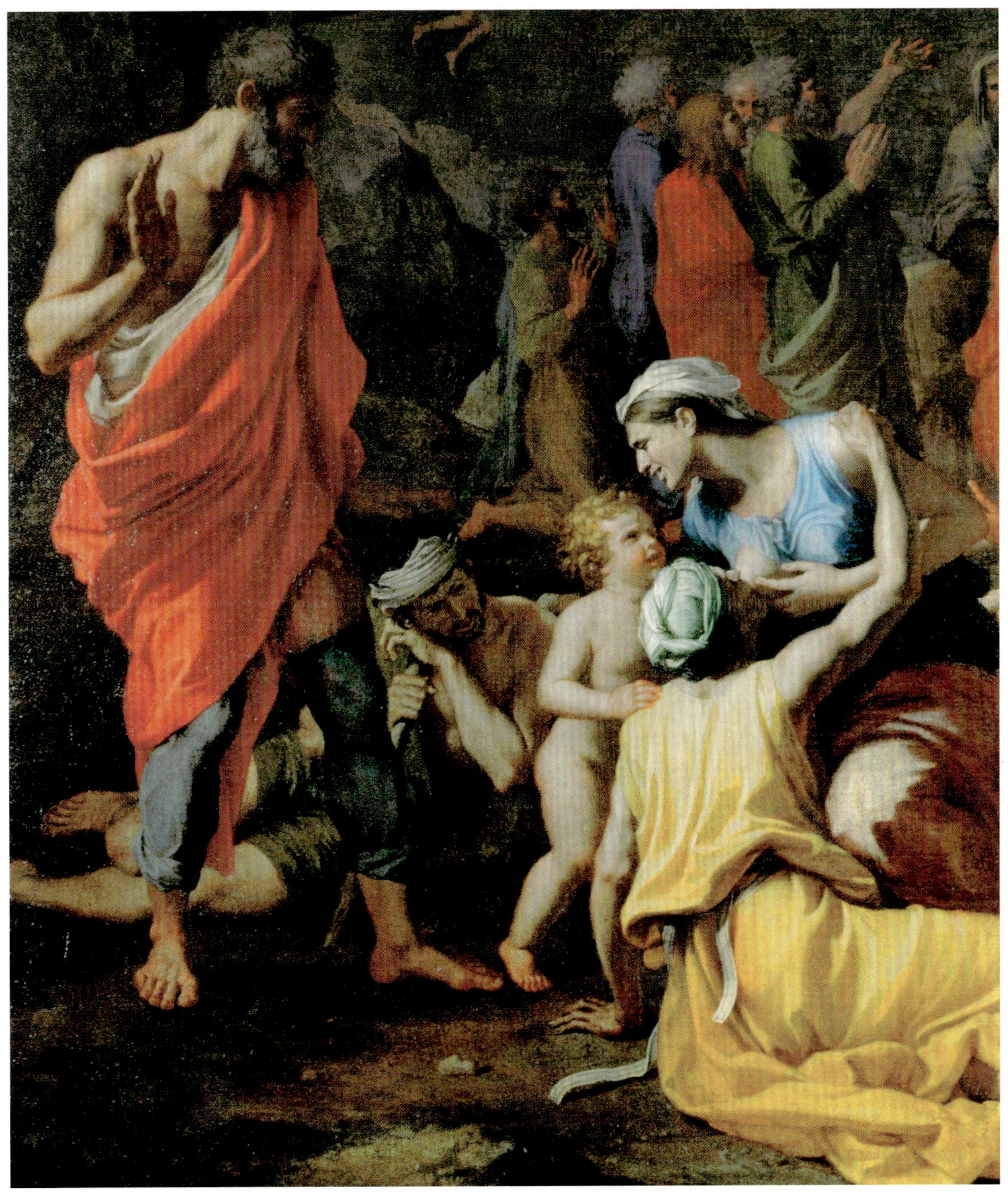

Pl. 1. Nicolas Poussin (French, 1594–1665)

The Israelites Gathering Manna in the Desert (detail), 1660–64, oil on canvas, 149 × 200 cm (58¾ × 78¾ in.)
Paris, Musée du Louvre

99

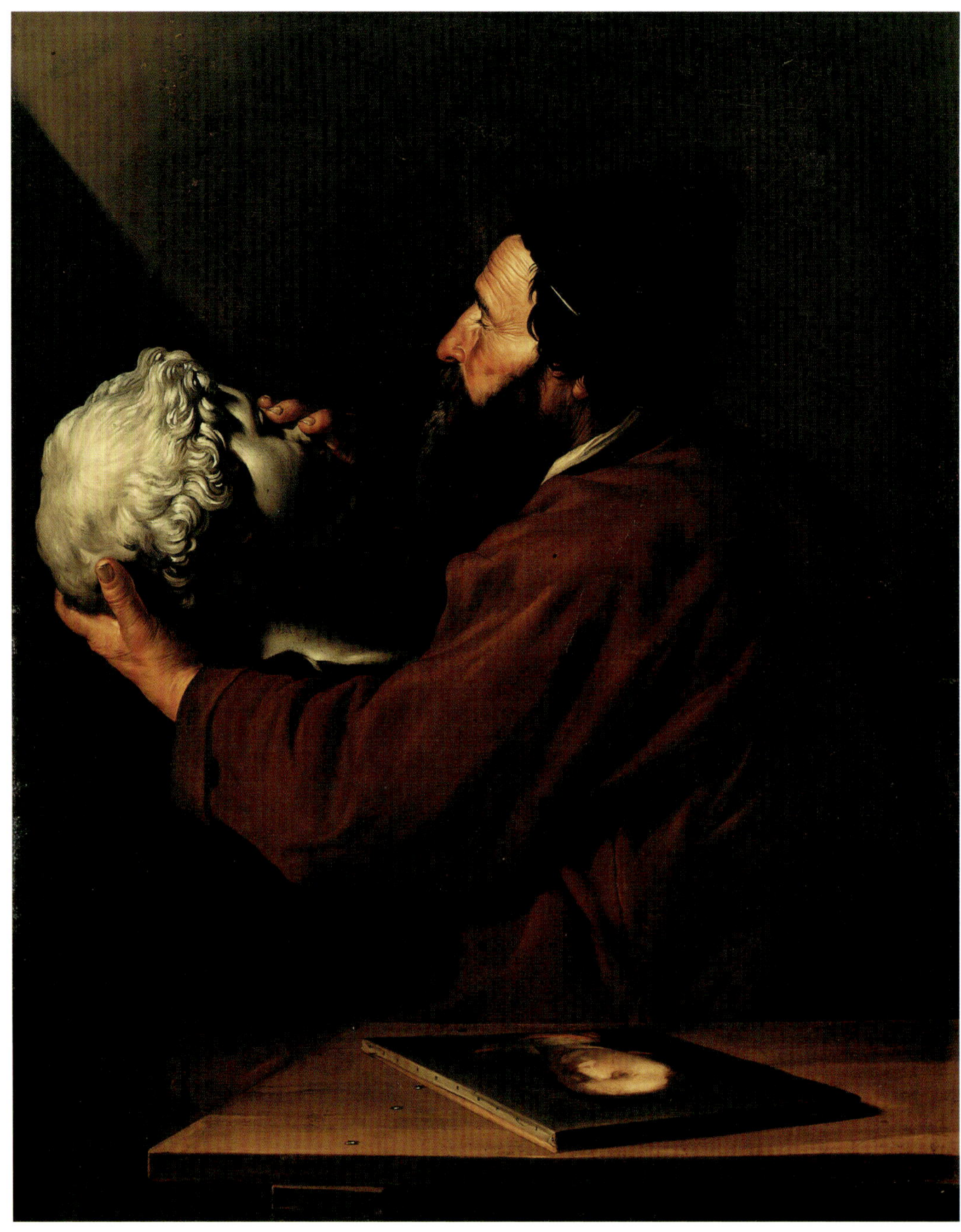

Pl. 2. **Jusepe de Ribera (Spanish, 1591–1652)**
The Sense of Touch, ca. 1615–16, oil on canvas, 115.9 × 88.3 cm (45⅝ × 34¾ in.)
Pasadena, Norton Simon Foundation

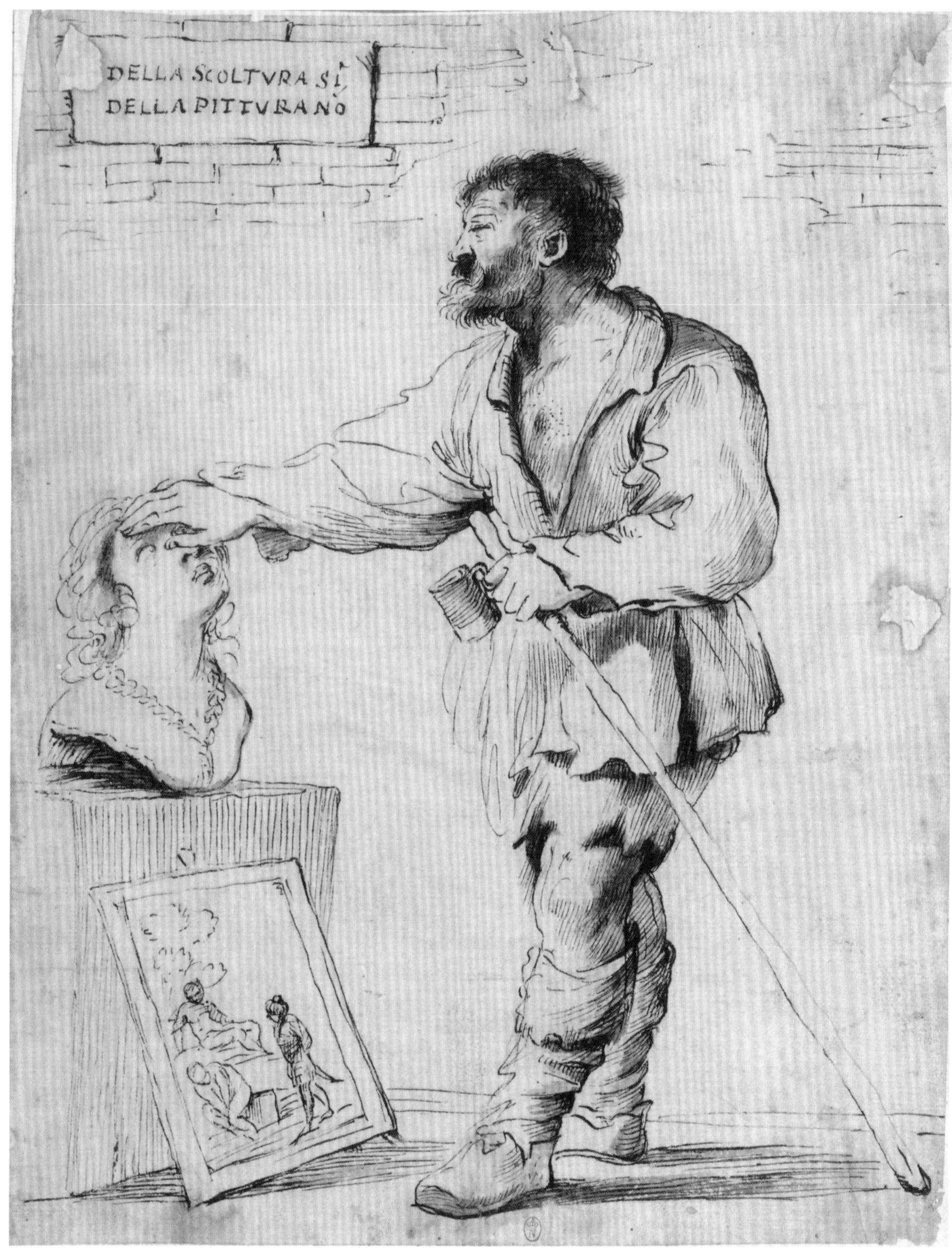

Pl. 3. **Attributed to Guercino (Italian, 1591–1666)**
Allegory of the Superiority of Sculpture over Painting, before 1621, pen, brown ink, brown wash, and black chalk,
26.9 × 20.1 cm (10⅝ × 7⅞ in.)
Paris, Musée du Louvre

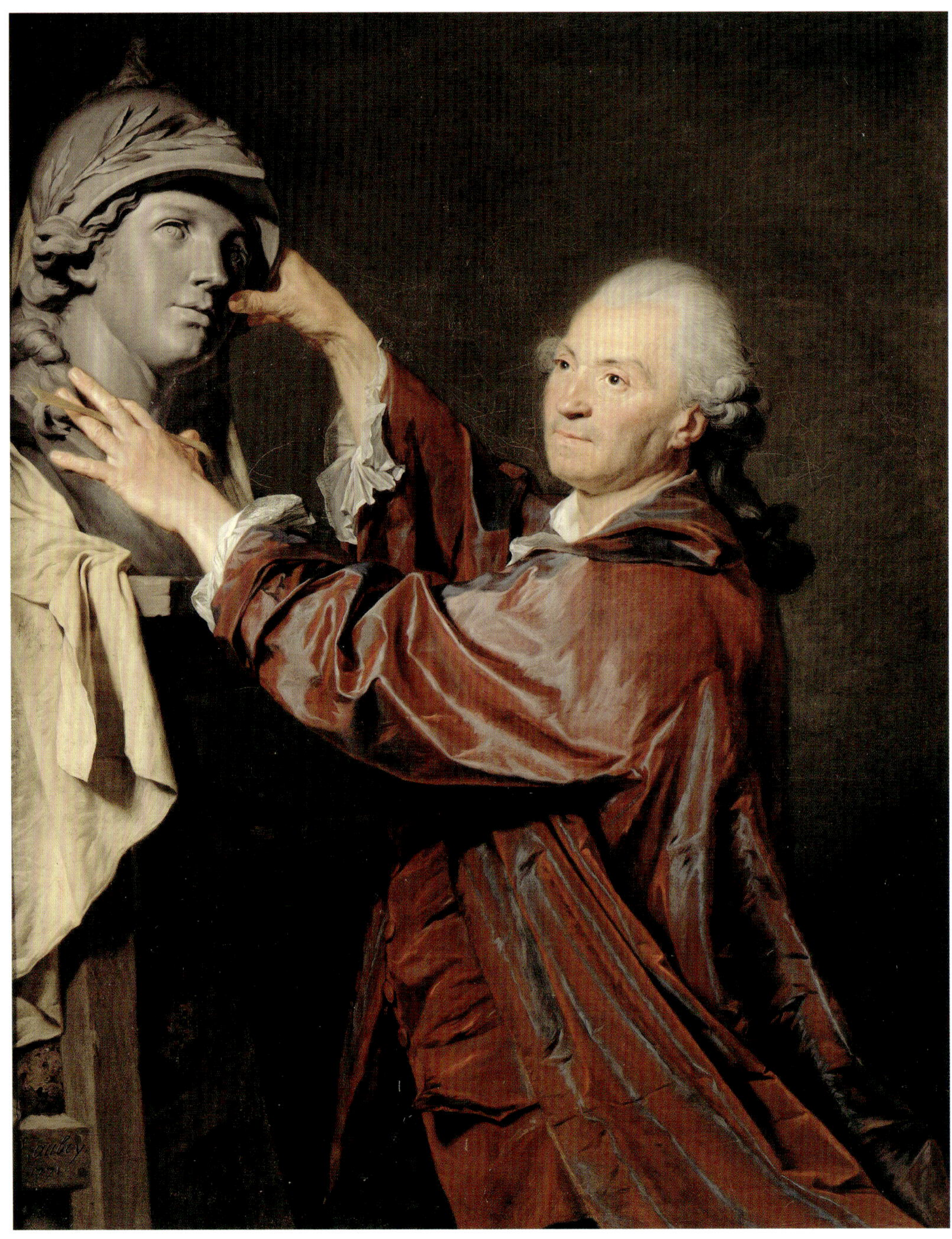

Pl. 4. **Etienne Aubry (French, 1745–81)**
Louis-Claude Vassé (1716–1772), 1771, oil on canvas, 119 × 97.5 cm (46⅞ × 38⅜ in.)
Versailles, Châteaux de Versailles et du Trianon

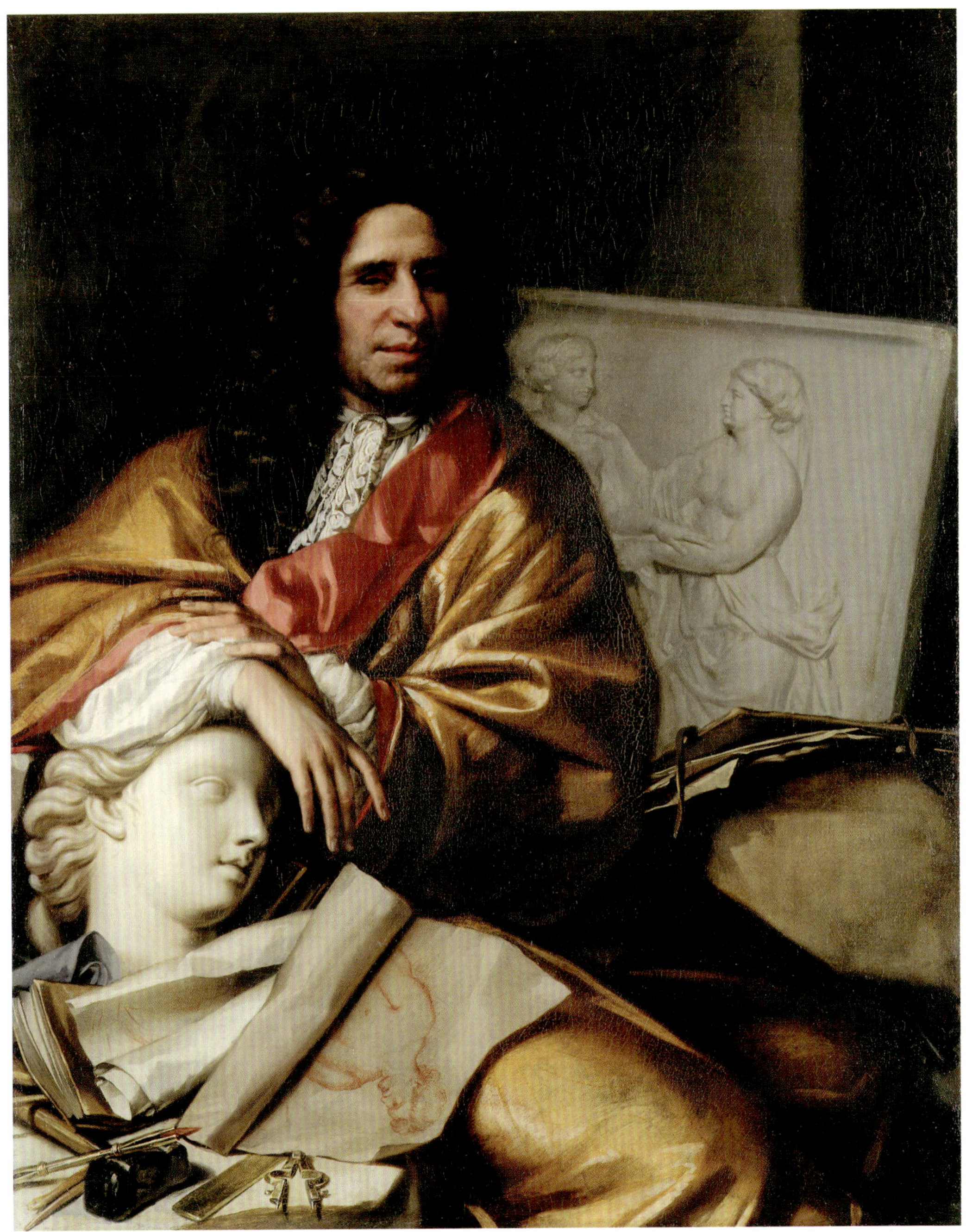

PI. 5. **Antoine Benoist (French, 1632–1717)**

Jacques Buirette (1631–1699), 1661, oil on canvas, 118 × 92 cm (45½ × 36¼ in.)

Versailles, Châteaux de Versailles et du Trianon

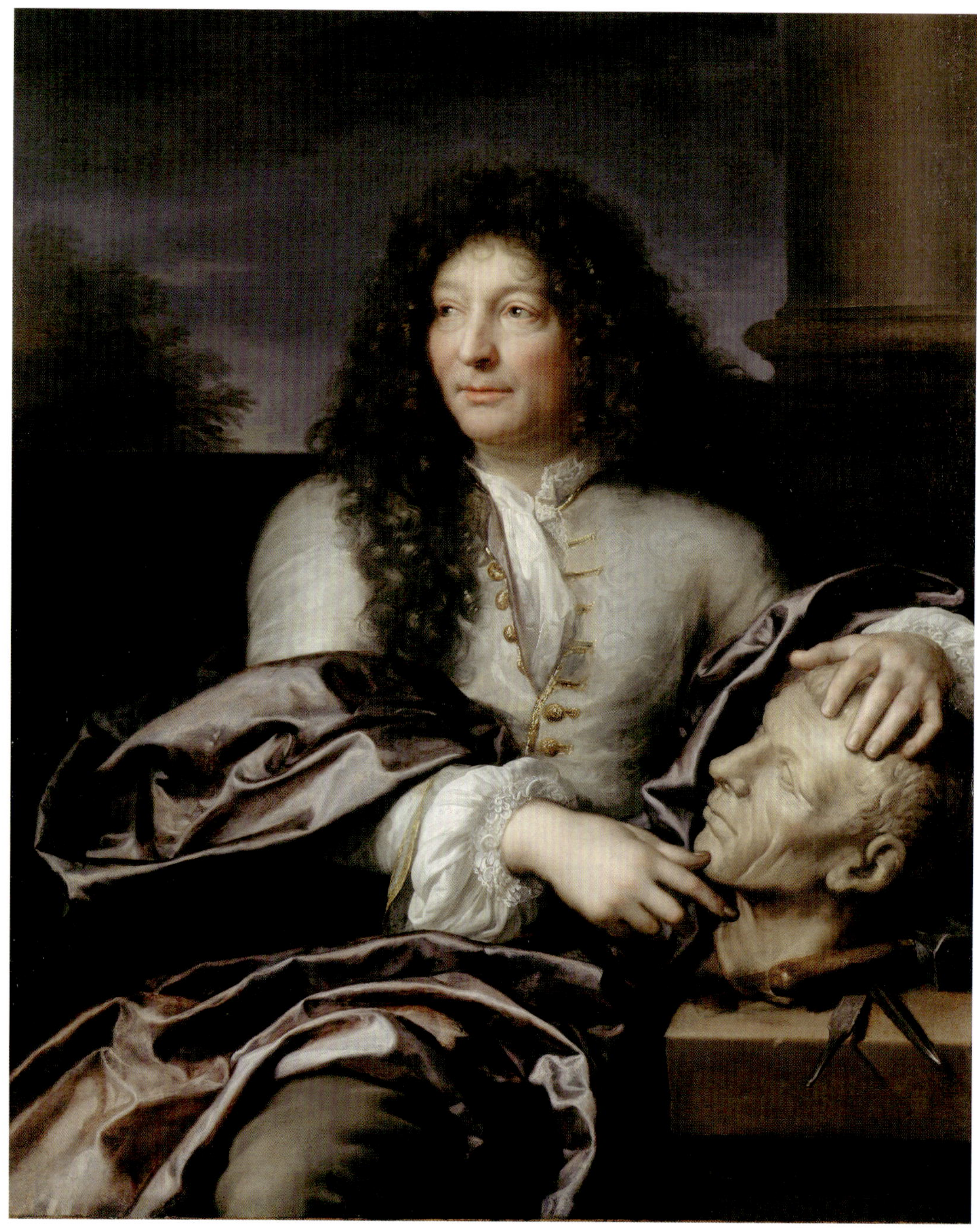

Pl. 6. Revel Gabriel (French, 1643–1712)
François Girardon (1628–1715), 1683, oil on canvas, 111 × 89.5 cm (43⅝ × 35¼ in.)
Versailles, Châteaux de Versailles et du Trianon

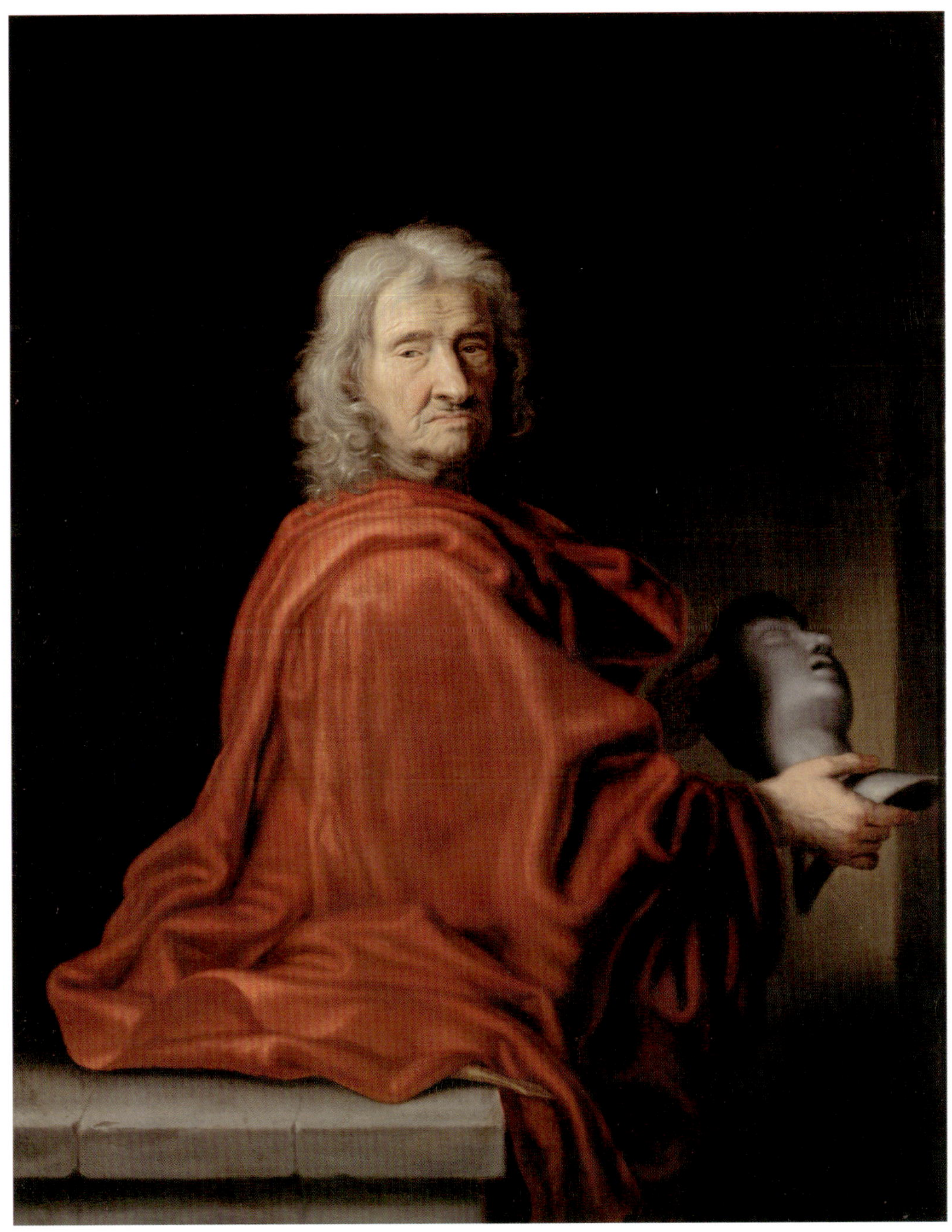

Pl. 7. **Philippe Vignon (French, 1638–1701)**
Philippe de Buyster (1595–1688), ca. 1687, oil on canvas, 115 × 89.5 cm (45½ × 34⅝ in.)
Versailles, Châteaux de Versailles et du Trianon

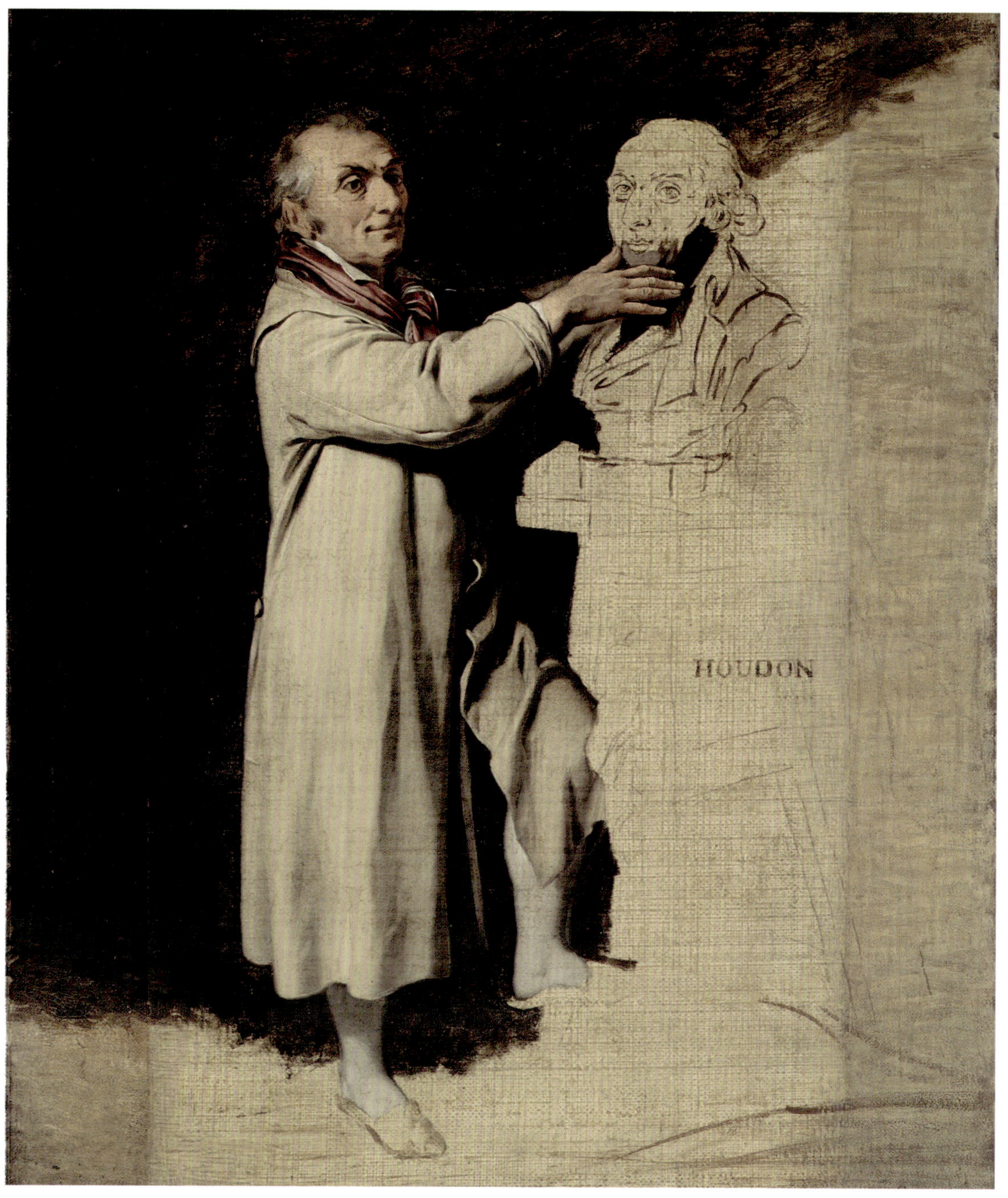

Pl. 8. **Louis Léopold Boilly (French, 1761–1845)**
Portrait of Houdon, ca. 1804, oil on canvas, 45 × 37 cm (17¾ × 14⅝ in.)
Lille, Musée des beaux-arts

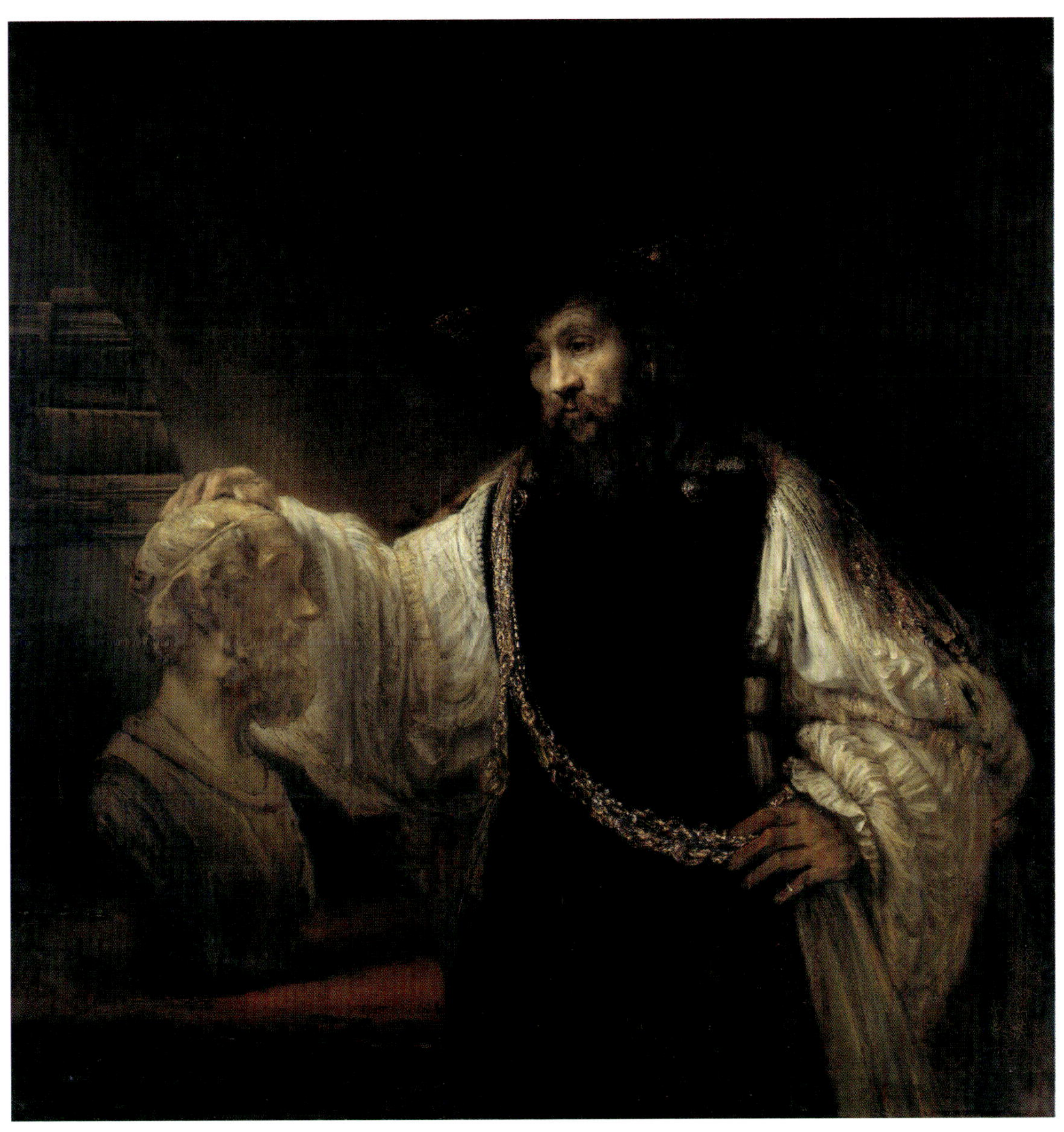

Pl. 9. Rembrandt van Rijn (Dutch, 1606–69)
Aristotle with a Bust of Homer, 1653, oil on canvas, 143.5 × 136.5 cm (56½ × 53¾ in.)
New York, Metropolitan Museum of Art

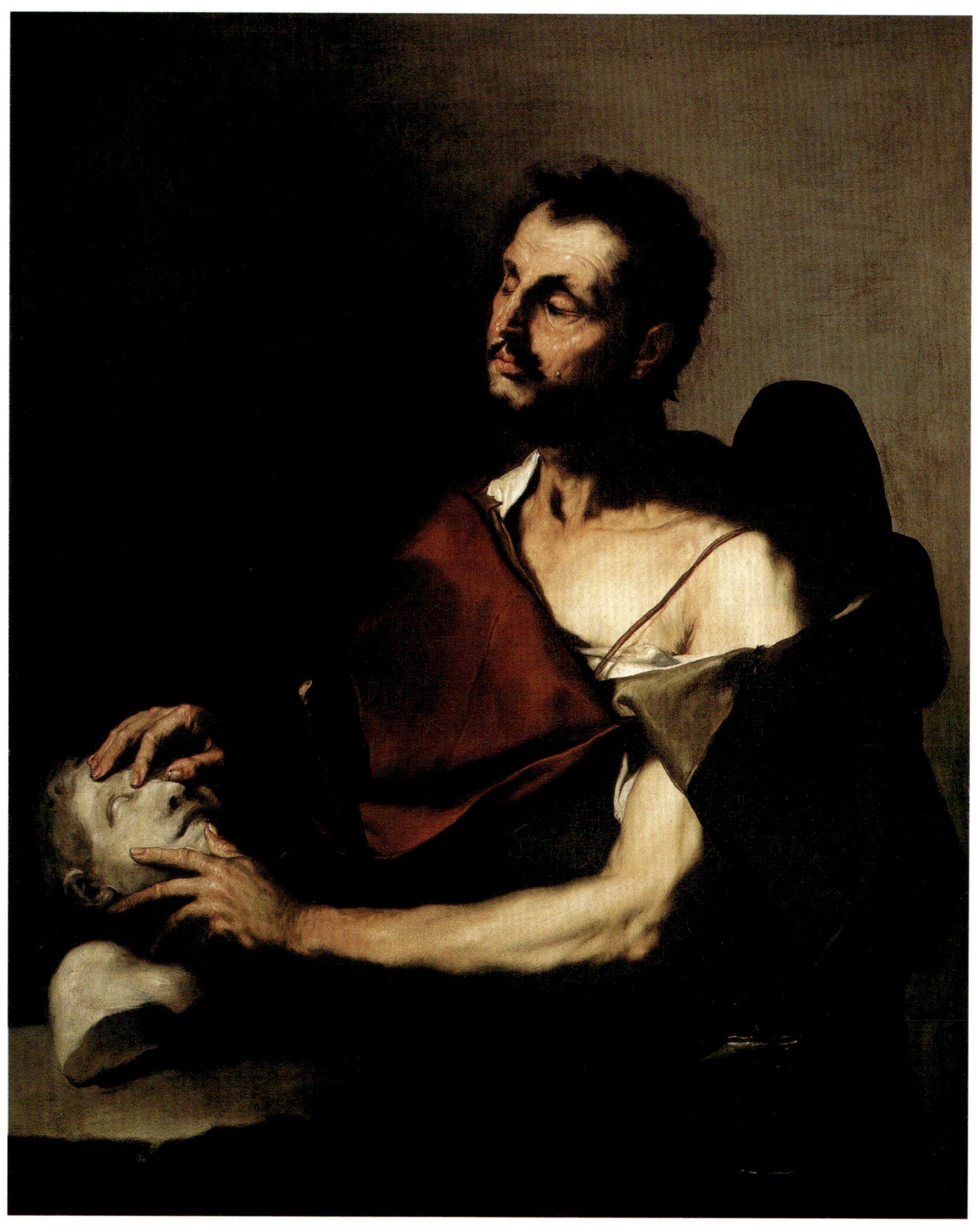

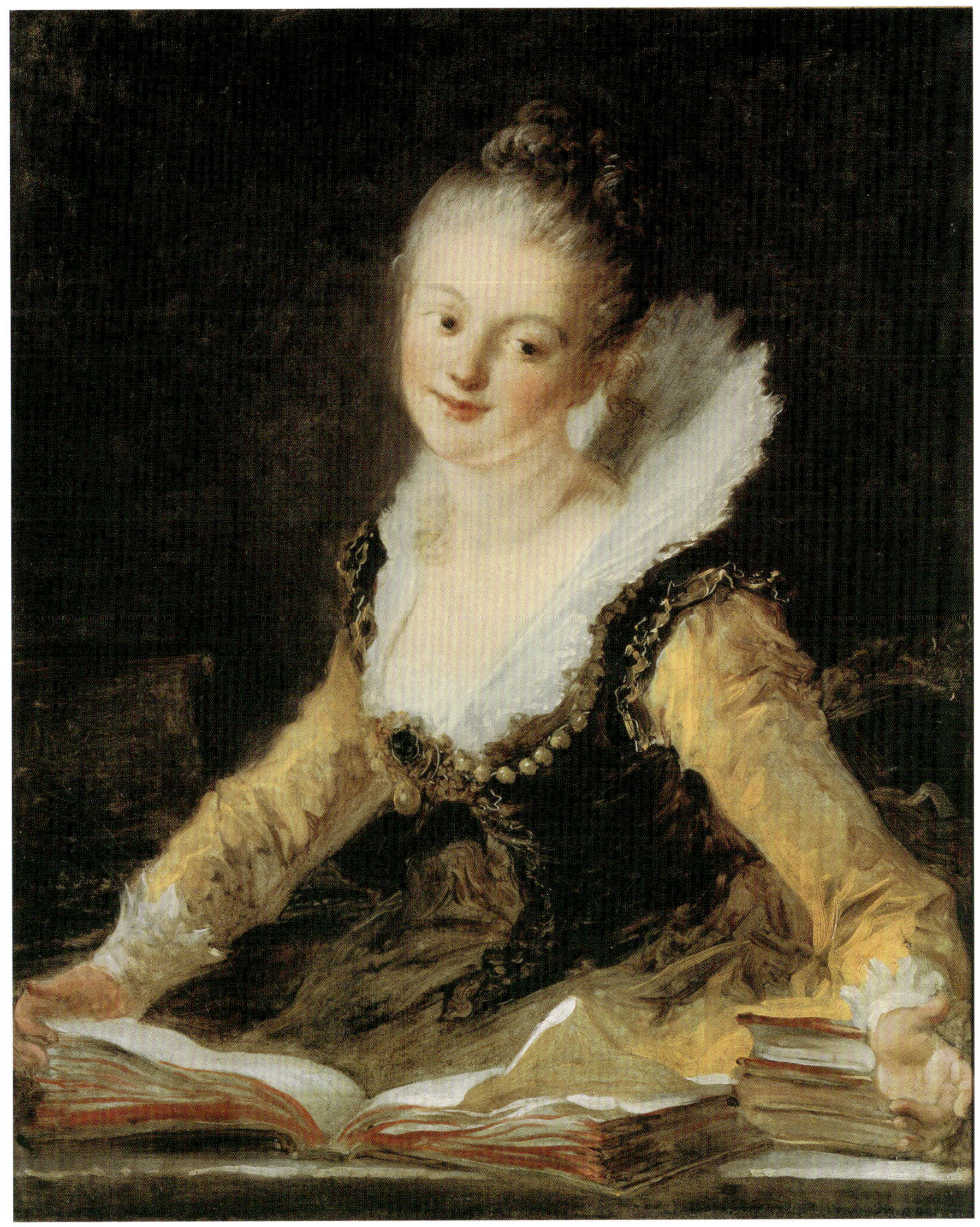

Pl. 11. **Jean-Honoré Fragonard (French, 1732–1806)**
Study, ca. 1769, oil on canvas, 81.5 × 65.5 cm (32 × 25¾ in.)
Paris, Musée du Louvre

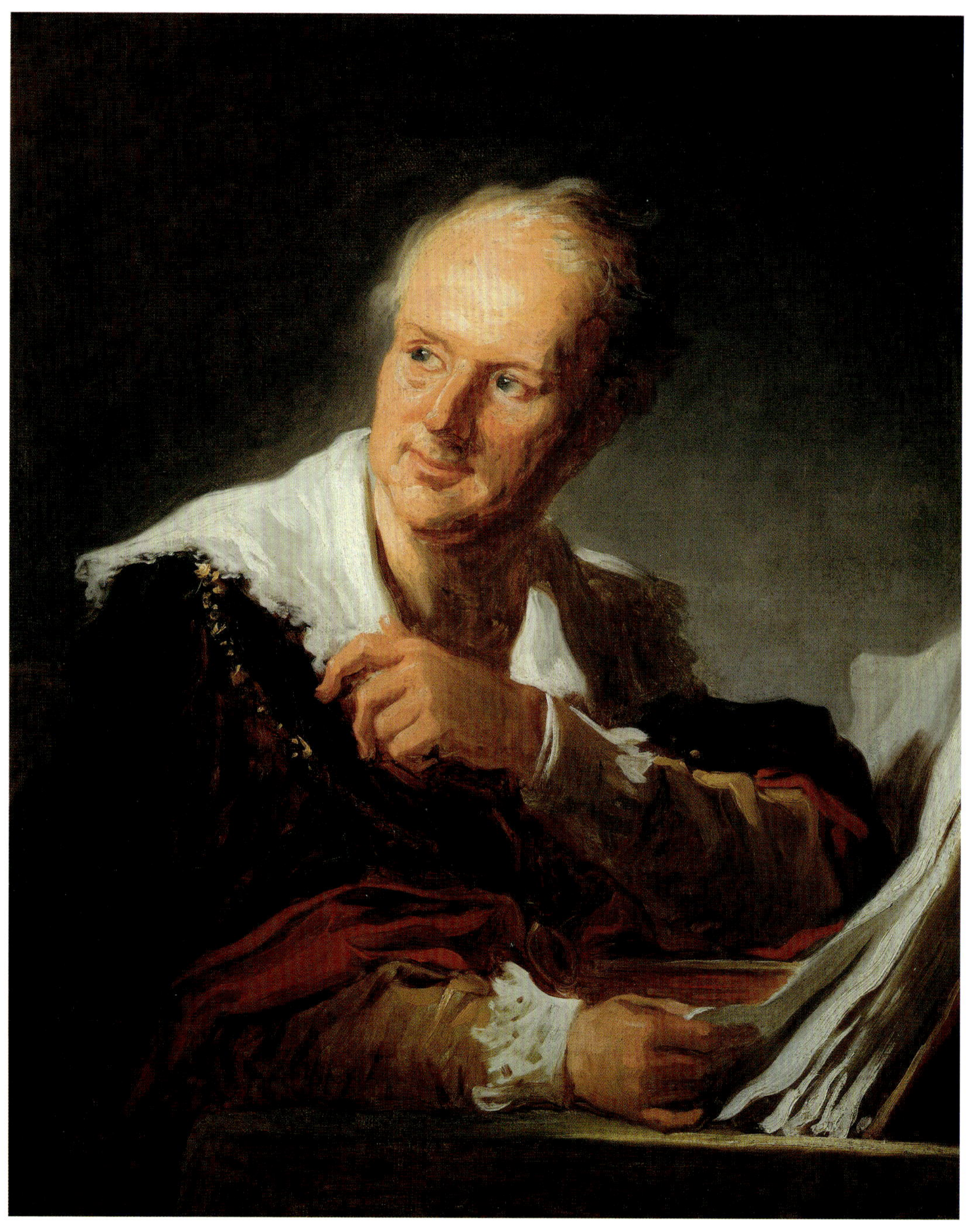

PL. 12. Jean-Honoré Fragonard (French, 1732–1806)
Portrait of Denis Diderot, ca. 1769, oil on canvas, 81.5 × 65 cm (32 × 25⅝ in.)
Paris, Musée du Louvre

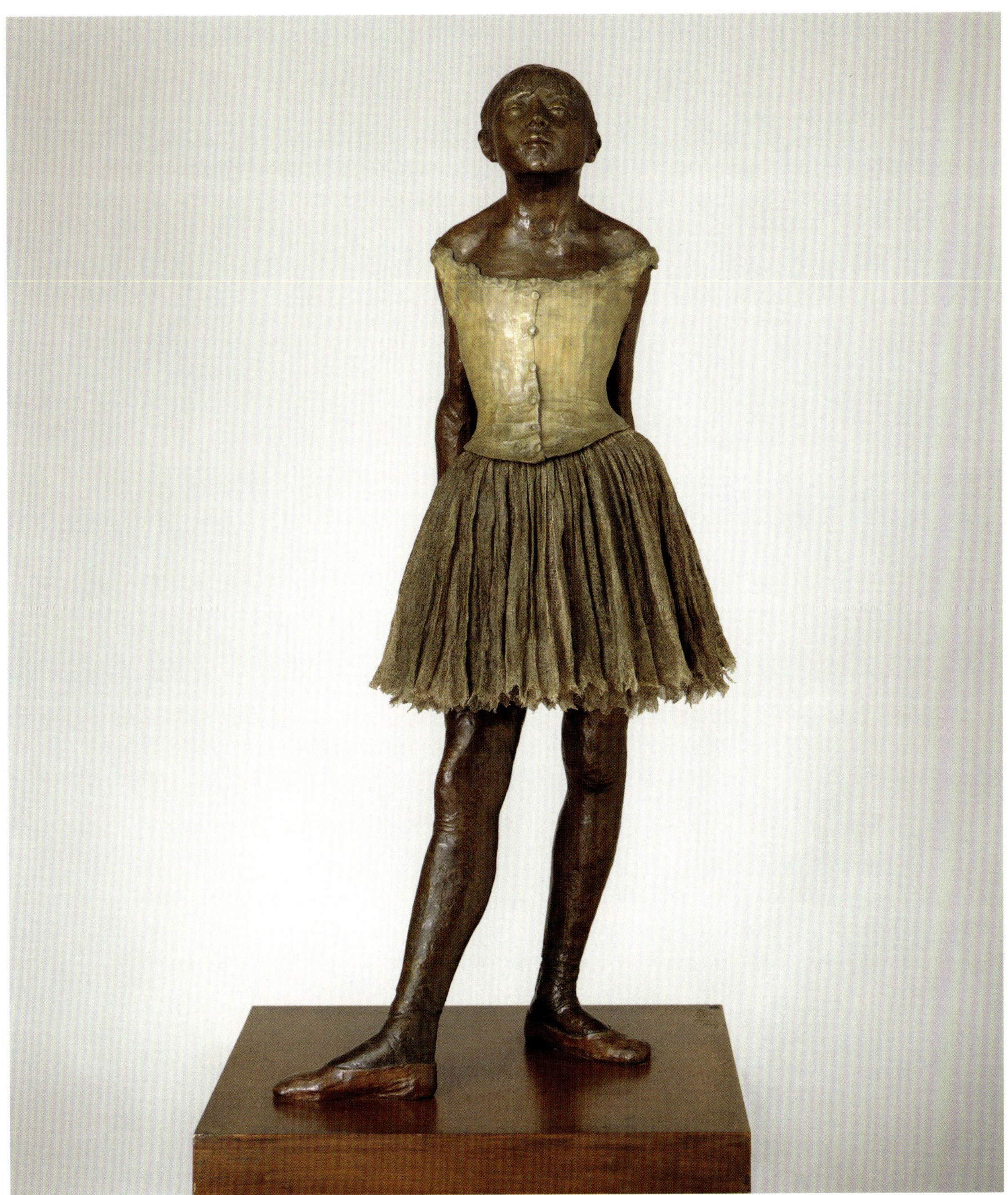

PI. 13. Edgar Degas (French, 1834–1917)
The Little Fourteen-Year-Old Dancer, executed ca. 1880, cast 1922, bronze, partially tinted, with cotton skirt and satin hair-ribbon, wood base, height (without base): 99.1 cm (39 in.)
New York, Metropolitan Museum of Art

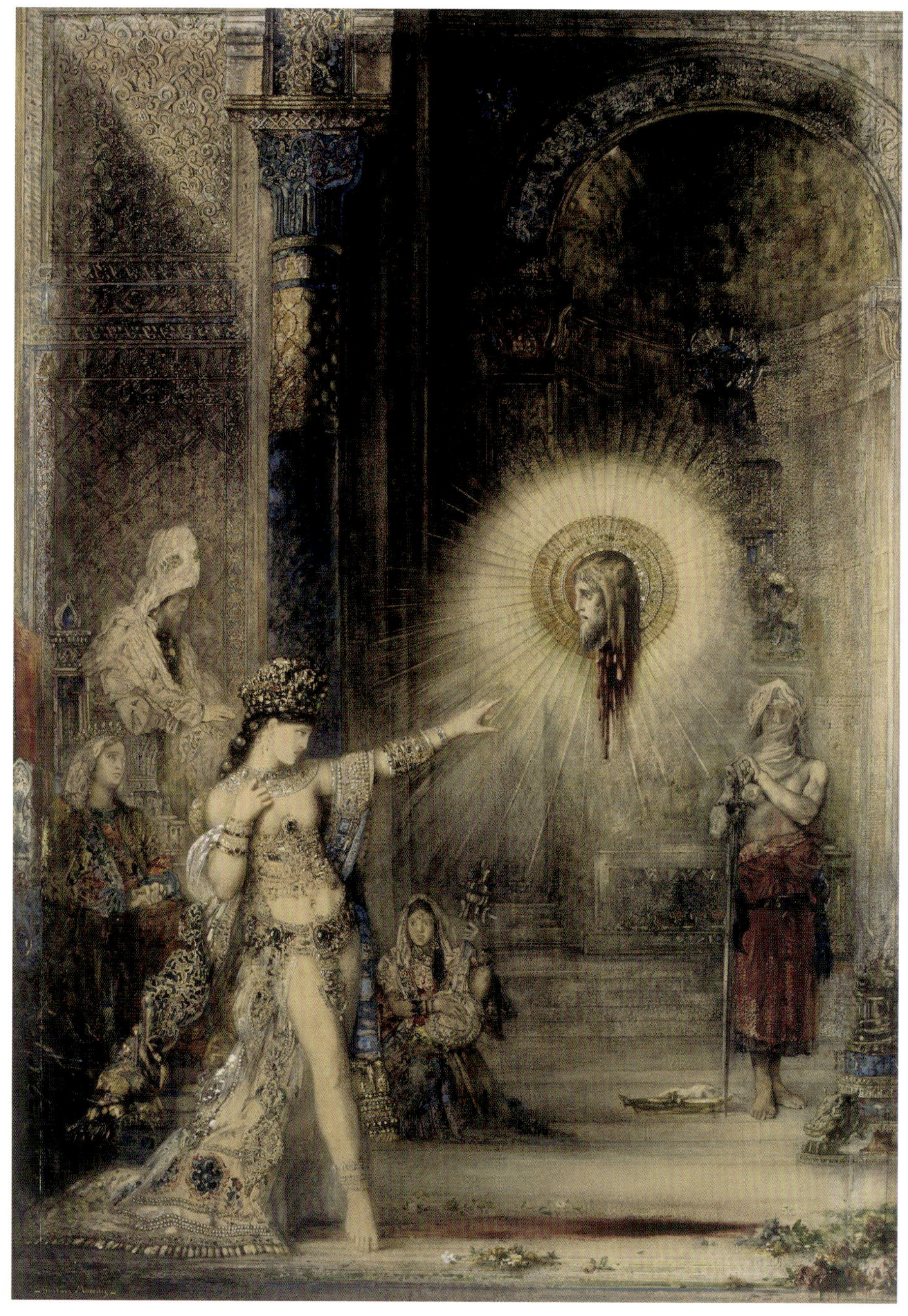

Pl. 14. **Gustave Moreau (French, 1826–98)**
The Apparition, 1876, watercolor, 106 × 72.2 cm (41¾ × 28⅜ in.)
Paris, Musée du Louvre

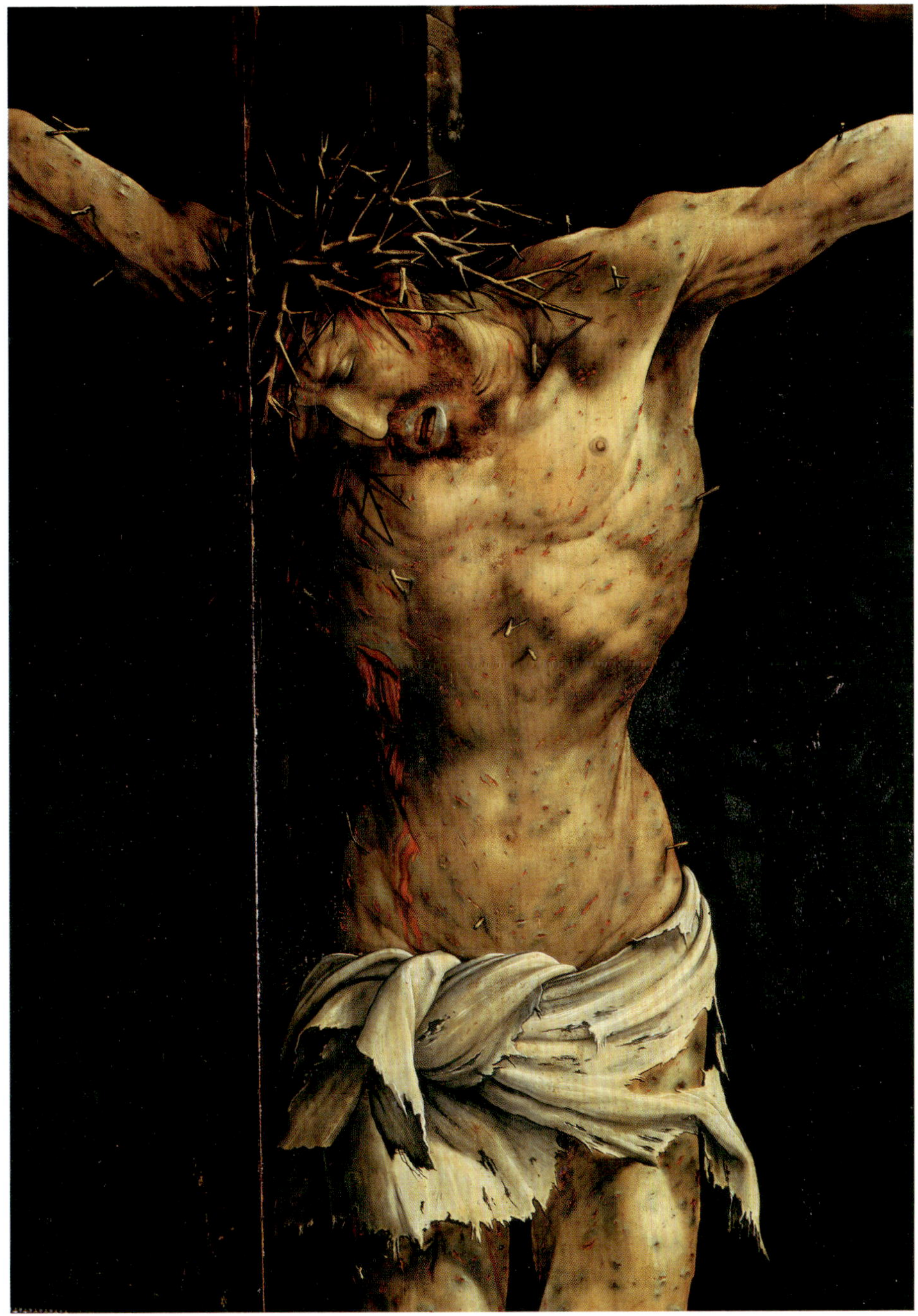

Pl. 15. **Matthias Grünewald (German, ca. 1480–1528)**
Detail of Christ, from the *Crucifixion,* the central panel of closed Isenheim altarpiece, ca. 1512–16, oil on panel,
Crucifixion panel: 269 × 307 cm (105⅞ × 120⅞ in.)
Colmar, Musée d'Unterlinden

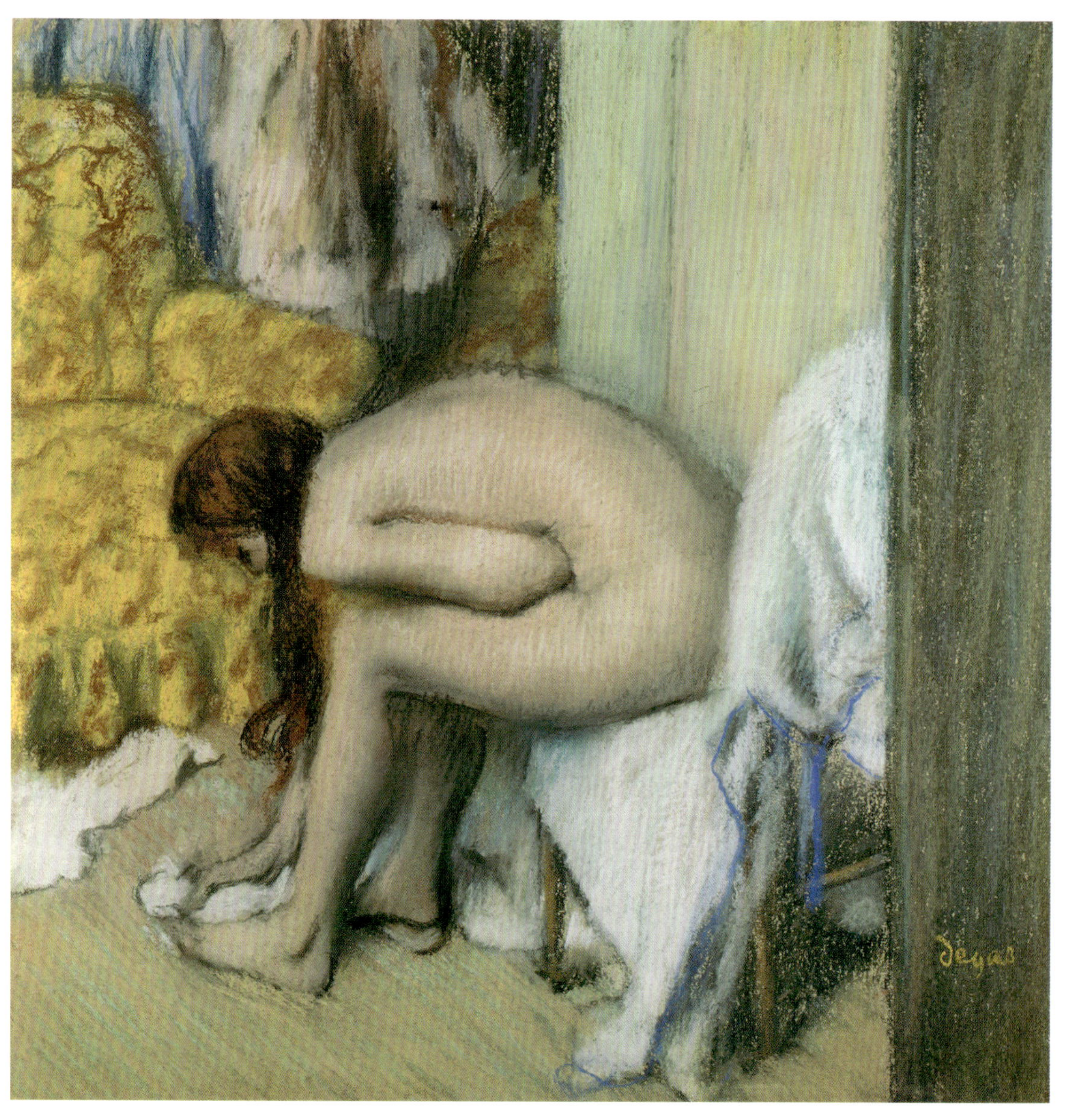

Pl. 16. **Edgar Degas (French, 1834–1917)**
  After the Bath: A Woman Drying Her Feet, pastel on cardboard, 1898, 62 × 65 cm (24⅜ × 25⅝ in.)
  Paris, Musée d'Orsay

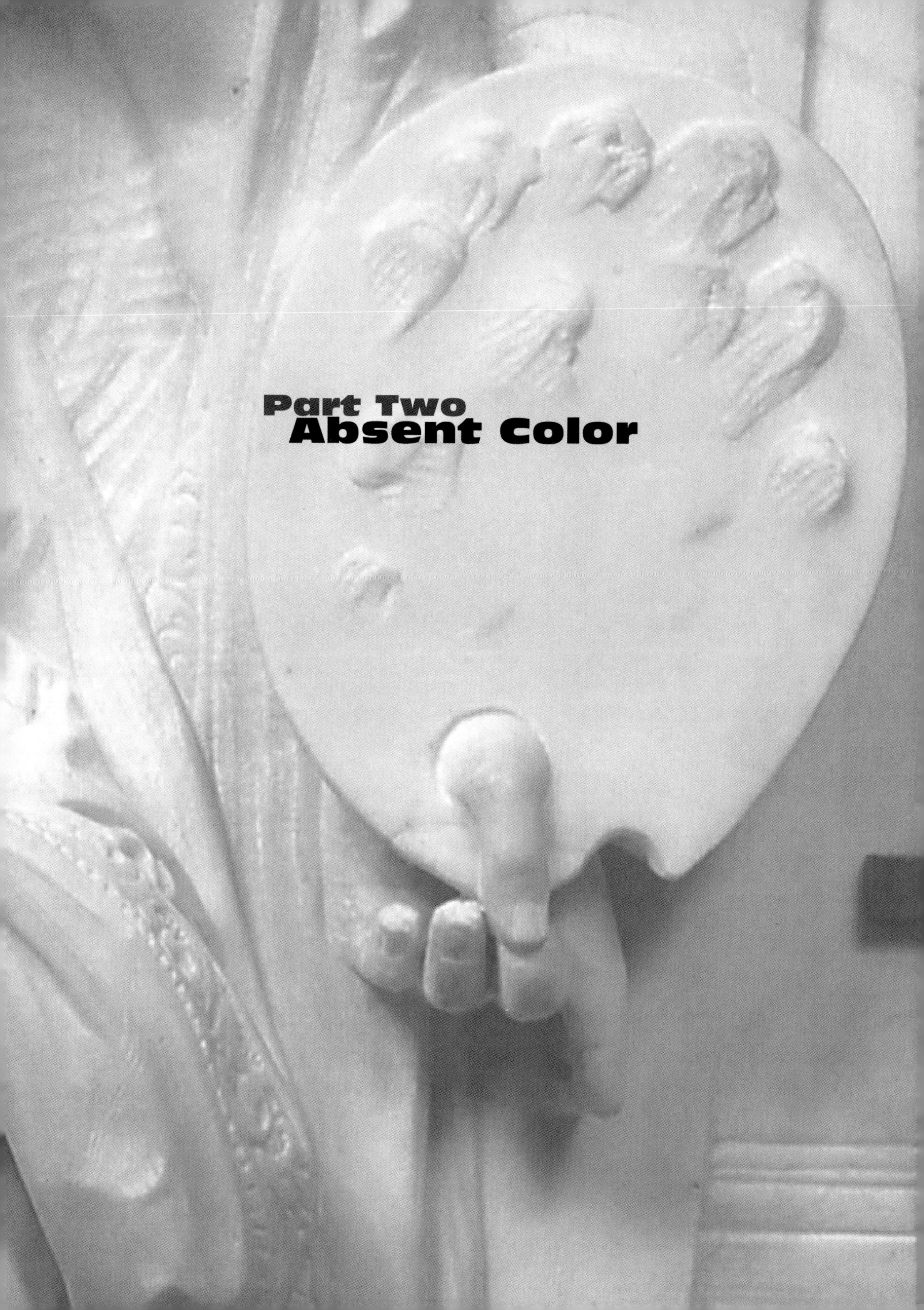
Part Two
Absent Color

The Inward and the Outward

Thoughts are the chisels with which poets mold
Beauty's virgin Paros marble, so immaculate and cold.

— Paul Verlaine[1]

A singular phenomenon comes to light in the history of the arts in France: under Louis XIV, sculpture took its lead from painting. At the very least, we can say that painting exerted a decisive influence over the character and progress of its rival. Le Brun was appointed inspector-general of all works of sculpture. And Le Brun was a painter with a great predilection for his own art.... This naturally drove the sculptors to encroach on the domain of the painters under whose direction they worked. Here was no doubt one of the reasons why they strove to inscribe into marble what could only be rendered by light- and color-effects on canvas: that vivacity, the fleeting but piquant expressions of French figures animated by the spirit of society and conversation. Irregularity of form and corruption of taste resulted from this. In statuary, the Greek qualities of beauty, simplicity, and naïveté disappeared, while sculptors proved unable to give their works the new character that they sought because, even allowing that it should ever have been the goal of one of the fine arts, it could never be appropriate to theirs. It was therefore because they were unaware of the nature of the two arts and the divisions between them that an inappropriate manner was cultivated by the sculptors.... Times have moved on; in the arts, what was exalted is now laid low, and sculpture no longer takes its lead from painting. On the contrary, painting takes its lead from sculpture.[2]

François Guizot was not yet the statesman but an art critic when he wrote these words for his Salon review of 1810. They testify to the major changes that had occurred in the fine arts in France. These had resulted from what Guizot calls "the felicitous revolution" effected first and foremost in the teaching of the École des beaux-arts by that "famous man," Jacques-Louis David. Since David's reform, says Guizot, the Greeks had again become "the true audience of the École." He writes, "It is among the marbles, which can, since it was the Greeks who made them, be considered their representatives, that [the École] seeks its models and its points of comparison—I might almost say its judges." [3]

The "felicitous revolution" was thus primarily a reaction against the taste—the bad taste—that had prevailed in France since Louis XIV: against the modern taste for an imitation of nature completely alien to the ancient ideal. Following Winckelmann, sculpture was considered the principal victim of this taste. The "naturalist" manner that Bernini had criticized in the French painters of the seventeenth century as "petty," "weak," and "mean" was now being identified and denounced in eighteenth-century sculptors, though in rather more virulent terms:

> To obtain some notion of the low and trivial in sculpture, one must bring to mind certain works in which a narrow, cramped system of imitation—exactly the opposite of the system of the ideal—had, in France, brought artists well known (though they shall be nameless) to seek realistic imitation in all the contingency and pettiness of the human body: in folds of skin, in wrinkles, in the mean-minded expression of these accessory animal details, which are minutiae that can do nothing but degrade and impoverish the image of mankind. [4]

As Guizot correctly observes, the return to the antique ideal of sculpture put an end to the domination that painting had exercised over sculpture since the seventeenth century. It allowed sculpture to free itself of a conception of mimesis entirely in thrall to the pictorial model. And it allowed painting to free itself, he says, of the simpering prettiness that was so fashionable under the ancien régime, for the return to the antique ideal in sculpture had been accompanied by a return to the ideal of the antique in painting. Whereas sculptors had till then striven to learn from painters, now the painters were schooled by the sculptors: "Study of the antique has become the foundation of all artistic activity." [5]

The "felicitous revolution" thus interrupted the course of a history that had begun with Le Brun and been characterized by the influence of painting over sculpture. That this revolution had come about through reforms instigated by a painter is something that Guizot, curiously, never adverts to. As in the seventeenth century, painting was still the art that determined the orientation of art-teaching in France.

Guizot was delighted by the pedagogical reforms that had "restored a true feeling for Art" but deplored their effect on painting. [6] The painters now painted like sculptors, he said. Their figures were stiff and cold like ancient marbles and therefore not lifelike; they lacked the truth that, in his view, painting could attain only through color. His judgment is categorical. Most of the artists from this new school of painting, having been trained by copying statues, were poor colorists:

"How can we expect the current school to abound in good colorists when we see masters who have graduated from it teach their pupils to paint from plaster models? The eye is quickly corrupted and learns to accept a cold, grey color as lifelike; it is unacquainted with variations in tone, the nuances of flesh and blood; this is no way to train a painter."[7]

Guizot's views about sculpture accord with neoclassical taste; he favors the imitation of ideal beauty. But in painting, he is a colorist and defends a point of view that the seventeenth century would have called naturalist. Indeed, his description of the paintings in the Salon of 1810 is somewhat reminiscent of de Piles's description of Poussin's pictures. The painters have, in his view, spent too much time studying the antique and not enough studying nature. This reproach belongs with another made by Guizot: the painters give excessive emphasis to the study of anatomy. Like Anguier, Guizot links the study of antiquity with that of anatomy. To imitate sculpture means at one and the same time to imitate the antique and prioritize anatomical representation. The focus of this criticism is the nude. One of the gravest defects in contemporary painters is, he says, to "anatomize" the body; they meticulously reproduce all the joints and muscles, multiplying anatomic detail till the nudes resemble skeletons or écorchés.[8] These nudes lack flesh. The painters fail in this way because they have adopted the style of the sculptors, who, in order to make the "inward sensible through the outward" must always begin by "shaping the inward":

> If the sculptor wants his figure to be accurate, elegant and true, he must, even when working with marble, concentrate on marking out the inward on the block before he so much as considers the outward. For the merit of a statue depends above all on the right structuring of the skeleton, its verticality, its curves, and its joints. In painting the same merit is required but it should be less obvious, since the painter presents but a single aspect of the outward. He can follow the same studies and undertake the same tasks as the statuary and his work will gain by the effort; but he must conceal them better and give greater attention to appearances, to the way in which the flesh and skin cover and hide the bones and muscles.[9]

We can see that Guizot does not at all share the view of Alberti, who recommended that painters should always begin by drawing a skeleton. Guizot is hostile to this method because it fails to take account of one of the essential attributes of painting, the fact that it is a two-dimensional art, a colored surface devoid of depth. Painted bodies have no inward dimension; they have but one aspect, the outer one. And this effect is not served by drawing outlines or delineating the joints and muscles. Making the inward structure of the body visible will not make the "inward sensible through the outward"; it will simply produce what

Guizot calls "veritable caricatures of the human body."[10] Nor is it enough simply to know how to distribute light and shade or how to shape things through the use of light. "All of that pertains to forms and three-dimensionality; their very academies [nude studies], painted from nature, often look like copies of statues; they look three-dimensional, but are all in gray and white. The color coming from within, from the transparency of the skin and the movement of the blood, is almost always absent."[11]

That very specific effect—making the inward sensible through the outward—can be attained in painting only through color, not by representing the internal nor by modeling forms, but by giving to flesh tones what Guizot calls "the color coming from within." Guizot's splendid formulation brings to mind Diderot's description of Chardin's paintings: "thick layers of color applied one over the next and whose effect transpires from the inside out."[12] This is an effect not of illusion but of sensation. The aim is not to make something visible, still less to make it credible; it is to make one feel the presence of something one cannot see. Moreover, it must be felt precisely as a hidden presence, a reality sensed but not seen. The art of painting is not to show the inward but the way in which the inward is manifested; to suggest its existence through the variations of color that make the skin pulse with the vein. It is to show how the inward transpires through the outward by which its presence is concealed.[13] Painting, says Guizot, is an imitation of colored appearances and rather than worrying about anatomical details, the painters should concentrate on rendering "the masses that form the flesh."[14]

Guizot's stance on painting is therefore very close to that of the colorists of the seventeenth and eighteenth centuries. But it is based on different premises and implies different conclusions. First and foremost, Guizot is a colorist only in painting. Unlike Diderot, he does not apply to sculpture the aesthetic criteria he recommends for painting. A colorist in painting, in sculpture Guizot holds to an aesthetic that we might describe as anti-colorist and that derives entirely from Winckelmann. This is why he condemns the eighteenth-century sculptors who sought to imitate with hammer and chisel flesh-effects that belong exclusively to the brush. But he is an anti-colorist in sculpture not because he believes (like Diderot and his predecessor de Piles) that sculpture is an art of line. On the contrary, Guizot considers sculpture an art of molding, not of line.[15] The privilege accorded to drawing in the training and practice of sculpture is for him a perfect illustration of the excessive influence that the painters—and Le Brun in particular—had long exerted over sculpture: "The sculptors—including Girardon himself—were forced to work bronze and marble from the drawings of the 'premier peintre du Roi.' On Le Brun's death, Girardon took his place; but the sculptors were still obliged to copy drawings, and Puget, furious at this ignominious servitude, left Paris rather than submit to it."[16]

Guizot predictably illustrates his critique with those bas-reliefs described by Anguier as "made in the modern manner."[17] In the dispute about bas-relief, whose origins in the seventeenth century we have already retraced, Guizot was clearly (in Perrault's terms) an ancient; his position is remote from Regnaudin's and still further from Falconet's.[18] Falconet believed that a bas-relief must resemble a picture, but Guizot does not: "Rather than make their pupils work in the round, they had them carve bas-reliefs, and these bas-reliefs were composed like pictures."[19]

When he criticizes the painters for imitating the sculptors, Guizot is not therefore accusing them of placing too great an emphasis on line. Their sin is to have strayed outside the bounds of painting. The fault he finds with them is exactly the same as that which he condemns in the sculptors of the seventeenth and eighteenth centuries; they fail to respect the specificity of their art. The idea of specificity underpinning his critique is by no means original in itself. We remember that de Piles had made it the keystone of his argument. But there it had a double function, specifying both a distinction and a hierarchy; the concept of specific difference served to establish both the priority of color over line in painting, and that of painting over sculpture. In Guizot, the idea of specificity is, on the contrary, entirely devoid of hierarchical value. Its function is exclusively that of distinction; it differentiates the arts within a relation of strict equality. The argument of specificity is no longer used as the colorists invariably used it, to demonstrate the hierarchy of the arts, but to challenge the notion of any such hierarchy.

This new way of thinking about the arts as different but equal no doubt testifies to the influence of political change. It is entirely consonant with the rejection of the artistic tendencies fashionable under the ancien régime. Guizot defends what one might surely call a republican conception of art. Yet this conception owes little to the democratic ideas that had come out of the French Revolution—the principal influence it exhibits is that of the German art theorists of the eighteenth century, since it is borrowed wholesale from Lessing. Guizot effectively does nothing more than apply to the *paragone* the analysis developed in Lessing's *Laokoon* about *ut pictura poesis*. Indeed, he refers explicitly to that work and quotes long extracts from it.

Guizot's views can, in this regard, be compared with Herder's; in other respects, they are very different indeed.[20] Guizot is not a philosopher but an art critic. The critique of the *paragone* derives in his case from reflection about works of art and is based on a real knowledge of art. Whereas Herder merely sought to determine what he described as the "subjective boundary" of the border separating painting and sculpture, Guizot strives to explain the very existence of this border, in other words, to describe the way in which it is expressed in art. Though he reaches the same conclusions, his method is exactly the opposite of Herder's. The latter was purely speculative, as we have seen; Guizot aspires to a descriptive method. So it is no surprise to find that he follows Lessing closely and includes most of the theoretical assumptions on the basis of which Lessing undermines the theory of *ut pictura poesis*. Guizot's analysis can be said to establish between the arts of space a separation systematically analogous to that which Lessing had established between the arts of space and those of time. Just as for Lessing there are things that one can say but not show, for Guizot there are things that one can paint but not sculpt. And it is, of course, on the basis of the distinction between sight and touch that he in turn justifies the existence of this separation: "Sculpture appeals to touch, painting to sight."[21]

Unlike Herder, Guizot does not give this distinction the status of a philosophical reason. He is content to use a topos, an argument traditional in the theory of art. But at the same time he integrates this topos into a fundamentally modern problem. The theoretical apparatus that he borrows from *Laocoon* is based on a new conception of space and time, since Lessing had adopted Leibniz's definitions of time as an order of succession and space as an order of simultaneity. This binary structure was founded on new criteria, but Guizot reintroduces the old line of division resting on the distinction of the senses. The arts representing their object according to the order of simultaneity are themselves divided into two categories: on the one hand, what one might call the arts of optical space, and on the other, the arts of haptic space. The traditional distinction between sight and touch now functions within a theory of artistic representation dominated by the modern idea of space, that is, a space in which elements are defined in purely differential fashion—on the basis of their respective positions and not hierarchically.

The reasons that made Guizot a colorist in painting are thus different from those that had previously been invoked by colorists. Whereas de Piles used the idea of specificity in Aristotelian fashion, as an ontological category allowing one to individuate an object and place it in the hierarchy of being, Guizot, like Lessing, makes it a sort of geopolitical concept. He uses it to mark out borders and establish limits, meaning that he is a colorist more on account of the separation of the arts than for the sake of color itself. When he criticizes the painters, the ideas he expresses are those that had always underpinned colorist discourse. But these ideas now relate to a new problematic and are therefore determined by new considerations. The many differences that we have detected between his arguments and those of his predecessors derive from the displacement undergone by the totality of the traditional concepts employed in thinking about art. If we take the elements of his argument one by one, we gain an idea of the wide-ranging consequences this entails. The first consequence concerns color, which is no longer defined in opposition to and therefore in relation to line. The application of Lessing's theoretical model to painting brings about what one might call the conceptual divorce of color and drawing. After several centuries of a sometimes harmonious but more often conflicted marriage with drawing, color becomes a "single" concept. This first breakup is followed by a second one, which affects the other half of the couple traditionally constituted by color and line. The family ties between sculpture and drawing, which had held strong since the Renaissance, are also broken. The agent of the separation here is the same principle of distinction, which states that, since the arts are different, they cannot depend on a common artistic procedure.[22] Within an overall framework defined by the distinction between the arts that appeal to sight and those that appeal to touch, these transformations ultimately make the notion of a comparison between painting and sculpture meaningless. With the passage of a few decades, the fall from favor of the doctrine of *ut pictura poesis,* undermined by Lessing's critique, had brought down with it that of the *paragone,* which had always been closely related to it. But the ground had already been prepared, as we have seen. One might say, plagiarizing Jean-Jacques Rousseau: "Things had then already come to such a pitch, that they could no longer continue as they were."[23]

When imported into the domain of the visual arts, the idea of a frontier or limit brings with it a further consequence, this one more curious and in a sense more paradoxical. It ultimately hardens the opposition between sculpture and painting as it was defined in seventeenth-century colorist doctrine, that is, in terms of an opposition between the models of antiquity and nature (in the "naturalist" sense of the word). The undermining of the *paragone* thus has no effect on the links established by de Piles between sculpture and antiquity on the one hand and painting and nature on the other. On the contrary, one might say that these links, thanks to Winckelmann, had been considerably strengthened. The new frontier between painting and sculpture faithfully follows the old one traced by de Piles on the basis of the opposition between color and line. It reproduces the same division between imitation of nature and imitation of the antique and, in relation to painting, identifies *nature* and *modern* in the same way. Guizot advises painters who must imitate nature to take what he calls "modern subjects": "Let the modern artists who have carefully studied antiquity strive to transport its beauties into modern subjects. When I say *modern,* I mean our history of the last few centuries: everything that belongs among the ideas, religion, and morals that we can consider our own."[24]

The adjective *modern* here does not mean new, current, or contemporary. It refers not to the opposition between the present and the past but to the division of history into periods: ancient and modern times. Guizot uses *modern* and *ancient* as purely descriptive historical categories, that is, in a value-neutral way. Their sense is not overdetermined by an ideological conflict, as it had been in the seventeenth century during the quarrel of the ancients and moderns and was again to be toward the end of the nineteenth century. Moreover, *modern* here is applied not to the imitation itself but to the object imitated. The word qualifies neither the art nor the artist but only the choice of subject. The way in which sculptors imitate the antique, particularly in the case of the nude, is no less modern for Guizot than the manner in which painters imitate nature in their modern subjects. These two forms of imitation express two different aspects of artistic modernity, neither of which is more modern than the other. And this difference is expressed in the choice of subjects, which should take into account the specificities that distinguish the two arts and the constraints these specificities imply. This is why Guizot has little to say in favor of the nude in painting, which he considers rather unrealistic in modern subjects and incapable of matching the sculpted nude in antique subjects. His criticism is explicitly targeted at David, whom Guizot accuses of introducing the nude into history painting:

> The absolute violation of truth and verisimilitude is one strong reason for condemning the famous author of *The Rape of the Sabine Women* [*sic*]. But there are other reasons based on the very nature of the art and its limits.... Compare the finest nude figures by Monsieur David, for example, the Romulus in his *Sabine Women* picture, with one of the more beautiful ancient statues, the *Lantin* or the *Meleager,* and tell me whether the nude has afforded the painter beauties as great as those it afforded the sculptor.[25]

For Guizot, the nude pertains to sculpture because sculpture aspires to ideal beauty, whereas painting aspires to nature and truth. Nudity is not a natural state for men who live in society and is always hidden in society and painting alike. The inward (or under) is never shown, nor indeed are the garments known as undergarments. Only outward garments can be shown. Stendhal takes up this same criticism a few years later, in his *Salon de 1824:*

> We are on the eve of a revolution in the fine arts. The great pictures composed of thirty nude figures copied from ancient statues...are most respectable works, by all means. But whatever people say, they are beginning to seem tedious and if the *Sabine Women* were to appear today, its characters would be found to lack passion and it would be observed that in any country it was absurd to go into battle unclothed. "Yet this is indeed the custom in ancient bas-reliefs!" exclaim the classicists of painting, the ones who swear by David and David alone, and who never say three words without mentioning style. Well, and what do I care about ancient bas-relief? Let us attempt to make good modern paintings. The Greeks loved the nude. But we never see it. I would go so far as to say: it repels us.[26]

Guizot and Stendhal would not go as far as Huysmans, who later remarked that "the nude, as understood by the painters, does not exist."[27] But they are not far from thinking it. Though their critique of the nude in painting belongs to a very different historical and therefore very different artistic context, it anticipates in many respects the one developed in the last few decades of the century by partisans of what is conventionally called modernity. It was in virtue of the same principle, the same logic, that Huysmans later contrasted the nude "as understood by the painters" with what he calls the "undressed." When he writes that there are no "nude women by Rembrandt who are not undressed women,"[28] his reasoning is basically the same. He, however, draws the implied conclusion and condemns the nude in painting when it does not present itself as an exception confirming the general rule: one is never nude except when one undresses. Therefore the nude, to be truthful, must be "undressed." For this reason Huysmans detests all these Venuses and hunting Dianas, with their "ivory" or—worse still—"porcelain" bodies, who clutter up the walls of the Salons; all these "stucco figurines" who manage instantly to convey, he says, that "for mythologizing painters nature and truth do not exist."[29] This is also why he has no greater affection for the sculptures exhibited at the Salon and why his assessment of contemporary sculpture as a whole is so negative. Clearly, this was not true of Guizot, who, on the contrary, praises the works of modern sculptors; nor is it true of Stendhal, who is already much more critical of modern sculpture yet unreservedly admires an artist like Canova.[30]

Some may perhaps be surprised at the importance accorded here to the views of Guizot, who will go down in history as a politician rather than an art critic.[31] We have dwelled at length on the work of an author who occupies a relatively insignificant place in art criticism because Guizot's critique seems to exemplify the transformation undergone in the early nineteenth century by the aesthetic logic whose course we are trying to trace. His critique stands at the confluence of three different sets of arguments whose intertexture was to determine the orientation of artistic theory in France for some time to come. The first concerned the definition of painting and belongs to the legacy of colorist doctrine as it had been elaborated in the seventeenth century. The second was an interrogation of the status of sculpture and derived from Winckelmann's theses. The third related to the differentiation of the visual arts and arose from Lessing's critique of *ut pictura poesis*. We can see how, in Guizot, these arguments, which had all arisen independently of each other, were combined, ultimately creating a new configuration of the artistic domain. The notion of frontiers, borrowed from Lessing, made it possible to be a colorist in painting and a Winckelmannian (an anti-colorist) in sculpture without self-contradiction. This aesthetic configuration prevailed throughout the nineteenth century, surviving a number of transformations in both art criticism and the philosophy of art. Baudelaire, Zola, Huysmans, Thoré, and the Goncourts all rejected *ut pictura poesis* along with the *paragone* in the name of specificity. Like Hegel or Taine, they are all colorists in painting and Winckelmannians in sculpture—not least when they condemn sculpture in the name of modernity. For what they reject is still the Winckelmannian image of sculpture. Whatever value they place on sculpture, whether they judge it positively or negatively, they all see it through Winckelmannian spectacles.

Winckelmann's conception of sculpture has a twofold aspect, which explains how it gave rise to such divergent or even opposing applications in two fields: that of artistic creation on the one hand and that of philosophical and literary reflection about art on the other. In one case it was the source of the neoclassical aesthetic of ideal beauty, that is, of a return to antiquity that restored sculpture to its past glory and raised it to the status of a model for painting. At the same time, it contributed to a discourse about the death of sculpture and more generally about the end of art. The paradoxical and very contradictory heritage of Winckelmann's thought resulted from the way in which it used the concept of antiquity, which it constructed from a dual perspective. It defined it in terms of both artistic properties and historical conditions. Winckelmann takes Greek sculpture to be a model that cannot be surpassed on the artistic front. At the same time, he inscribes this model in the past. From the coexistence of these two points of view, the aesthetic and the historic, arises a tension that pervades the whole of Winckelmann's analysis and imparts a painful and even tragic tone to his writing. For ancient art is not, for him, simply an object of historical knowledge, it is also—and perhaps above all—an object of love that overwhelms and exalts his imagination. Hence his twofold determination of sculpture. Winckelmann defines it both in terms of art, and thus from the point of view of the artist and art lover, and in terms of history, that is, from the point of view of reflection and knowledge. According to the first point of view, ancient art should be studied and imitated by the modern artists. But the second point of view excludes the idea that this model can be reborn from the rubble of history and experience a new artistic life.[32] The historian knows that the golden age of sculpture lasted only a short time, from the reign of Pericles to that of Alexander, and that this golden age will never come again. He knows that the perfection of ancient sculpture belongs to the ancient world. Unlike the idea of the antique, which has always functioned as stylistic category implying reference to a past posited as a timeless model, and therefore constantly reactivated over the course of time, antiquity is a historical category designating the period of our history furthest removed from modern times. The antique model is thus for the first time detached from the present, removed into the distance so that it can be reinscribed in the times that witnessed its birth, that is, "times gone by." Historical consciousness as expressed in Winckelmann pushes the antique back into a distant past of which only traces remain. It places it in a world that has disappeared and survives only in the form of fragments and ruins. The antique no longer has any other locus than that of antiquity. For the idea of the revival of the antique, an idea dear to artists and art theorists, the historian substitutes knowledge of the antique, a knowledge based on our awareness of its irremediable and definitive loss, on the painful recognition that "the beautiful days of Greek art … are gone," as Hegel puts it.[33] Returning to the antique was the foundation of the theory of art. But the death of the antique, that is, for Winckelmann, the death of art, is what presides over the birth of the discipline called art history. *Geschichte der Kunst des Alterthums* (*History of the Art of Antiquity*) is no doubt the most beautiful paean of praise for the antique ever written, but it is a funeral oration.[34] The author's voice fills with sadness and nostalgia as the book draws to a close. In the last lines, the historian compares himself to a lover abandoned on the shore, reduced to following with his eyes the vessel that carries off into the distance the object of his desire. It is an image that evokes not only the legends of Ariadne and Iseult but also the story of the daughter of the potter Dibutades, which recounts the invention of painting and sculpture:

> Just as a beloved stands on the seashore and follows with tearful eyes her departing sweetheart, with no hope of seeing him again, and believes she can glimpse even in the distant sail the image of her lover — so we, like the lover, have as it were only the shadowy outline of the subject of our desires remaining. But this arouses so much the greater longing for what is lost, and we examine the copies we have with greater attention than we would if we were in full possession of the originals. In this, we often are like individuals who wish to converse with spirits and believe they can see something where nothing exists.[35]

Speaking of the death of God, Nietzsche said that it took a while for very important news to reach the ears of mankind. And this was no less true of the death of the antique. It required a certain time for the theory of art to register the fact. It began by being unaware of the news and behaving as if the antique were still there. From Winckelmann's history it at first retained only the eulogy of the ancient, making of it the basis of a new school of art. Only after many years was Winckelmann's encomium recognized as a funeral oration. His influence came as it were in two successive waves moving in opposite directions, each matching one aspect of his conception of the antique. The artistic and the historical perspectives that constituted the two sides of one and the same thought were developed separately, each in its turn. The first wave helped re-cement the links between sculpture and the antique, which had started to come apart over the course of the eighteenth century in both art and art theory. The second ultimately led to the notion that sculpture had, as Huysmans put it, become alien to the modern world. Of course, there were many incidents along the way. The progression of the idea was paradoxical in the extreme. Thus, though the aesthetic of ideal beauty undeniably derived from Winckelmann, the aesthetic of modernity also owes him a great deal. Of course, this was clearly not, as it was in the case of the *beau idéal,* an artistic debt. Modern art was radically opposed to the neoclassical ideal and therefore to the Winckelmannian conception of art. The debt was theoretical. It related not to the idea of modern art, which was profoundly alien to Winckelmann's thought, but to the modern idea of art, that is, the orientation taken in the nineteenth century by modern reflection on art. The influence exerted by the strictly historical aspect of Winckelmann's account is obviously attributable to the new theoretical perspectives emerging from the philosophy of history. The second wave cannot be separated from its context any more than the first. It was carried along on a powerful philosophical tide whose effects gradually made themselves felt in discourse about art. They gave birth to a new theoretical and critical attitude, which was, in its turn, modified by transformations in the artistic domain: by the emergence of new forms of art.

The application of a historical grid to the analysis of art resulted in a radically new inflection of the aesthetic configuration that we have seen in Guizot, who encountered the first wave. In Guizot's analysis, the differences between painting and sculpture, nature and the ideal, modern subjects and ancient models, functioned as purely structural models. They were considered exclusively from the point of view of the system; that is, defined in terms of and on the basis of the system of the fine arts. In the authors of the following generation, they were also considered from a historical point of view; that is, they were historicized. But the consequences of this historicization, in a Winckelmannian sense, were very different from those that Winckelmann himself had drawn. A nostalgic vision of history haunted by the idea of ruin, destruction, and decadence was succeeded by an artistic valorization of all the artistic forms embodying a rejection of antique models, in other words, an artistic desire to be rid, once and for all, of the antique model. The past whose disappearance Winckelmann lamented—but that remained for him beyond compare—soon came to be considered an outmoded artistic past, a dead past that it was time to bury.

So radical a change of perspective undeniably constitutes a break in the history of artistic thought. It was not, of course, a general phenomenon in the nineteenth century, and it was ignored or rejected by many art critics. And those who adopted it did not always or from the outset express it in its most radical form. A certain Winckelmannian vision of history persisted in the writers of the romantic generation, in whom its expression is melancholic rather than nostalgic. It was not until the advent of a generation of critics who argued for what Zola called "a new manner in painting" that it completely disappeared, to be replaced by a progressive vision of the historicity of art.[36] But however it was achieved and whatever the diversity of its effects, this change of perspective testified to a new relationship between art and history, a new conception of the historic destiny of art. And it was the common feature of all the many and different strands comprising the aesthetic trend of modernity. It completely transformed the sense and value attributed since the seventeenth century to the categories of the ancient and modern in the field of art. The normative value was transferred from the idea of the antique to that of the modern, thus determining a new sense of the word *modern* that in fact attains the status of a veritable semantic mutation. After Baudelaire, this word no longer served simply to assign individuals to a particular temporal configuration, as it did even as late as Guizot; it had come to describe a certain way of painting, writing, composing, and building with which the champions of modernity identified. Its sense had till then been essentially historical and now became aesthetic and artistic. People no longer spoke of the art of the moderns but of modern art. What was thus described was no longer confused with the art of the moderns nor reduced to choosing modern subjects. What makes it possible to unite many different artists under a single head by describing them as "modern" is not the fact that they belong to the modern epoch, nor indeed that they represent subjects borrowed from the modern world, but that they practice a modern art, that is, an art reflecting the aesthetic values and meeting the artistic requirements of modernity. This new use of the word *modern* in the artistic field constituted a complete break with the system of oppositions that had determined its meaning in the preceding centuries.[37] The division was no longer between modern and ancient, as it had been in the seventeenth century, nor between modern and classical, as with the romantics, but between the two senses of the word *modern,* its aesthetic and historical senses, in other words, between the partisans of modernity and most of their contemporaries. The modern artist works against the grain of the present and not just of the past. When the modern artist succeeds in "raising himself to the heights," it is always "despite his century," as Baudelaire declared of Delacroix in his *Salon de 1859.*[38] To be modern no longer meant being at one with one's own times but declaiming against them; it meant defending what Nietzsche called "untimely" (*unzeitgemäße*) ideas and values, that is, being antimodern in the historical and cultural sense of the word. The modern artist wanted to be everything that modern man was not. For him, the representative modern man was Flaubert's Monsieur Homais.[39]

1. Paul Verlaine, epilogue 3, from *Poèmes saturniens* (1866), in idem, *Oeuvres poétiques complètes* (Paris: Gallimard, 1962), 96.

2. François-Pierre-Guillaume Guizot, *Salon de 1810*, in idem, *Études sur les beaux-arts en général* (Paris: Didier, 1851), 5–7.

3. Guizot, *Salon de 1810* (note 2), 7, 8.

4. Antoine-Chrysostôme Quatremère de Quincy, *Essai sur l'idéal dans ses applications pratiques aux oeuvres de l'imitation proper des arts du dessin* (Paris: Adrien Le Clère, 1837), 10, 49–50; the quoted text is on p. 10. One of the more notable paradoxes of the antinaturalist critique deriving from Winckelmann's views was the fact that it was often turned against Bernini, who the German historian considered largely responsible for the corruption of art and taste. As we have seen, when Bernini visited France, he preached the imitation of the antique and the adoption of the grand manner and was unsparing in his criticism of French naturalism.

5. Guizot, *Salon de 1810* (note 2), 7.

6. Guizot, *Salon de 1810* (note 2), 7.

7. Guizot, *Salon de 1810* (note 2), 95.

8. The two men in Girodet's picture *The Deluge* "are overloaded with anatomical details," says Guizot; in Girodet's *The Cairo Revolt*, "The nude Arabs, the arms of the seated Turk, etc., are anatomized as if for an écorché." This fault, he adds, "which in the master is merely an abuse of knowledge and talent, becomes a ridiculous error in the student." He cites as evidence Pierre Dorcy's picture *A Hunter and His Mistress by the Tomb of Two Lovers*: "At first one is not expecting to find an excess of anatomy here…but all of a sudden one perceives, in the man's shoulder, a collarbone so strongly outlined that one is tempted to believe that the artist wanted to make it clear that he knew where in the body it came"; Guizot, *Salon de 1810* (note 2), 42–43.

9. Guizot, *Salon de 1810* (note 2), 40–41. Guizot borrowed his analysis of sculptural methodology, the idea of proceeding from the inward to the outward, from Toussaint-Bernard Émeric-David, *Recherches sur l'art statuaire: Considéré chez les anciens et chez les modernes…* (Paris: Nyon aîné, 1805), referring to it frequently in his *Salon de 1810*.

10. Guizot, *Salon de 1810* (note 2), 43.

11. Guizot, *Salon de 1810* (note 2), 96.

12. Denis Diderot, *Salon de 1763*, in idem, *Arts et lettres (1739–1766)*, ed. Jean Varloot, vol. 13 of Denis Diderot, *Oeuvres complètes* (Paris: Hermann, 1980), 380.

13. The logicians of Port-Royal had already noted this. In words easily applicable to painting, they observed: "Those who state that nothing ever appears by means of that by which it is concealed are on very shaky ground"; Antoine Arnauld and Pierre Nicole, *La logique ou l'art de penser: Contenant, outre les regles communes, plusieurs observations nouvelles, propres à former le iugement* (1662; Paris: Gallimard, 1992), 81.

14. Guizot, *Salon de 1810* (note 2), 41.

15. This definition of sculpture is surely influenced by Winckelmann, who did not consider drawing the primordial form of art. As he says in the very first lines of *Geschichte der Kunst des Alterthums,* if art began with sculpture, sculpture did not begin with drawing: "Art began with the simplest form, and probably with a kind of sculpture, because even a child can give a distinct shape to a soft mass, though he cannot draw anything on a flat surface. For sculpture, the mere conception of a thing suffices, but drawing requires many other kinds of knowledge—though painting later was used to adorn sculpture"; Johann Joachim Winckelmann, *History of the Art of Antiquity,* trans. Harry Francis Mallgrave (Los Angeles: Getty Research Institute, 2006), 111.

16. Guizot, *Salon de 1810* (note 2), 5.

17. Michel-Andre Anguier, "La maniére de Paris les bas reliefs" (9 July 1673), in Jacqueline Lichtenstein and Christian Michel, eds., *Les conférences de l'Académie royale de peinture et de sculpture,* vol. 1, *De 1667 à 1679: Les conférences au temps d'Henry Testelin* (Paris: École nationale supérieure des beaux-arts, 2007), bk. 2, 515–18.

18. Cf. chap. 1, n. 53.

19. Guizot, *Salon de 1810* (note 2), 5–6.

20. It is very unlikely that Guizot had read Herder's book.

21. Guizot, *Salon de 1810* (note 2), 95.

22. My use of the expression "family ties" does not simply reflect a taste for metaphor. After all, Vasari had defined drawing as the "father" of all the visual arts: painting, sculpture, and architecture.

23. Jean-Jacques Rousseau, "A Discourse on the Origin of Inequality," in idem, *The Social Contract; and, The Discourses,* trans. George Douglas Howard Cole (London: Knopf, 1993), 84.

24. Guizot, *Salon de 1810* (note 2), 67.

25. Guizot, *Salon de 1810* (note 2), 44–45.

26. Stendhal, *Salon de 1824,* in idem, *Mélanges d'art et de littérature* (Paris: Lévy, 1867), 152.

27. Joris-Karl Huysmans, *Salon de 1879,* in idem, *L'art moderne, Certains* (Paris: Union générale d'éditions, 1975), 36.

28. Huysmans, *Salon de 1879* (note 27), 36.

29. Huysmans, *Salon de 1879* (note 27), 36–37.

30. Unlike Guizot, Stendhal attacks the influence exerted by David over both sculpture and painting. On Canova's death, he wrote: "It is superfluous to add that this illustrious man is the execration of the French school; he possessed *expression,* as the Sommariva Magdalene proves; he had *grace*—people still remember the *Hebe* exhibited four years ago; these are things in which the school of David is somewhat lacking. This illustrious painter, the most able of the eighteenth century, has perhaps had greater influence over the art of sculpture than that of painting"; Stendhal, *Salon de 1824* (note 26), 233.

31. Guizot, who soon abandoned his first career as a journalist and art critic to go into politics, was not the only French politician to adopt this career path in the nineteenth century. Adolphe Thiers did the same.

32. There follows from this an ambiguity in Winckelmann's conception of imitation, which has often been noted in the literature.

33. Georg Wilhelm Friedrich Hegel, *Aesthetics: Lectures on Fine Art,* trans. T. M. Knox (Oxford: Clarendon, 1988), 1:10.

34. Édouard Pommier uses the very beautiful expression "funeral lament" (*lamento funèbre*) to describe the *Geschichte der Kunst des Alterthums.* Cf. Philippe Hoff and Paul-Louis Rinuy, eds., *Antiquités imaginaires: La référence antique dans l'art moderne, de la Renaissance à nos jours* (Paris: Presses de l'École normale supérieure, 1996); and *Winckelmann: La naissance de l'histoire de l'art à l'époque des lumières: Actes du cycle de conférences prononcées à l'auditorium du Louvre du 11 décembre 1989 au 12 février 1990* (Paris: Documentation française, 1991). See also Alex Potts, *Flesh and the Ideal: Winckelmann and the Origins of Art History* (New Haven: Yale Univ. Press, 1994); and Élisabeth Décultot, *Johann Joachim Winckelmann: Enquête sur la genèse de l'histoire de l'art* (Paris: Presses universitaires de France, 2000).

35. Winckelmann, *History of the Art of Antiquity* (note 15), 351.

36. Émile Zola, "Une nouvelle maniére en peinture: Édouard Manet," *Revue du XIXe siècle: Les lettres, les arts, la philosophie, romans et voyages* 4, no. 10 (1867), 43–64.

37. On this question, see Hans Robert Jauss, "Modernity and Literary Tradition," trans. Christian Thorne, *Critical Inquiry* 31, no. 2 (2005): 329–64. Cf. Marc Fumaroli, "Les abeilles et les araignées," introduction to Anne-Marie Lecoq, ed., *La querelle des anciens et des modernes: XVIIe–XVIIIe siècles* (Paris: Gallimard, 2001), 5–218.

38. Charles Baudelaire, *Salon de 1859,* in idem, *Curiosités esthétiques: L'art romantique et autres oeuvres critiques,* ed. Henri Lemaître (Paris: Éditions Garnier frères, 1962), 338.

39. The pharmacist in Flaubert's *Madame Bovary.*

The Death of Sculpture

These white poems of marble, their broken stanzas dug from the earth,
constitute at once the admiration and the despair of modern art.

— Théophile Gautier[1]

WE HAVE SEEN how a certain aesthetic logic created an image of sculpture as a philosophical art, or more precisely as an art for philosophers: one that met the requirements of reason, its bare purity of form wholly at one with philosophical criteria of truth. This image is present in both Diderot and Winckelmann, and reaches its most extreme form in Herder. But it was not always perceived in the same way by the Germans and the French. The same representation gave rise to radically opposed aesthetic assessments in the two countries, the former judging positively what the latter took a dim view of. For the Germans, that image justified the undeniable superiority of sculpture; for the French, starting with Diderot, it was one of the arguments advanced against it. As of the seventeenth century, a second comparison was proposed, one that mapped onto the analogy of sculpture and philosophy that of sculpture and poetry. Given the privileged link between sculpture and the antique, it comes as no surprise that reference to the antique played a determining role in the second comparison. Since the Renaissance, ancient literature had been a model for writers, just as ancient sculpture had guided the sculptors. Like their statues but unlike their pictures, the literary works of the ancients had come down to us. And they had survived the ravages of time much better than the statues, of which there often remained little but fragments. Moreover, even these fragments were for the most part known only through copies. Unlike sculptures, the texts handed down from antiquity not only were original works but were often intact. But the comparison between poetry and sculpture, because it was based on sculpture rather than poetry, curiously tended to efface this essential distinction. In the *ut pictura poesis* of the Renaissance, poetry had afforded a model by which to define painting. The doctrine of *ut sculptura poesis* reversed this, applying the model of sculpture to poetry; and in this new variant of the parallel between the arts, sculpture was the term of reference. The image of poetry was made to derive from the image of sculpture, and its relationship to antiquity was conceived by analogy with that of sculpture. This meant that not only was poetry, like sculpture, connected with antiquity, it was connected in the same way. Poets were now expected to behave toward antiquity in the same way as sculptors, in other words, to treat the antique as an aesthetic element and embed specimens of it in their own works. Dubos strongly recommends inserting "ancient fragments" into poems, even comparing such quotation with the ancient statues placed in the *galerie des glaces* (hall of mirrors) at Versailles: "These new [architectural] works gain a new grace by being ornamented with ancient fragments. Lines by Horace and Virgil, well translated and aptly put to work in a French poem, have the same effect in that poem as the ancient statues in the gallery at Versailles. Readers are pleased to discover, recast in a new form, a thought that once pleased them in Latin."[2]

Dubos immediately cites the names of Corneille, Molière, and La Fontaine, who "often did this." But it must be observed that his perspective on antiquity is profoundly alien to the thinking of seventeenth-century authors. True, they often borrowed entire passages from the ancient authors, as Molière did, employing, as Dubos rightly says, "ten successive lines from Ovid in the second act of *Le misanthrope*."[3] But ancient literature was not, in their view, for quoting, it was for appropriating. Their borrowings were not exhibited as such but fused with and integrated into the unity of original work. The theory of imitation implied a living relationship with the ancient. This is very different from the ornamental use of quotation described by Dubos, whose effect is inseparable from the exercise of memory, since he attributes it in large measure to the pleasure taken by the reader in remembering what he once loved and learned. This aesthetic effect still belongs within the problematic of mimesis, to the extent that the pleasure is one of recognition. But recognition does not here have the sense it had in Aristotle, a sense that the theorists of the seventeenth century had retained. The immediate pleasure of recognition, which Aristotle linked to the imitation of nature, is here transformed into a scholarly pleasure of reminiscence appealing to one's knowledge of art. By applying to literature the idea of the "ancient fragment" borrowed from sculpture, Dubos performed a twofold operation. The first consisted of generalizing to the poetic arts the characteristics of a mode of representation belonging to the visual arts, since the hierarchy between the arts of image and language posited by *ut sculptura poesis* runs in the opposite direction from the tradition established and codified since the Renaissance as *ut pictura poesis*. The second operation bore on the status of the antique and was a direct consequence of the first. By becoming an object inserted into a representation, antiquity, hitherto considered a living source of inspiration, now became an object of representation. The fragment shows the antique as antique. But it shows it at the same time as a fragmented whole, like a body broken into pieces of which there remain only a few scattered vestiges, precisely in the image of all these bodies of ancient sculpture reconstructed on the basis of a leg, an arm, or a torso. The way in which Dubos thus establishes a comparison between poetry and sculpture, focusing on the relationship with antiquity, prefigures an aesthetic transformation clearly perceptible only in the following generation, particularly in Germany. Dubos would probably have rejected the consequences of this transformation. It already contains in embryo the idea of the death of antiquity. It is therefore no surprise to find it again in Winckelmann, though in a slightly different form, since there it is based on an analogy between the arts of language and those of the image: "Painting and sculpture related to each other like oratory and poetry."[4]

Winckelmann's comparison, unlike that of Dubos, bears on the relationship between the terms rather than on the terms themselves. It involves establishing between them relations of proportionality according to a pattern not unlike the famous line of book 7 of Plato's *Republic:* if painting is to sculpture what eloquence (oratory) is to poetry, then painting is to eloquence what sculpture is to poetry. In Winckelmann, the comparison between sculpture and poetry matches the one firmly established since the Renaissance between painting and rhetoric. It challenges *ut sculptura poesis* with *ut rhetorica pictura.* This opposition perfectly summarizes the disparity between Winckelmann's and Diderot's aesthetics. Whereas Winckelmann clearly preferred the poetry of sculpture, Diderot responded more readily to the eloquence of painting. His aesthetic of the visual arts, like that of de Piles, to whom he owed so much, was entirely determined by a rhetorical model. Precisely what he reproved in sculpture was its lack of eloquence, in the sense given to this term by the theorists of rhetoric: its inability to move one, attested in his view by the fact that it generally left him indifferent and rarely touched him or excited his enthusiasm. Diderot preferred painting to sculpture because he expected a work of art to act on the person who gazes at it; he expected it to bring him out of himself, to speak to him. And these statues with their blind eyes did not speak to him. They spoke, for statues also speak.[5] But—here is the point of contrast with painting—Diderot did not feel that their silent speech was addressed to him. We have seen that this was one of the reasons why he was so "brief" with painting. Without rehearsing this aspect of his critique of sculpture, which we have already examined, we should simply like to underline the fact that it presents strange analogies with certain arguments developed since antiquity in the field of rhetoric. In fact, it is reminiscent of the way in which Cicero contrasts two kinds of speech: a speech that is in some respects autarchic, introverted, and indifferent to others, and an effective speech addressed to others and that seeks to reach its audience. The first of these characterizes, in his view, the words of poets and philosophers and the second that of orators. Unlike orators, Cicero says, the poet and philosopher can do without the assent of the public. And this kinship between poetic and philosophical discourse explains in his view why a philosopher may not be deterred by the reading out loud of a poem that everyone else finds repellently boring. He illustrates this with the story of Antimachus, who continued to read out his poem when no one but Plato was any longer listening: "When reading that long and well-known poem of his before an assembled audience, in the very midst of his reading all his listeners left him but Plato: 'I shall go on reading,' he said, 'just the same; for me Plato alone is as good as a hundred thousand.'"[6]

Sculpture for Diderot is like poetry for Cicero—it is destined primarily for philosophers. But the comparison between the two authors extends no further. Indeed, whereas Diderot sees affinities between the activity of the sculptor and that of the philosopher, he very often opposes poetry and philosophy, as he does in his *Lettre sur les sourds et muets,* his correspondence with Falconet, or again in his *Salon de 1767.* In the latter, indeed, he describes the philosophical cast of mind as fatal to poetry: "Everywhere verve and poetry decay as the philosophical cast of mind progresses."[7]

This distinction between poetry and philosophy is pregnant with consequences on the aesthetic level and in large measure determines the system of correspondences that governs the comparison of the arts in Diderot. If poetry is pitted against philosophy, it is also necessarily pitted against sculpture, which is closely linked to philosophy. Comparing sculpture with poetry, as Winckelmann does, therefore makes no sense from a strictly Diderotian point of view, not because Diderot has a different definition of sculpture—we have seen that they are entirely at one on this topic—but because he has a quite different idea of poetry, which brings in its train a quite different idea of art. In the figure of poetry, it is the very nature of artistic activity in general—indeed, what one might call the artistic cast of mind—that Diderot contrasts with the philosophical cast of mind. The opposition between poetry and philosophy implies a more fundamental distinction between art and philosophy, which affects the whole range of his aesthetic assessments in literature, painting, and sculpture. In a number of respects, this distinction maps onto one made by the theoreticians of rhetoric between rhetoric and philosophy. And it makes use of a series of interconnected analogies very different from those that we find in Winckelmann. For Diderot, painting is to sculpture not what eloquence is to poetry but what both eloquence and poetry are to philosophy. *Ut rhetorica pictura* is for him simply a variant of *ut pictura poesis.* And his conception of the comparison between painting and poetry—which dominates his entire vision of art—makes any comparison between sculpture and poetry if not impossible then at least logically contradictory, that is, incompatible with the principles that underpin his aesthetic. The eloquent poetry of painting, like the eloquent painting of poetry, is contrasted in the same way and for the same reasons with the cold, abstract philosophy of sculpture. If we adopt his point of view, a comparison between sculpture and poetry—that is, understanding the philosophical language of sculpture as a poetic language—would bear witness to undeniable progress on the part of the philosophical cast of mind, which he accuses of annihilating poetry. We have said that *ut sculptura poesis* contained in embryo the idea of the death of the antique; we now see that it also contains the seeds of another idea, that of the death of art. This is not in the Hegelian sense of art being transcended by philosophy but in the Diderotian sense of art falling into decadence under the impact of philosophy. Considered in the light of Diderot's aesthetic philosophy, *ut sculptura poesis* rests on a vision of poetry and of art in general permeated with philosophy: in other words, on a mistaken notion of art.

Should we conclude from this that Winckelmann's conception of sculpture is based on a mistaken notion of art? Diderot did not, of course, go so far. Although he did not share Winckelmann's enthusiasm for sculpture, he did not attack his ideas; he did not even question them. But, even if Diderot himself did not draw this conclusion, it follows directly from his line of thought. And he would probably have applied it without hesitation to Herder if he had known the latter's work on sculpture, in which a purely philosophical approach to art concludes by celebrating sculpture precisely as a philosophical art, that is, by defending the aesthetic value of a philosophical art.

Did Germans like sculpture—and ancient sculpture in particular—because they were more inclined to poetry and philosophy than the French, who undoubtedly preferred painting? Or was it because they were more philosophical than artistic and therefore thought about art only in terms of philosophy? The second thesis was adopted by the French in the nineteenth century, when many of them denounced philosophical art as a typically German idea. They saw it as deriving from a mistaken vision of art fueled by metaphysical abstraction, a vice that German artists were, alas, unable to shake off. This accusation was directed above all at the painters. For the French, painting was the first and principal victim of the wrongheaded notion of art prevailing in Germany. In his unfinished article, "L'art philosophique," Baudelaire writes: "As we all know, and as it would be all too easy to guess if we did not, Germany is the country which has sunk deepest into the error of Philosophic Art."[8]

The judgment is unanimous and recurs throughout the second half of the nineteenth century: German painting is a painting of ideas, a literary art that claims to express poetical and philosophical ideas.[9] As Théophile Gautier puts it, German painters do not paint pictures. They write mythological, religious, and metaphysical poems:

> Germany seems to relish the aesthetics of art.... It does not make pictures so much as poems; in these cyclical inventions are unfolded the destinies of the human race, the migration of the races, the myths and apocalypses of religion, or again symbolic and philosophical systems in which figures come forward as hieroglyphic signs rather than as representations of individuals. This entirely intellectual school scorns color, technique, and the pleasure of the brushstroke. It does not so much paint as write the idea. This way of envisaging art is entirely new to us.[10]

The expression "aesthetics of art" immediately designates this new perspective on art as German. The word *aesthetics,* which was beginning to make its way into the French language in the nineteenth century, is simply a translation of the German *Äesthetik* and refers exclusively to a philosophical approach to art.[11] Now, in France as in Germany, the image of philosophy tended to be inseparable from that of the philosophy teacher. But in France, unlike Germany, the image of the teacher was a negative one. Since the seventeenth century, teachers, tutors, and indeed pedagogues of all kinds had been numbered by artists and art lovers as among the enemies of art. Coming from an art critic like Gautier, the expression "aesthetics of art" was therefore doubly pejorative. It designated not only the way in which Germans envisaged art but more generally the dogmatism and excessively methodological approach of teachers in general. It suggested a kind of pedantry inherent in their way of thinking, especially when they took it upon themselves to speak of art. Stigmatizing the twin evils of "pédantisme et philosophisme," Baudelaire openly avowed the horror inspired in him by "these modern self-appointed aesthetic pedants, as Heinrich Heine . . . calls them,"[12] thereby contriving to suggest that there were some Germans—for the most part Francophiles—who shared his point of view.

The idea that German artists were under the sway of teachers is a leitmotiv of French criticism over the following few decades. Thus the poet Jules Laforgue, writing in 1886 about a sculpture exhibition that had just opened in the Dresden gallery: "As tradition so clearly requires in Germany—as it has done for the last hundred years—here too the teachers have provided the impetus and prepared the field for the plow."[13]

And though Laforgue's terms are somewhat different, his description of German painting is very similar to Gautier's: "I would remind the reader that the German school remains an improvised one, hastily engrafted by the national vanity of a very intellectual and sensitive race. The German is as yet artistic only in respect of his brain and ear, excelling only in poetry and music, the two abstract arts."[14]

His point of view is shared by Taine, who writes about Germany:

It is the land of metaphysics and system. But the superabundance of higher meditations has been harmful to the arts that derive from drawing. German painters strive to express humanitarian or religious ideas in their canvases or frescoes. They subordinate color and form to thought; their work is symbolic; they paint courses of philosophy and history on walls; and if you go to Munich, you will see that the greatest of them are philosophers who strayed into painting, better equipped to appeal to reason than to the eye and suited rather to the pen than the paintbrush.[15]

Criticism of philosophical art began with German art but was not confined to it. French critics were quick to denounce the influence exerted on French painters by this erroneous German notion of art and did so in exactly the same terms. Baudelaire was one of the first to broaden his critique of the German school to include French painting and to suggest that philosophical art was an aberration not, alas, confined to the Germans: "What is Philosophical Art according to the ideas of Chenavard and the German school? It is a plastic art which sets itself up in place of books, by which I mean as a rival to the printing-press in the teaching of history, morals and philosophy."[16]

The case made against the German school is therefore nothing other than the expression of a more radical and fundamental critique that transcends the frontiers of nations as it does those of painting. Beyond or rather through painting, the dispute concerns what Gautier very properly calls a way of envisaging art. A significant part of French artistic thought has always been very hostile to the idea that one art could obey the norms and rules imposed by another. De Piles, Anguier, Diderot, Falconet, and Guizot, to cite only those authors on whom we have focused, have all in their various and sometimes mutually contradictory fashions defended the idea of the autonomy and still more the specificity of the different forms of art. What Gautier calls the German "manner" was on a collision course with this tradition, which had survived in France (not without controversy) for two centuries. Paradoxically, the influence of the German Lessing had only reinforced it. The critique of philosophical art and thus of German painting is merely another aspect of the combat that the French have always waged against mixing genres and confusing the arts or the discourses about them. They were hostile to the confusion of the visual and the literary arts, of painting and sculpture within the visual arts, of theater and poetry within the literary arts, and, of course, of art and philosophy. Their hostility was based on the principle of distinction, which is ultimately very Cartesian and therefore philosophical in itself. But this principle of distinction has surely never been applied to the arts with such strength and stubbornness as in the nineteenth century. It lies at the heart of all the critiques made of philosophical art, beginning with that of Baudelaire, as we can see from the lines that follow the two sentences cited above attacking Chenavard and the German school:

> In fact, there have been periods of history in which the role of the plastic arts was to paint the historical archives of a people and its religious beliefs.
>
> But for several centuries now, the history of art has been marked by an ever-increasing division of powers, some subjects becoming the special preserve of painting, others of music and others of literature.
>
> Is it by some fatal consequence of decadence that today each art should evince a desire to trespass on the next, so that we have the spectacle of musical scales being introduced into painting, colour into sculpture, plastic devices into literature, and, by other artists — those indeed with whom we are specially concerned today — a sort of encyclopedic philosophy into plastic art itself?[17]

It was in the name of this same principle of distinction, the idea of frontier or limitation, that Baudelaire also condemned the poetic and sentimental painting of Scheffer ("it dawned on Ary Scheffer, a little late no doubt, that he was not a painter born")[18] and indeed all forms of this — in his view, typically modern — ailment with which so many artists were afflicted. He called it eclecticism: "the encroachment of one part upon another, the importation of poetry, of wit and sentiment into painting, all these trivialities of our day are vices peculiar to eclectics."[19]

And it is in the name of this same principle that he deprecates the use of color in sculpture, rehearsing a criticism that had first entered the tradition in the eighteenth century: "Oh sculptor, you who once upon a time made fine statues, are you ignorant of the great difference between drawing on canvas and modeling clay? Are you unaware that color is a melodic science whose secrets cannot be discovered by pummeling marble? — A musician who wished to ape Delacroix, that we could understand — but a sculptor, never. Oh mighty carver of stones! Why do you insist on playing the violin?"[20]

Note that Baudelaire gives a slightly different twist to the argument about specificity found in Diderot and his contemporaries. Introducing color into sculpture is, he says, like wanting to play the violin with a stone. Saying that color is musical and that it is therefore incompatible with sculpture (which means that for him, sculpture, unlike painting, has no musical aspirations) surely contradicts the principle of distinction by reintroducing a comparison between the arts. The analogy between music and color is not original — it had been used since antiquity and has long since entered the language. One speaks of a coloratura voice and of color harmony in painting. And this analogy is one of the forms in which the comparison between painting and music has been expressed over the course of the centuries.[21] The novelty of Baudelaire's argument consists precisely in detaching it from any sense of comparison or parallel, inscribing it instead into a theory of correspondences. In contrast with comparisons between the arts themselves, which had always consisted of comparing their so-called essences or definitions, Baudelaire's correspondence applies exclusively to their effects. It establishes a completely different relationship between the arts based on the analogous nature of the reveries that they inspire, the ideas that they suggest, and the sensations that they excite in the listener, reader, or spectator.[22] This relationship, far from abolishing the distinctions between the arts, maintains their separation; it never eliminates their differences or their singularities. "Perfumes, colors, and sounds correspond"[23] in the imagination, but the arts from which they derive do not on that account resemble one another. In his critique of Scheffer, Baudelaire writes: "Painting is interesting only by colour and form; it resembles poetry only in so far as the latter awakens in the reader ideas of painting."[24]

Perceiving correspondences does not therefore imply comparing objects but the ideas and sensations that these objects give rise to, in other words, approaching them exclusively from the point of view of the subject. The most faithful expression of Baudelaire's idea of correspondence is no doubt that of Huysmans. Speaking of Gustave Moreau's paintings, he writes: "There is no analogy between these works and those of the past unless in literature. Seeing these pictures, we experience a sensation barely inferior to those elicited by certain bizarre and charming poems, such as the dream that Charles Baudelaire dedicated to Constantin Guys in *Les fleurs du mal.*"[25]

These new ways of thinking about the relationship between the arts constitute an undeniable break with the tradition of *ut pictura poesis,* a break that grew clearer over the following few decades. In the wake of Baudelaire, there came ever more violent denunciations of what the Goncourt brothers called "the disastrous influence of literature on painting,"[26] bringing together under a single head of condemnation painter-poets, literary paintings, musician-painters, and philosopher-painters: all those who "paint from the brain," driven astray by "casual contact with ideas and aesthetics,"[27] as the Goncourts put it, or who subordinate painting to the tutelage of the book and art in general to the norms of bourgeois society. For Baudelaire and his successors, these two aspects were self-evidently linked. The painters so much appreciated by the bourgeoisie were worthy representatives of a society founded on the twin pillars of trade and marriage. They behaved toward art like shopkeepers and married men; they imported art and "shacked up" with it, to adopt an expression (*se mettre à la colle*) then at the height of its vogue. In the eyes of those who defended what one might call a bachelor notion of art, whose model of art was the unique, independent, singular individual, and who were for the most part celibate artists, there was nothing to be said in favor of such painters. This relationship between the critique of literary painting and that of bourgeois values is fully articulated by the Goncourts, those paragons of celibate art. In *Manette Salomon,* as in their *Journal,* the brothers declare open season on those "dry fruits of literature,"[28] the literary painters whose art so easily falls in with the norms of prevailing taste. The list of French painters so condemned is particularly long, going from Poussin to Delaroche via David, and Baudelaire would no doubt have been scandalized to see the name of Delacroix placed alongside that of Ingres. According to the Goncourts, "With Raphael begins allegory, which is so much to the taste of serious critics: common or garden fellows on whom grand names are bestowed — 'Socrates,' 'Phidias,' or 'Homer' — and women inscribed with titles like 'Jurisprudence,' 'Law,' 'Philosophy,' 'History'; so there it is, Raphael is the first literary painter, the father of all those painters who cannot paint, call them Ingres or Delacroix or what you will."[29]

First directed against the German school, this critique of the painting of ideas is now synonymous with that of literary painting, which is itself synonymous with critiques of romanticism or more precisely romantic ideas about painting. Though these displacements broaden the target to include new names like that of Delacroix, they change neither the nature of the critique nor what was at stake; it persists unaltered till the turn of the century. We hear it in Zola, for example. He too makes fun of painters who, as Gautier put it, made poems instead of pictures:

> Our artists are poets. This is a grave charge to bring against people of whom thought is neither expected nor desired, but one that I maintain. Look at the Salon: it is all stanzas and madrigals. Here a painter rhymes an ode to Poland; his fellow composes an ode to Cleopatra; here one sings in the mode of Tibullus and another attempts to wind the sonorous trumpet of Lucretius. I leave aside the warlike hymns, the elegies, the salacious songs and fables.
>
> What a mess!
>
> For goodness sake, gentlemen, since you are painters, no singing please! Just paint.[30]

Or again, when he inveighs against the painting of ideas: "Only, for goodness sake, no painting of souls! There is nothing so tedious as the painting of ideas."[31] Now these same writers, up in arms against the invasion of the Salon by paintings oozing poetry and philosophy, were also unanimous in condemning the sculpture of their time. It is as if sculpture exemplified in their eyes everything that they rejected in painting. It feeds on abstractions — such as truth, virtue, justice, and beauty—loves big ideas and noble principles, aspires to be poetic and philosophical, serves morality and politics, and never avoids the pedagogical.[32] To this must be added a further trait, the final straw that makes it completely odious to the defenders of modernity: sculpture strives desperately to perpetuate the antique ideal and will only grudgingly adapt it to the prevailing taste.

We must begin with Baudelaire if we are to understand the reasons for so massive and unanimous a rejection of sculpture by the partisans of modernity. As we know, Baudelaire's position relative to sculpture changed considerably between the *Salon de 1846* and the *Salon de 1859*. In the *Salon de 1846,* it is for the most part very negative. In the chapter devoted to Delacroix, contemporary sculptors, who had so disparaged the painter's draftsmanship, were described as "prejudiced and one-eyed people…whose judgment is worth at most half that of an architect,"[33] while the chapter on sculpture is entitled "Pourquoi la sculpture est ennuyeuse" ("Why Sculpture Is a Bore"). The critique is of course primarily directed at contemporary sculpture, which is in a "pitiful state."[34] But its intended target is broader yet and includes not simply contemporary sculpture but sculpture in general. Unlike painting, "which is an art demanding deep thought and one that requires a special initiation merely to be enjoyed,"[35] sculpture is, he says, "an art of the Caribbees,"[36] a primitive art, an art made by primitives. Even when "it had emerged from its primitive period and attained its most magnificent development," that is, today, it is "only a complementary art," a "drawing-room or bedroom art" in which the "Caribs of lace, like M. Gayrard, and the Caribs of the wrinkle, the hair and the wart, such as M. David" reign supreme.[37] Then come "the Caribs of the andiron, the clock, the writing table and so on."[38] The attacks on contemporary sculpture continue in the *Salon de 1859.* Indeed, the way in which Baudelaire begins his description of the sculpted works is not unlike that of Diderot, who, it will be remembered, said that he was going to be "short with the sculptors": "And so you will not be surprised to find me brief in my examination of this year's works" (fig. 20).[39]

But in the *Salon de 1859,* this remark follows an important passage about "the divine role of sculpture."[40] Far from being insensitive to sculpture, Baudelaire claims to love the "mysterious priestly art of Egypt and Nineveh," the art of the Greeks, that of Michelangelo ("precise as science, prodigious as dream"), the works of Guillaume Coustou and those of the sculptors of the eighteenth century. Different as they are, each of these forms of artistic expression illustrates in its own way the divine role of sculpture. Modern sculpture does not: "But if you will stop to think how many different types of perfection must be brought together to achieve this austere magic, you will not be surprised at the exhaustion and discouragement which often takes possession of our minds as we

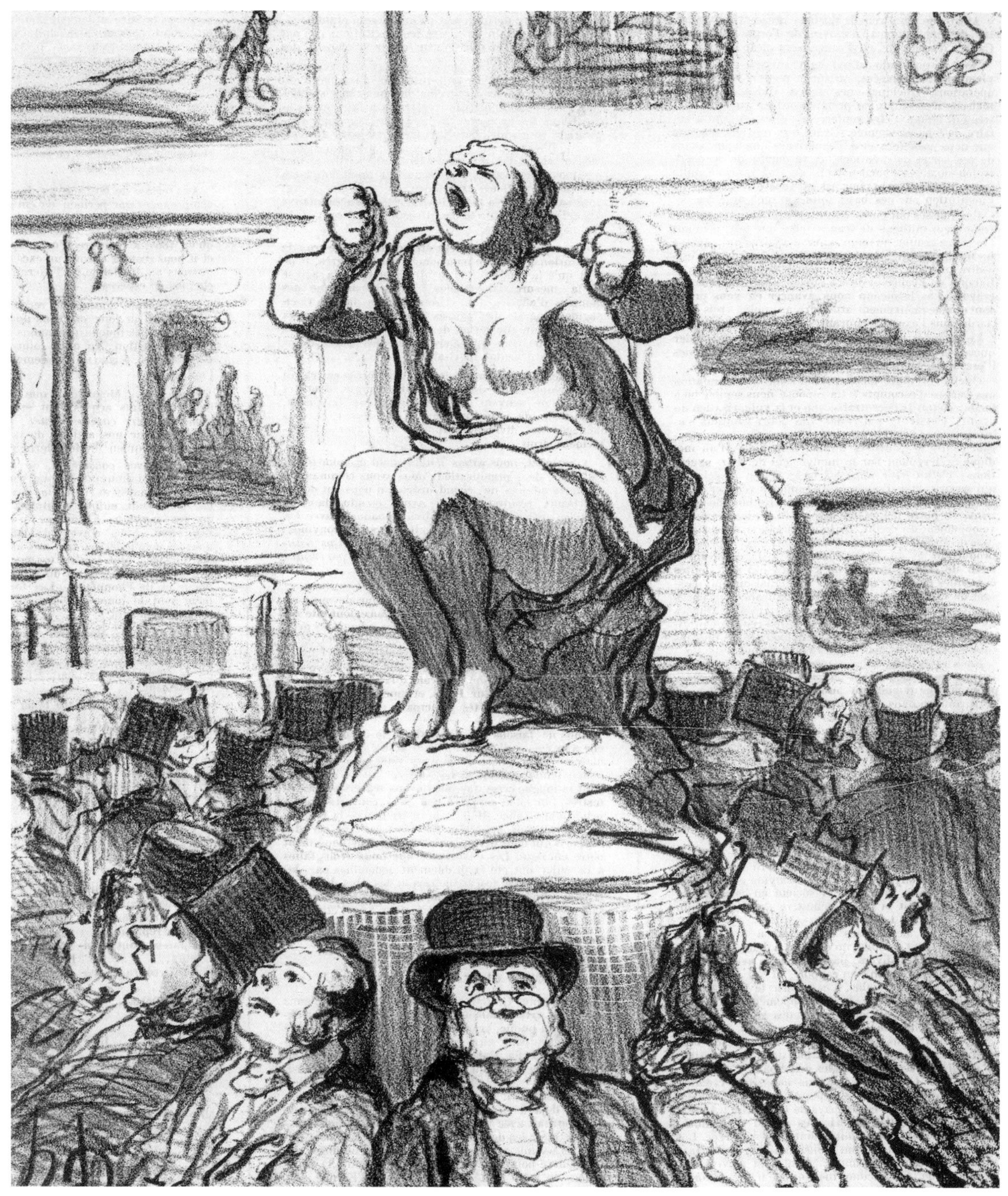

Fig. 20. Honoré Daumier (French, 1808–79)
Sculpture's Dismay at Being Surrounded by Painting
From *Le charivari*, 22 July 1857
Los Angeles, Getty Research Institute

hasten through these galleries of modern sculptures, in which the divine aim is nearly always misunderstood and a trifling prettiness is indulgently substituted for grandeur."[41]

In the *Salon de 1859,* Baudelaire's negative judgment of modern sculpture is counterpointed by his encomium of sculpture as a divine art. The exceedingly ancient origin of the art is no longer invoked against it but adduced as a proof of its greatness: "It is indeed a strange art, whose roots disappear into the darkness of time and which already, in primitive ages, was producing works which cause the civilized mind to marvel!"[42]

The long poetic evocation that prefaces the text of the *Salon de 1859,* preceding the critique as such, bears witness to this new way of understanding sculpture. It is described there as an immemorial art, an art of memory, dream, imagination, giving birth to a solemn and silent world peopled with sublime figures that evoke feelings of melancholy. These "imperious phantoms" encountered in the depths of an ancient library, glimpsed from within a grove or in the darkest corner of a little chapel or confronting one in a public square, "urge you on to the sublime," writes Baudelaire, and implore you, "a creature of passage, to think of eternity." This is surely not the "Carib" art described in the *Salon de 1846.* It has now become an allegory of poetic inspiration. It expresses eternal and immutable beauty, such as Baudelaire describes in the poem "Beauty" in *Les fleurs du mal:*

> I am lovely, o mortals, a stone-fashioned dream,
> And my breast, where you bruise yourselves all in your turn,
> Is made so that love will be born in the poet —
> Eternal, and silent as matter is timeless.
>
> I reign in the air like a puzzling sphinx;
> My heart is of snow and is pure as the swans,
> I hate only impulse, the breaking of line,
> And I never will cry, nor will ever show smile.
>
> The poets, in view of my lofty design —
> The style, as it seems, of the finest of statues —
> Will spend all their days in their painstaking studies
>
> Since I have a charm for these suppliant suitors:
> Pure mirrors, which transform to beauty all things —
> My eyes, my wide eyes, clear as air, clear as time.[43]

This woman — beautiful as a dream of stone — white, monumental, impassible, impenetrable, whose wide eyes are pure mirrors without the shadow of a pupil, has all the characteristics of sculpture. "Beauty" is a sculpture or rather a "sculptural dream," to adopt the expression Baudelaire uses in the *Salon de 1859*. And the way in which he describes the "divine forms" of sculpture in the *Salon* reminds us insistently of his poem "Beauty": "Just as lyric poetry makes everything noble — even passion; so sculpture, true sculpture, makes everything solemn — even movement. Upon everything which is human it bestows something of eternity, which partakes of the hardness of the substance used."[44]

This poetic vision of sculpture, in which one recognizes all the themes integral to Baudelaire's imagination — including his image of woman — is nonetheless very Winckelmannian. It is like a transfiguration of Winckelmann's image of sculpture. As in Winckelmann, sculpture is for Baudelaire an object of poetic and philosophical meditation:

> And at the corner of that flowery pathway which leads to the burial-place of those who are still dear to you, the prodigious figure of Mourning, prostrate, disheveled, drowned in the flood of her tears and crushing the powdered remains of some famous man beneath her heavy desolation, teaches you that riches, glory, your country even, are pure frivolities compared to that great Unknown which no one has named, or defined; which man can only represent by mysterious adverbs such as 'Perhaps,' 'Never,' 'Always!'; — and which contains, as some hope, the infinite beatitude which they so much desire, or else an anguish without respite, whose image is rejected by modern reason with the convulsive gesture of a death-agony.[45]

This cold, ideal Beauty — a "sculptural dream" exhaling a funereal scent, its appearance that of a disturbing sepulchral dream — is contrasted with a completely different figure of beauty incarnated in painting. The first is a beauty of stone, the second a beauty of flesh. The beauty of painting is excessively given to cosmetics, whereas sculpture has the whiteness of the swan. The former is not even slightly averse to the movement by which lines are displaced. Antithetical and complementary, these two beauties correspond to the two halves of art as defined in *Le peintre de la vie moderne:* "Modernity is the transient, the fleeting, the contingent; it is one half of art; the other being the eternal and the immovable."[46]

On the one side, painting; on the other, sculpture. But the correspondence is not as close as our first glance might suggest. True, in Baudelaire's eyes painting also possesses the share of eternity inscribed in his definition of art. But it is difficult to discover anything in his description of sculpture that suggests the characteristics of modernity. Baudelaire pays homage to sculpture but does not rank it as high as painting. Immovable and eternal, sculpture only partially realizes his definition of art, whereas painting realizes it completely, that is, in respect of both halves. The essence of painting is, for him, synonymous with the essence of art: it expresses the contents of modernity in the forms of eternity. In this regard, one cannot help but be struck by the extraordinary proximity of Hegel and Baudelaire. The conceptual distinction between sculpture and painting established by Hegel's philosophy rests on the same criteria of difference as in Baudelaire. But the contrast between eternity and modernity, immutability and movement, white and color, stone and flesh—that is, between sculpture and painting—is historicized in Hegel. He sees not two contemporary halves of a single definition of art but two successive moments in the gradual development of the history of art: classical art and modern or romantic art. Sculpture is not, in Hegel, the symbol of an eternity suited to melancholy and dreams but an outmoded figure of art, a form of artistic expression that had found its fullest expression in the past. But when Baudelaire says of sculpture that it is "an art in which color is difficult and movement impossible," does he not proceed as Hegel does, that is, negatively? Does he not define it in terms of the very attributes that prevent it from becoming painting? There are many differences between Hegel's philosophical methodology and Baudelaire's artistic analysis, but we must acknowledge that the two authors take the same view both of sculpture and of the difference between the two arts. They both have a Winckelmannian vision of sculpture and a colorist conception of painting. And though "modern" does not have precisely the same sense in both, they both assimilate painting to modern art and modern to romantic art. Whether it expresses the life of the spirit or the transports of the imagination, the movement of subjectivity or the infinite variations of the soul, in both authors color is at once what "makes a painter a painter," as Hegel puts it, and what makes painting a modern art.[47]

Only this identification between painting, color, and modernity—so clearly visible in Baudelaire and which we also find, in a different guise, in Hegel—can explain the multiplicity of critical reactions to sculpture during the second half of the nineteenth century. The principal reason given by all the partisans of modern art is the mediocrity of contemporary sculptors, but this is not an adequate explanation. These reactions are the more or less inevitable result of an aesthetics of modernity, one that immediately became synonymous with an aesthetics of painting and that Baudelaire's successors developed in ever more radical form. If, in sculpture, movement is difficult and color impossible (as Baudelaire says), should we be surprised that the sculptural art seems increasingly alien to the partisans of modernity? Sculpture as they see it is too antipictorial to be perceived as anything other than antimodern. In Zola as in Huysmans, rejection of sculpture and defense of the new forms of painting are two sides of the same coin. The love that they feel for the sickly glow of Olympia's undressed body or the blue-tinged flesh of Degas's dancers is incompatible with a similar esteem for the whiteness and nudity of bodies represented in the timeless immobility of ancient poses.

The critique of sculpture grew ever harsher over the following decades. No longer confining themselves to denouncing the feebleness of contemporary sculptors, critics began to doubt whether sculpture could ever progress and therefore came to envisage its complete disappearance. Such radical doubts were unprecedented in the history of artistic ideas. The critique of sculpture had till then been linked to a body of thought about the hierarchy of the arts and had developed along essentially theoretical lines. People wondered about the place of sculpture, its role and its influence, not about the intrinsic value of the art itself and still less about the artists who practiced it. Diderot has reservations about sculpture but does not denigrate it; he does not rank it with painting but recognizes that it has its own qualities and is often very sensitive to its beauty. As to Baudelaire, his stance on sculpture remained, as we have seen, qualified, not to say ambiguous. He loved sculpture but detested what it had become. The tone changes in the second half of the nineteenth century, when the critique of sculpture gradually becomes more virulent. As we noted, some even contested the art's right to exist, wondering whether sculpture was not simply and basically incompatible with the conditions and requirements of what they called "modernity." Could sculpture ever become modern? Were not *sculpture* and *modern* antithetical, indeed mutually exclusive terms? In "Le Salon de 1879," Huysmans posed the question openly: "Let us be clear about this. Either sculpture can acclimatize to modern life or it cannot. If it can, let it essay contemporaneous subjects, and we shall soon know what to think. If it cannot, it is clearly futile to rehearse ad nauseam subjects better treated in previous centuries; the sculptors should confine themselves to ornamental functions and stop cluttering the Salon with their products."[48]

Huysmans tended to believe that sculpture could not thus "acclimatize." Viewing the state of contemporary sculpture, he found it nigh impossible to imagine such a thing as modern sculpture—almost as impossible as imagining a square circle. Short of a miracle, the future of sculpture seemed to him severely compromised by the modern evolution of the arts. He thought the same about poetry. Poetry, like sculpture, was dying. Huysmans brought painting and sculpture together for one last time in a funeral oration that gives its final form to the comparison between the two arts and more or less concludes the career of *ut sculptura poesis*. The two arts die simultaneously of the same cause: their tendency to immobility.

> Today we clearly see the course mapped out for literature and painting. We can also guess what a modern conception of architecture might be.... Music too has advanced; in the entire field of art, then, only poetry and sculpture have remained static. Poetry is dying;

　　　　　　　　　　　　　　　　　　　CHAPTER FOUR

that much is certain. Great as Victor Hugo was, technically and artistically able as Leconte de Lisle may be, they are even now losing and — this is the main thing — will shortly have altogether lost all influence over the new generation of poets. Following the example of Musset cannot possibly rescue poetry from the muddy ditch in which it is currently wading up to its knees. Without the birth of a man of genius, then, I do not see what can become of the art that Flaubert termed an art of amenity. Still less do I see where that other art called sculpture is heading. No more dreadful state of stagnation can be imagined than the one in which we now find it. It is high time we removed to the attic that old cliché spouted year after year: "Sculpture is France's glory. Painting is not making much progress, but sculpture!" Well, no and again no. True, I hate with all my heart most of the paintings exhibited in the annual Salons. I hate the painting of Bonnat and his ilk. I hate the mystifications of great art, those green cheeses that the combined cowardice of the public and the press contrive to pass off as the moon; but I hate even more, if such a thing is conceivable, those other green cheeses constituted by contemporary sculpture. The official painters are veritable geniuses beside the official plasterers.[49]

By now, art critics were not the only ones announcing the death of sculpture. "Like Monsieur Renan, Monsieur Taine adopts a graveside manner to speak of sculpture," noted Laforgue, citing a phrase from Renan's *Dialogues philosophiques:* "The reign of statuary is at an end."[50] The phrase makes clear what "the death of sculpture" meant to all these writers and philosophers of the second half of the nineteenth century. Questioning the future of sculpture meant questioning that of the statuary art; the two had been firmly identified since antiquity. This in turn meant questioning the permanence of the model laid down by ancient sculpture. Saying that the reign of the statuary was at an end came down to saying that the reign of Greek sculpture was now finished. Everyone was in agreement on this point: one could no longer sculpt like the Greeks. This form of artistic expression, Zola said, speaking of the Salon of 1868, had become a dead language, an artificial language that no one any longer knew. It could no longer be spoken naturally: "Sculpture as Greece understood it is a dead language for us, an artistic expression that we can no longer make any natural use of. Our artists speak Greek art the way fifth-graders speak Latin, with much recourse to the dictionary, no real accent, and a revolting lack of idiom."[51]

The idea was not wholly new. Zola was taking up an image that Gautier had used some ten years previously: "The statuary art now exists only as Sanskrit, Greek, and Latin do: as a dead language."[52]

From the middle of the nineteenth century, then, certain critics were agreed that, as Renan put it, "the reign of statuary was at an end."[53] But unlike the writers of the following generation, they shed tears over the death of the art, signing its death certificate with something like nostalgia. They were still, one might say,

Winckelmannians. Sculpture was dead—alas! Zola and Huysmans thought much the same but could not bring themselves to add the "alas." Yet they were no less in thrall to the Winckelmannian image of sculpture than their predecessors. One of the main reasons why sculpture was dying was, in Zola's view, the incompatibility of the nude with the reality of the modern world: "If there is one art that suffers from the modern context, it is undoubtedly sculpture. It was born in the dawn of humanity among people who lived their lives half-naked and is therefore ill at ease in our aging societies with their dark, somber clothes."[54]

Formulated in less systematic and theoretical fashion, Zola's ideas are not unlike Taine's. Zola too thought that the birth and development of an art—and therefore its decadence—could be explained by concepts such as those set out by Taine: race, environment, and historical moment. "In Greece," Zola said, "sculpture must have found a particular context that was to impart its characteristics of grandeur and simplicity. The Greek sculptor was a poet, a dreamer, a son of Plato, who lived in the gymnasia where the perfect limbs of the athletes were always on display. A statue was a poem, an act of faith, a tendency to reach divine beauty through that of humanity."[55]

Clearly Zola is completely faithful to the double image of sculpture as a poetical and a philosophical art. His Greek sculptor—at once poet and philosopher, a dreamer living in the gymnasia surrounded by young athletes with perfect bodies—is not just a son of Plato, he is also a son of Winckelmann. Nor does Zola depart from the Winckelmannian theory that "the nude is the essential condition of statuary,"[56] as Gautier put it and as the authors of the neoclassical period had put it before him. It will be remembered that the definition of sculpture as the art of the nude had gained, in Guizot, a distinctive function, serving to mark the frontier between sculpture and painting. Now it served to explain the death of sculpture. What had defined the essence of sculpture was seen as precisely the attribute that condemned it to death. Sculpture was dying because the ideal nude had become incomprehensible and was profoundly alien to the modern sensibility. The same idea is repeated in every register during the later decades of the century: modern man is too civilized, too refined, too profound, too artificial—Nietzsche would say, too sick—to be able to love the nude: not nudity as such but the nude, that is, the representation of an ideal body, with perfect proportions and well-drawn muscles. His vision of corporeal beauty was no longer that of the Greeks. And everyone agreed to see in this transformation the effect of historical necessity. Thus the decline of the ideal of the nude was for Taine an inevitable consequence of the progress of civilization: "High civilization, complete development, and the profound elaboration of the soul cannot be combined with an athletic nude body acquired in the life of the gymnasium."[57]

But why should the death of sculpture "as Greece understood it" (Zola's words) necessarily entail the death of sculpture? To say that the reign of statuary and therefore of the nude had come to an end was one thing; to conclude that sculpture was dead was quite another. That conclusion implied that the image of sculpture was completely identified with that of Greek sculpture. It meant, in other words, that it was impossible to understand sculpture in ways other than the Greeks had understood it.

Though the death of sculpture was widely reported, the identity of the deceased was not always clear. A certain confusion remained in this respect, which testifies to the persistence of the Winckelmannian image of sculpture. What was dying? Was it sculpture or was it a certain historically determined idea of sculpture, whose forms of expression now appeared historically outmoded?[58] The question asked by all these critics about the possibility of modern sculpture therefore came to be synonymous with another question: could sculpture survive the dissolution of the antique ideal? This question was in a sense more radical. Although, like the first, it was based on an empirical observation, it was not in itself empirical in kind. It implied that the mediocrity of contemporary sculpture might not be a contingent fact but a necessary one; in other words, that it was not simply because the sculptors were bad that sculpture was dying but because things could not be otherwise. This was what Victor Cousin believed. He thought that there could be no modern sculpture and that sculpture was exclusively an ancient art, linked to paganism. The Goncourts said no such thing but sometimes seem to have been thinking it. Visiting the Glyptothek in Munich in 1860, they made this entry about the *Barberini Faun* in their *Journal*: "Do you realize that the absolute, inimitable perfection of antique sculpture is a formidable argument against progress."[59]

In 1867, at the Museo Vaticano, they again noted the "crushing superiority of Greek sculpture" not only over Greek painting (about which they were clearly very skeptical)[60] but over all other forms of sculpture too. They again insisted on this absolute and inimitable perfection, though they somewhat perfidiously recorded "one beauty in Greek beauty—a beauty that we know from the poets is much appreciated."[61] For the Goncourts, too, antique sculpture was an art destined for those of a poetic cast of soul.

But on 3 September 1865, they wrote about Carpeaux in their *Journal*: "For him, the finest specimens of today's human body afford examples as beautiful as those of Greece."[62]

Their interest in the sculpture of Carpeaux continued to grow, throwing up ever more admiring and enthusiastic judgments. On 16 March 1865, Carpeaux was as yet only "a sculptor of great talent," as Edmond de Goncourt specified in a note added in 1887 (by which time he alone was continuing to write the *Journal*, which had for so long been kept by two hands):[63] "I give our first impression of Carpeaux such as I find it in our journal. But I should add that this impression has been greatly modified by the relations we have since had with him and that we consider him the greatest French artist of the second half of the nineteenth century."

Though the forecast remained, for the most part, very pessimistic—notably among the most radical critics, those who placed their pens at the service of modern art, such as Zola and Huysmans—some had begun to detect the dawning of a little ray of hope. In 1879—the very year in which Huysmans, writing about the Salon, had wondered whether a modern sculpture was really possible—Armand Silvestre perceived, "not without a fond anxiety," he writes, the signs of a renewal in sculpture:

> If I were looking for the secret of this renewal, I would, I believe, find it in the maturing of a feeling of naturalism unknown to the preceding period. The word is too pregnant with stormy controversy for me to do other than explain at once the sense that I attach to it. Naturalism in sculpture does not attack, indeed respects as it should be respected, the impeccable nobility of proportions assigned to the human body by Greek art—which shall, till the complete abasement of the races, remain an eternal model. The modern element that naturalism tends to substitute for the indefinite imitation of antiquity lies elsewhere. It lies in movement, for movement changes with the times, and forms, as it were, the visible imprint of living habits, thus transforming not merely gait but gestures and folds of clothing. The marble of the gods of ancient Olympus has melted away like snow and the immortal myths reappear with the same whiteness now inhabited by a new soul.[64]

Silvestre was not a fanatical supporter of modern art, and he was above all a circumspect critic. He wants immediately to reassure those who might be frightened by the word *naturalism,* which he knows to be "pregnant with stormy controversy." The naturalism of this new school of sculpture does not at all seek, he says, to question the ideal of antiquity. On the contrary, for all these young artists, Greek art remains an "eternal model" and they persist in respecting it "as it should be respected." The modern element that they have introduced into sculpture does not concern proportions; it concerns movement and movement alone. Silvestre thus takes great care to specify that this naturalism is a temperate one and respectful of the authorities, one that restores a new vigor to art without on that account breaking with the past. In short, it is a renewal and not a revolution. The text manifests a clear unease. Silvestre's precautions—his care to show that the new can accord with the ancient, and naturalism with the Greek ideal— combine to suggest the contrary. It is as if he obscurely perceived that it was no longer possible to save the ancient model even by modernizing it and adapting it to both the taste of the day and the new forms of sensibility. To think that confining naturalism to the question of movement was sufficient to reconcile it with an ideal vision of the human body, and thus make it acceptable, was a complete illusion. The introduction of movement did a great deal more than add a little touch of modern to an eternal model that might thus survive unchanged. It struck at the heart of the Winckelmannian ideal of noble simplicity and calm grandeur.

Some critics, like Silvestre, perceived signs of a renewal in sculpture and hailed the existence of a new school; some, like Zola or Huysmans, were still awaiting the birth of a modern art of sculpture. But they were all in agreement on one point: modernity in sculpture would consist of movement and expression. The idea is given very clear expression by Eugène Véron in his *Esthétique:* "If we want sculpture to become a genuinely modern and independent art, we must apply ourselves above all to developing it in accord with the modern spirit, that is, in the direction of expression and movement."[65]

Véron's "movement and expression," without which there could be no modern sculpture, must themselves be understood in a modern sense. He is not talking about purely physical movement, as exemplified in the *Discus Thrower* or the *Borghese Gladiator,* or about the expressive movement exemplified by the *Laokoon.* As in the seventeenth century, expression was a priority, but it was no longer understood in the same sense. The classical theorists conceived of bodily movement — what they called the actions of the body — as a visible translation of the invisible passions of the soul. Expression was the expression of passions; it referred to feelings common to human nature, to states, emotions, and affects common to all humans, such as fear, anger, love, jealousy, and pity. Art offered an exemplary and distilled representation of these with which everyone could identify. For the moderns, on the contrary, art had to be the "expression of the subjective"; it had to express "the changing and the contingent in empirical individuality," to adopt one of Hegel's formulas about painting. Thus it was no longer expressing universal passions but a particular subjectivity, a feeling, state, or intention private to a particular individual placed in a particular situation. It is just this lack of expression in the modern sense that the Goncourt brothers disliked in ancient art, even when the latter had attained its culminating perfection, as it had in sculpture: "We find this art unsympathetic. There is nothing personal about either the people or the works. The beautiful remains impersonal and so does the artist. It has periods but no artists. The sublime, the perfect, the most absolute beauty — these things antiquity discovered and attained in sculpture. But even there, ancient art abolished the human face; it abolished physiognomy and expression. It is a decapitated art."[66]

The ancient works that they most admired were precisely those in which they discovered personal beauty, an expression of real life such as to answer the requirements of the modern sensibility or what Véron calls "the modern spirit." One such work was the *Belvedere Torso*—paradoxically a paradigm of the decapitated work of art:

> The only work of art in the world to have given us the complete and absolute sensation of a masterpiece [is]…the *Torso.*… Yes, here in this *Torso,* so admirably human, is the divine sublimity of art; it draws its beauty from the representation of life: this breathing fragment of chest, these muscles at work, these palpitating entrails in a stomach that is digesting. For its beauty is that it is digesting, despite Winckelmann's imbecilic encomium; he thinks he is honoring the masterpiece by saying that it does no such thing.[67]

Winckelmann understood nothing about Greek sculpture. At a stroke of the pen, the Goncourts, with their customary insolence, shatter the image of Greek sculpture consecrated as self-evident by the previous hundred years. They show that one can admire Greek sculpture while rejecting the ancient ideal and that one can like it for modern reasons entirely antithetical to those invoked by Winckelmann. If Greek sculpture had become a dead language, as Zola said, the Goncourts were not alone in thinking that the fault was mainly Winckelmann's; Winckelmann had killed it. It could be brought back to life simply by rescuing it from the rubble in which he had buried it.

Véron, too, believed this. Greek sculpture was, he said, infinitely more rich and diverse than the sycophants of ideal beauty could bring themselves to acknowledge. They sought to reduce it to the solitary genre of monumental statuary. But a vivid, naturalist, and realist art had also existed in Greece, giving rise to what Véron called "lay statuary":

> Besides religious and heroic sculpture, there always existed in Greece another and completely different genre, which one might call "realist." Instead of seeking to express a quality, character, or sentiment, it worked toward individual exactitude and at times demonstrates a very close study of the model. There are many monuments of this kind of sculpture. Multitudes of them have been discovered in recent times…their infinite diversity cannot easily be reconciled with the narrow-mindedness of academic admiration, nor with the code that the latter claims to impose on all the arts, in the name of the ideal it claimed to have discovered in Greek sculpture. It ultimately imprisoned Greek sculpture in that ideal, heedless of the refutation implicitly inflicted by the many works of completely different character.[68]

For Véron, then, what he calls "the despotism of academic taste" was based on a mistaken and truncated view of antique sculpture, and the best way to combat it was to reestablish historical truth. The critique of Winckelmann's image of sculpture had already begun to develop in a somewhat diffuse fashion through conflicting interpretations, but in Véron it takes on a political and institutional dimension. It is explicitly directed against the "official aesthetic," which defends a conception of sculpture that is both completely wrong on historical criteria and desperately sterile on the artistic plane:

> We cannot too emphatically point out the facts about this great art-historical epoch. For, let there be no mistake, the metaphysical prejudices that in large measure constitute the official aesthetic derive from the idealist and literary interpretation of Greek sculpture. They have not even taken the trouble to study the corpus of works left to us by antiquity. A constricted mindset has confined itself to three or four statues that seemed best to lend themselves to this Platonic fantasy, and the entire theory was built on those foundations. Anything that did not relate to it, which is the great majority of ancient works, was simply eliminated or considered in the light of accidents of no theoretical importance. Once the absolute rules were proclaimed, any attempt to take another approach was condemned as decadent and tainted. Over the course of the last century, when Winckelmann was invested with dictatorial powers over public taste, the eternal models of immutable beauty were the *Apollo Belvedere,* the *Medici Venus,* and the *Laokoon* group. Today they have been replaced by the *Venus of Milo* and the Parthenon marbles. The models may have changed, but the rules have remained the same and are no less eternal and infallible today. Though they wield the scepter under other names, it is still Winckelmann and Plato who preside over criticism today.[69]

This vision of sculpture, contested by Véron in such virulent terms, exactly corresponds to the mistaken idea of art whose disastrous effect on painting the writers had been denouncing for some fifty years. Véron merely applies to sculpture a critique hitherto elaborated mainly in respect to painting. The transfer demonstrates not only that the influence of new ideas in painting had begun to be felt in the domain of sculpture; it was also an essential component of Véron's defense of a new notion of sculpture. For here was the principal obstacle to envisaging the existence of modern sculpture, and Véron had found a way to remove it. Thanks to this transferred application of an existing critique, it became possible to think of sculpture in ways not deriving from the Winckelmannian model and so to break with the traditional image of sculpture as a philosophical art. These two divorces were in fact one, as Véron clearly understood when he dismissively yoked Winckelmann to Plato.

Denouncing Winckelmann's image of Greek sculpture was, however, only a first step in the process that led to the complete dissolution of the conceptual framework that for several centuries had determined how people thought about Greek sculpture. A second step had to be taken, that of questioning the trump card of Greek sculpture — ideal beauty. To dispose of Winckelmann, it was not enough to destroy his image of Greek sculpture; one had also to bring Greek art down from the pedestal on which he had placed it, or, in other words, to demonstrate that the idea that sculpture had reached its culminating point in Greece was also mistaken. Having shown that Greek art was not confined to monumental statuary, Véron now set about describing the extreme diversity and above all the great wealth of forms of expression that were alien to Greek art, in the first rank of which he placed medieval sculpture. Thus he spoke with enthusiasm of these "poor master masons" and "modest carvers of images" who were "scorned by the established regulators of modern taste and art," writing extensively about the "marvelous conceptions, both sculptural and architectonic" of French sculpture of the twelfth and thirteenth centuries: those of Moissac, Vézelay, Bourges, and Chartres, the portal of the Cathédrale Notre-Dame d'Amiens, and the facade of Notre-Dame de Paris. In each case, he analyzed with great precision the properties that distinguished these sculptures from those of ancient works. Even when they are large, like the kings of Notre-Dame d'Amiens, such sculptures do not seek the appearance of *colossi*. The figures are always grouped "so as to produce striking scenic effects at certain points." Véron is particularly interested in this type of composition, which he feels embodies an approach very like that taken in modern painting: "Unlike the Greek or the Egyptian, the French artist does not seek to develop sculpture along broad frontals or long friezes. On the contrary, he tries to concentrate it on certain points, whose excessive detail and brilliant effects contrast with the other, more tranquil parts. This opposition—a contrast that awakens sensation by exciting or relaxing the eye—is the prevailing character of modern art and had already, in medieval art, taken on unprecedented importance."[70]

Véron states that instead of endlessly attempting to imitate Greek sculptors, today's sculptors would do better to find their inspiration in medieval sculpture. Huysmans says the same but goes much further when he enjoins sculptors to turn away from the ancient world toward the Middle Ages. Reference to medieval art means something else to him, something of which Véron says little, namely, a return to materials that sculpture had long ignored, such as wood:

> For thousands of years, sculptors have neglected wood, which would, in my view, be marvelously suited to a real, living art; the painted sculptures of the Middle Ages, the altarpieces of the Cathédrale Notre-Dame d'Amiens and Hall Museum, for example, are there to prove it. The statues that stand in Sainte-Gudule and in most Belgian churches—for example, the life-size statues by Verbruggen of Antwerp and by other old sculptors of Flanders—are even more striking evidence, if such a thing is possible.
>
> In these realistic and humane works, there is a play of features and a carnal life never since rediscovered in sculpture. And see how malleable and supple, how docile, almost

unctuous, wood becomes at these masters' behest. See how light and precise is the cloth of these garments carved in solid oak, how it cleaves to their poses, how it assists in the expression of their role and character.[71]

Huysmans is not content simply to reject the model of the antique statuary and substitute, as Véron does, that of the medieval statuary. His critique is more radical because ultimately it questions the very model of the sculptor and undoes the identification between sculpture and statuary. If sculpture wishes to become modern, he argues, it must give up some of its traditional materials: "Indeed, I do not see what path this art can follow without resolutely repudiating both the study of the antique and the use of marble, stone, and bronze."[72]

And it must also return to the polychrome, "combining elements of painting and sculpture" as it had not only in the Middle Ages but in Greece. Huysmans writes:

> Either the inescapable necessity of employing certain materials in preference to others and the despotic need to ally the two arts — a need recognized since antiquity, given that the very Greeks adopted painted sculpture — will be understood and acknowledged by today's artists, who can then attempt scenes of modern life; or else, withered and spent, sculpture will year by year suffer a progressive ossification till it eventually collapses into a state of permanent, driveling paralysis.[73]

At the sixth impressionist exhibition of 1881, Huysmans saw Degas's *Little Fourteen-Year-Old Dancer* (see pl. 13). This painted wax figure wearing a real skirt, real blouse, real stockings, and real ballet shoes, its horsehair locks knotted with a real ribbon and wearing another ribbon around its neck, filled him with enthusiasm:[74] "This statuette is the only really modern attempt that I know of in sculpture. At his first attempt, Monsieur Degas has overthrown the traditions of sculpture just as he has long shaken the conventions of painting."[75] Winckelmann and Plato are now dead and buried.

But topoi are hardy, irrepressible creatures, no doubt because they contain a partial truth. Degas had been gradually losing his eyesight for several years, and the painter became a sculptor as he grew blind. "I can't see much," he said, "so I look with my fingers." Valéry described the aged Degas: "But his hands were still groping for form. He would finger things: as the sense of touch grew more important, he was apt to describe things in terms of it; he would praise a picture by saying 'It has the smoothness of really fine painting.'"[76]

What did Diderot tell us? Sculpture is an art for the blind.

1. Théophile Gautier, *Les beaux-arts en Europe, 1855* (Paris: Michel Lévy, 1855), 1:119.

2. Jean-Baptiste Dubos, *Réflexions critiques sur la poésie et sur la peinture* (Paris: École nationale supérieure des beaux-arts, 1993), pt. 2, sec. 8, p. 197.

3. Dubos, *Réflexions* (note 2), pt. 2, sec. 8, p. 197.

4. Johann Joachim Winckelmann, *History of the Art of Antiquity,* trans. Harry Francis Mallgrave (Los Angeles: Getty Research Institute, 2006), 191.

5. This phrase was suggested to me by the title of an article by René Démoris, itself an homage to a movie by Chris Marker: "Peinture et belles antiques dans la première moitié du siècle: Les statues vivent aussi," *Dix-huitième siècle,* no. 27 (1995): 129–42.

6. Cicero, *Brutus,* in idem, *Brutus, Orator,* trans. George Lincoln Hendrickson (*Brutus*) and Harry Mortimer Hubbell (*Orator*) (Cambridge, Mass.: Harvard Univ. Press, 1971), 163.

7. Denis Diderot, *Salon de 1767,* in idem, *Ruines et paysages: Salons de 1767,* ed. Else Marie Bukdahl, Michel Delon, and Annette Lorenceau (Paris: Hermann, 1995), 215.

8. Charles Baudelaire, "Philosophic Art," in idem, *The Painter of Modern Life and Other Essays,* trans. and ed. Jonathan Mayne (London: Phaidon, 2005), 206.

9. It should be noted that a very similar critique of German painting was elaborated in Germany and occurred early enough to be found in Hegel. Careful always to distinguish the arts from the point of view of what he calls their "concept," Hegel condemns descriptive poetry, which attempts to compete with painting, just as he does lyrical painting, which seeks to "master the special character of poetry; but if it ventures on an attempt at such mastery, it merely falls into aridity or insipidity"; Georg Wilhelm Friedrich Hegel, *Aesthetics: Lectures on Fine Art,* trans. T. M. Knox (Oxford: Clarendon, 1988), 2:856. This last criticism is specifically targeted at the Nazareans, to whom Hegel devotes a few pages of remarkable accuracy and acuity: "In the Berlin Art Exhibition last year (1828) several pictures from the so-called Düsseldorf school became very famous.... Their subjects were for the most part poems by Goethe or were drawn from Shakespeare, Ariosto and Tasso, and were especially made up of the inner feeling of love. Each of the best pictures generally portrayed a pair of lovers, e.g. Romeo and Juliet, Rinaldo and Armida, without any more definite situation, so that the two do nothing and express nothing except being in love with one another and so, having an inclination for one another, regard each other as true lovers and look one another in the eye as true lovers.... When so much has been said in recent times about poetry in painting, this ought to mean only conceiving a subject with imagination, making feelings explicable by an action, and not proposing to adhere to a feeling in the abstract and expressing it like that. Even poetry, which can express a feeling in its inner depth, spreads itself in ideas, images and descriptions. For example, if it is proposed to go no further in expressing life than saying 'I love you,' and always just repeating 'I love you,' this indeed might be agreeable to those gentlemen who have had much to say about the 'poetry of poetry,' but it would be the flattest prose"; Hegel, *Aesthetics* (this note), 2:856–58. This critique of the Nazareans is one example among many illustrating the originality of Hegel's analysis of art and his singularity in the field of philosophical discourse. Of all the philosophers who have written about painting, Hegel is perhaps one of the few to take an interest in individual works—including those of his contemporaries—and to defend the specificity of painting. The idea has gained currency that Hegel sought to subordinate painting to philosophy and force painters to philosophize or poeticize. This idea is completely alien to his philosophy of art—one can hardly imagine a less speculative concept of painting than Hegel's. This is precisely what distinguishes his philosophy of art from most philosophical aesthetics—including those of today.

10. Gautier, *Les beaux-arts* (note 1), 1:6.

11. In the *Supplément à "l'Encyclopédie"* (1776), the word *esthétique* appears under the heading "Terme nouveau" and the accompanying article is an almost literal translation of the article "Äesthetik" from J. G. Sulzer's *Allgemeine Theorie der schönen Künste* (1771). The German word *Äesthetik* was itself formed from the Latin neologism *aesthetica,* created by Baumgarten. But use of the term began to spread into France only toward the mid-nineteenth century, as confirmed by the publication of Théodore Simon Jouffroy's *Cours d'esthétique* in 1843.

12. Charles Baudelaire, "The Universal Exhibition of 1855," in idem, *Selected Writings on Art and Artists,* trans. P. E. Charvet (Harmondsworth: Penguin, 1972), 117.

13. Jules Laforgue, *Gazette des beaux-arts,* 1 February 1886, in Mireille Dottin, ed., *Jules Laforgue: Textes de critique d'art* (Lille: Presses universitaire de Lille, 1988), 80.

14. Laforgue, *Gazette des beaux-arts,* 1 October 1886, in Mireille Dottin, ed., *Jules Laforgue: Textes de critique d'art* (Lille: Presses universitaire de Lille, 1988), 95.

15. Hippolyte Taine, *Philosophie de l'art* (Paris: Hachette, 1909; reprint, Geneva: Slatkine, 1980), 145–46. In 1864, Taine had replaced Viollet-le-Duc in the chair of aesthetics at the École des beaux-arts; he held the post for twenty years. The extraordinary success of his lectures led him to publish them; the first volume appeared in 1865 and was based on notes taken by his students. After these little volumes had been reprinted several times, he decided to collect them in a book he published in 1881 under the general title *Philosophie de l'art.* His ideas were therefore very widely known and accepted well before the 1880s.

16. Baudelaire, "Philosophic Art" (note 8), 205.

17. Baudelaire, "Philosophic Art" (note 8), 205.

18. Charles Baudelaire, *Salon of 1846,* in idem, *Selected Writings on Art and Artists,* trans. P. E. Charvet (Harmondsworth: Penguin, 1972), 91.

19. Baudelaire, *Salon of 1846* (note 18), 91.

20. Charles Baudelaire, *Salon de 1845,* in idem, *Curiosités esthétiques: L'art romantique et autres oeuvres critiques,* ed. Henri Lemaître (Paris: Éditions Garnier frères, 1962), 40.

21. The comparison of painting and music is less frequently encountered than that of painting and poetry. Nevertheless, it has been an important topos of art theory since the Renaissance. We find it in the classical age, particularly in Poussin's theory of modes or de Piles's idea of harmony, but its popularity reached a high point in the nineteenth century. In different forms, it can be seen in the work of twentieth-century painters such as Klee and Kandinsky.

22. It is in his essay on Wagner, at the end of which he quotes the two first stanzas of his poem "Correspondances," that the idea of analogy or correspondence is most forcefully stated: "For the only really surprising thing would be that sound could not suggest colour, that colours could not give the idea of melody, and that both sound and colour were unsuitable as media for ideas; since all things always have been expressed by reciprocal analogies, ever since the day when God created the world as a complex and indivisible totality"; Charles Baudelaire, "Richard Wagner and *Tannhaüser* in Paris," in idem, *Selected Writings on Art and Artists,* trans. P. E. Charvet (Harmondsworth: Penguin, 1972), 330–31.

23. Charles Baudelaire, "Correspondances," in idem, *Les fleurs du mal* (Antwerp: Éditions Moorthamers frères, 1927), 22, line 8.

24. Baudelaire, *Salon of 1846* (note 18), 92.

25. Joris-Karl Huysmans, "Le Salon officiel de 1880," in idem, *L'art moderne, Certains* (Paris: Union générale d'éditions, 1975), 145. It is interesting to note Nietzsche's reservations about this idea of correspondence: "This century in which the arts have recognized that each can produce the effect of the others *is perhaps ruining the arts!* For example, *painting* with poetry (Victor Hugo, Balzac, W. Scott, etc.); eliciting *poetic* sentiments with *music* (Wagner); eliciting poetic sentiments and even *philosophical ideas* with painting (Cornelius); practicing anatomy and psychiatry with novels, etc."; Friedrich Nietzsche, *Fragments posthumes (printemps–automne*

1884), vol. 10, *Oeuvres philosophiques complètes,* ed. Giorgio Colli and Mazzino Montinari, trans. (German to French) Jean Launay (Paris: Gallimard, 1982), 60.

26. Edmond de Goncourt and Jules de Goncourt, *Manette Salomon* (Paris: Union générale d'éditions, 1979), 29.

27. Goncourt brothers, *Manette Salomon* (note 26), 29.

28. Edmond de Goncourt and Jules de Goncourt, *Journal: Mémoires de la vie littéraire* (Paris: Robert Laffont, 1989), entry for 16 January 1859, 1:435.

29. Goncourt brothers, *Journal* (note 28), entry for 17 April 1867, 2:76.

30. Émile Zola, "Mon Salon" (1866), in idem, *Écrits sur l'art,* ed. Jean-Pierre Leduc-Adine (Paris: Gallimard, 1991), 110–11.

31. Émile Zola, "Peinture," *Le figaro,* 2 May 1896, in idem, *Écrits sur l'art,* ed. Jean-Pierre Leduc-Adine (Paris: Gallimard, 1991), 472.

32. Albert E. Elsen insists on the fact that in the second half of the nineteenth century, sculpture was "viewed as a branch of philosophy" and had its place in national educational systems; Albert E. Elsen, *Origins of Modern Sculpture: Pioneers and Premises* (London: Phaidon, 1974), 4.

33. Baudelaire, *Salon of 1846* (note 18), 67.

34. Baudelaire, *Salon of 1846* (note 18), 100.

35. Baudelaire, *Salon of 1846* (note 18), 98.

36. Baudelaire, *Salon of 1846* (note 18), 97.

37. Baudelaire, *Salon of 1846* (note 18), 98, 99.

38. Baudelaire, *Salon of 1846* (note 18), 98–99.

39. Charles Baudelaire, *Salon of 1859,* in idem, *Art in Paris 1845–1862: Salons and Other Exhibitions Reviewed by Charles Baudelaire,* trans. and ed. Jonathan Mayne (London: Phaidon, 1965), 206.

40. Baudelaire, *Salon of 1859* (note 39), 206.

41. Baudelaire, *Salon of 1859* (note 39), 205.

42. Baudelaire, *Salon of 1859* (note 39), 204.

43. Charles Baudelaire, *The Flowers of Evil,* trans. James McGowan (Oxford: Oxford Univ. Press, 1993), 39.

44. Baudelaire, *Salon of 1859* (note 39), 205.

45. Baudelaire, *Salon of 1859* (note 39), 203.

46. Charles Baudelaire, "The Painter of Modern Life," in idem, *Selected Writings on Art and Artists,* trans. P. E. Charvet (Harmondsworth: Penguin, 1972), 403.

47. Hegel, *Aesthetics* (note 9), 2:838.

48. Huysmans, "Le Salon de 1879," in idem, *L'art moderne, Certains* (Paris: Union générale d'éditions, 1975), 93–94.

49. Huysmans, "Le Salon de 1879" (note 48), 92–93.

50. Jules Laforgue, "Notes d'esthétique," *La revue blanche,* 1 December 1896, reprinted in Mireille Dottin, ed., *Jules Laforgue: Textes de critique d'art* (Lille: Presses universitaire de Lille, 1988), 153.

51. Émile Zola, "Mon Salon," in idem, *Écrits sur l'art,* ed. Jean-Pierre Leduc-Adine (Paris: Gallimard, 1991), 225.

52. Gautier, *Les beaux-arts* (note 1), 1:170.

53. Ernest Renan, "Dieuxième dialogue.—Probabilités," in *Dialogues et fragments philosophiques,* in idem, *Oeuvres complètes de Ernest Renan,* ed. Henriette Psichari (Paris: Calmann-Lévy, 1947), 1:600. See also Laforgue, "Notes d'esthétique" (note 50), 153.

54. Zola, "Mon Salon" (note 51), 224.

55. Zola, "Mon Salon" (note 51), 224–25.

56. Gautier, *Les beaux-arts* (note 1), 1:117.

57. Taine, *Philosophie de l'art* (note 15), 301. This critique of the athletic body is reminiscent of Plato's contrast between cosmetics and gymnastics in *Gorgias* (465). As we have already noted, this contrast seems to run through the entire history of theories of artistic representation. The modern vision of the body of modern man is decidedly anti-Platonic and on the side of cosmetics rather than gymnastics.

58. Taine himself does not really answer this question. He takes it for granted that ancient sculpture is a thing of the past. It communicates to the spectator, he says, "a thought that is almost null and void, because it is from another age and belongs to another moment of the human mind"; Taine, *Philosophie de l'art* (note 15), 164. But this does not lead him to conclude that the art of sculpture is dead: "One should not therefore say that the art is now exhausted. It is true that certain schools are dead and cannot be reborn; for certain arts languish and the future into which we are going does not promise them the sustenance that they need"; Taine, *Philosophie de l'art* (note 15), 106.

59. Goncourt brothers, *Journal* (note 28), entry for 18 September 1860, 1:612.

60. For the Goncourt brothers, painting was a northern European art. This was a conviction they shared with all the nineteenth-century colorists, first and foremost Baudelaire, though they rejected his tendency to identify color and romanticism. (In the *Salon de 1846*, Baudelaire wrote: "Romanticism is a child of the North, and the North is a colourist; dreams and fairy tales are children of the mist"; Baudelaire, *Salon of 1846* (note 18), 53. So they did not believe in the mythical perfection of Greek painting. Immediately after proclaiming the "crushing superiority of Greek sculpture," they add: "As to painting, I do not know; it may have been a very great ancient art, but painting is not drawing. Painting is color and in its triumphal state, I see it only in the countries of hot and cold fog, in the countries where a certain prismatic [effect] comes off the water and rises through the air, in Holland or Venice. I do not see it in the clear ether of Greece any more than in the clear blue of Umbria"; Goncourt brothers, *Journal* (note 28), entry for 23 April 1867, 2:79.

61. Goncourt brothers, *Journal* (note 28), entry for 23 April 1867, 2:77.

62. Huysmans shared the Goncourt brothers' predilection for Carpeaux, one of the few contemporary sculptors for whom he had some respect.

63. Jules de Goncourt died in 1870.

64. Armand Silvestre, "Le monde des arts," *La vie moderne,* no. 1, 10 April 1879, and no. 4, 1 May 1879, in idem, *La promenade du critique influent: Anthologie de la critique d'art en France, 1850–1900,* ed. Jean-Paul Bouillon et al. (Paris: Hazan, 1990), 213.

65. Eugène Véron, *L'esthétique* (Paris: Alfred Costes, 1921), 239; recently reissued with a preface and notes by Jacqueline Lichtenstein (Paris: J. Vrin, 2007). Published by Charles Reinwald in 1878, this volume was read by Huysmans and does not merit the oblivion into which it subsequently fell. It is a remarkable work both for the breadth of its philosophical reflection and the precision of its historical analyses; it has few equivalents in the field of the philosophy of art.

66. Goncourt brothers, *Journal* (note 28), entry for 13 May 1862, 1:816.

67. Goncourt brothers, *Journal* (note 28), entry for 6 May 1867, 2:83.

68. Véron, *L'esthétique* (note 65), 234–35.

69. Véron, *L'esthétique* (note 65), 235–36.

70. Véron, *L'esthétique* (note 65), 247.

71. Joris-Karl Huysmans, "L'exposition des Indépendants en 1881," in idem, *L'art moderne, Certains* (Paris: Union générale d'éditions, 1975), 230–31.

72. Huysmans, "L'exposition des Indépendants en 1881" (note 71), 230.

73. Huysmans, "L'exposition des Indépendants en 1881" (note 71), 232.

74. The original appearance of the statuette can be approximately reconstructed with the aid of reviews published at the time.

75. Huysmans, "L'exposition des Indépendants en 1881" (note 71), 228. Shortly afterward, Huysmans celebrated (in *À rebours,* 1884) the birth of a modern poet in the person of Mallarmé. In Huysmans's view, poetry and sculpture, whose death he had predicted in the *Salon of 1879,* were reborn more or less simultaneously.

76. Paul Valéry, *Degas, Manet, Morisot,* trans. David Paul (London: Routledge & Kegan Paul, 1960), 99.

The Hospital of Painting

A love of Painting implanted in the very fibre of his being.
— Charles Baudelaire[1]

It is the sun fallen into Hades, the dazzling palette of the flesh.
— Edmond de Goncourt and Jules de Goncourt[2]

TO MARK THE PUBLICATION of *À rebours* (*Against Nature*), Huysmans published an apocryphal interview with himself under a pseudonym. This is how he introduced the author of the novel: "Only the last descendant, the writer of whom we speak, has abandoned the paintbrush for the pen; he has, in order to remain true to his pedigree, written an art book that would certainly astonish his ancestors, for their sole preoccupation was meticulously painting onto an ultramarine background the parsley-form foliage of the trees."[3]

The scion of a family of painters, Huysmans was trained in painting by his father and discovered his vocation in the Musée du Louvre while contemplating the pictures of the seventeenth-century Dutch school. Standing before them, he suddenly found himself thinking "that he should do that with a pen."[4]

Pictorial representation has held writers in its thrall since the Renaissance. Fénelon had written: "One should write as the Carracci brothers, the Raphaels, and the Poussins painted."[5] But the spell of painting was never so strong as in the second half of the nineteenth century. One indication of this is the abundance and diversity of works about painting: novels, letters, poems, and extended Salon reviews. Another is that art criticism was never a secondary activity, still less a vocation to which writers came late in life. They often began with art criticism; some even began with painting. The Goncourt brothers initially wanted to be painters, and Gautier registered his profession on his passport as "man of letters and painter." Huysmans's first publication was an article on the French landscape painters in *La revue nouvelle* in 1867, and his first book, *Le drageoir aux épices* (*The*

Comfit Box), contains innumerable references to painting: to Rembrandt, Rubens, and all the great Italian, Dutch, and Flemish colorists. Laforgue published an art-critical column early in his career, and we know from his friend Ernest Froissac that "he considered his poetic efforts fantasies and entertainment and did not conceal his ambition to be an art critic."[6] Another of his friends, Jules Kahn, said of him that he was "a devotee of the picture and the image."[7] The same might be said of the Goncourt brothers and Huysmans. All of these writers had an idolatrous passion for painting and proclaimed it loud and strong. They openly adopted the path that Baudelaire had traced in his *Salon de 1859*—"even when I was very young, my eyes, although steeped in images painted and engraved, were always eager for more, and I verily believe that the end of all worlds would come, 'impavidum ferient,' before ever I became an iconoclast."[8] Each of these men might have taken for his own the iconolatrist's profession of faith made by Baudelaire in "Mon coeur mis à nu" ("My Heart Laid Bare"): "To glorify the cult of images (my great, my unique, my primitive passion)."[9]

Lovers of painting, these writers likewise all declared their allegiance to the same pictorial aesthetic, one that the seventeenth century had first designated "colorist." Again following Baudelaire, all these partisans of "modernity" insisted that there was a close fit between the qualities inherent in color and the modern idea of the beautiful, between colorist painting and modern forms of art. They shared most of the themes developed in the seventeenth century by the Rubenists in their quarrel with the Poussinists, from an admiration of the northern paint-ers to paeans in praise of flesh, artifice, cosmetics, and toilette. Foremost among these was celebration of Rubens himself, whose name is the opening word in Baudelaire's poem "Les phares" ("The Beacons"): "Rubens, garden of sloth, stream of oblivion."[10] Of course, the Rubenism of the nineteenth century should not be confused with that of the seventeenth century. It had been reworked and revised in many ways, and the artistic issues at stake were new. But over and above these differences, one cannot help noting that Baudelaire's aesthetics constituted the triumph of the colorist doctrine so dear to de Piles. It marked the sometimes sur-prising endpoint of a concept of representation worked out in the classical period. Baudelaire's aesthetics took the logic of that concept to an extreme and—this was entirely new—did so in the literary field too. This colorist aesthetic found expres-sion not only in the writers' declarations of support for "modern" painting but in their style, above all in the way they described things. Color was triumphant in the writing of precisely those who, in their reviews of the Salons, were campaign-ing for the triumph of the "dot" or "dash" (*tache*) of color in painting.[11]

But none of these writers was so strangely and profoundly enthralled by color as Huysmans. For him, the beauty of literature, like that of painting, rested above all on color effects, or more precisely on the effect of the patches and specks in which it is found. Thus, in *À rebours* he praises the "the superb, spotted tongue spoken by Claudian, Rutilius, and Ausonius"[12] and again the "superb, speckled style of the Goncourts."[13] And in *L'art moderne,* he writes about Degas: "He too had to borrow from all the vocabularies of painting, combine all the various elements of solvent and oil, watercolor and pastel, distemper and gouache, to forge color neologisms and break down the accepted organization of subjects."[14]

In Huysmans's prose, color neologisms, discrepant components worked into a new visual syntax, and a comprehensive disregard for the rules of composition forge a style that itself seems to borrow from all the vocabularies of painting.[15] His description of Goya's painting of a bullfight, exhibited in 1887, is particularly telling in this respect:

> The Goya: a crush of red, blue, and yellow; commas in white; brightly colored impasto slapped down pell-mell, pulped and digested by the palette knife, rubbed, smeared with the thumb, the whole lot leveling out into more or less wrinkly patches from top to bottom of the canvas. You look for things in vain. Vaguely, amid the riot of these faculae, you make out a wooden toy shaped like a cow, slices of sealing wax barred with black and crowned with brown umlauts; then, as you look up, chevrons and periods, an entire punctuation of color ventilating the tawny-colored page. You step back and it is suddenly extraordinary: as if by magic, everything delineates and declares itself, everything comes to life, the impasto teems, the commas neigh; toreadors appear, brandishing red cloths, striving, jostling one another, yelling into the searing sunlight. . . . In the depths of the arena, horses are trampling one another, and this crush of colors, smeared with a thumb or scrubbed across the canvas with a rag, becomes a pullulating, unbridled crowd, hurling insults and threats and yelling deafening hurrahs. It is just wonderful. Out of this unfathomable mess, clear figures emerge: the umlauts are sparkling eyes; the bars are gaping mouths; the chevrons are clenched hands. It is the wildest uproar that has ever been set down on canvas, the most intense jostling a palette has ever created.[16]

The organizing principle of this text is an issue central to Diderot's aesthetics, that of the distance between the spectator and the picture. From a distance, forms and figures appear and delineate themselves, but up close we see paint: patches and lines of color. This color is evoked under its two aspects, as material substance and graphic form. Up close, we see now a "crush," impasto, flat areas of color, patches of color pulped, smeared, and rubbed, now commas, umlauts, chevrons, and periods: "an entire punctuation of color" on a "tawny-colored page." Specks and dots make an image out of paint, but they also make a discourse legible, make it into a written text. On the one hand, color as matter: dense, compact, and formless, crushed onto the canvas by various sizes of brush. On the other, color as sign, which can be made out among the masses and volumes by marks analogous to those traced on paper by a pen. Unlike color-matter, color-signs belong to the category of the mark, the inscription, the trace left by writing or drawing—though in this case a drawing made of nothing but colors.

Close up, a painting resembles a page of writing seen at such close range that the eye cannot decipher the text and elicit its meaning. Close up, the picture is like a page whose sense can no longer be made out, leaving only its material existence perceptible. Spots of ink alternate with blanks and are interspersed with bars or dots; it resembles a text decomposed into its graphic elements, which no one can any longer read but only see or hear—a writing in which words explode deafeningly into sight like patches of color. For Huysmans also speaks of the *vacarme,* the "uproar" or "racket" of color, thus returning to another topos of art theory and colorist aesthetics: the analogy between sound and color. He speaks of Grünewald "bellowing colored orisons in an original dialect, a language apart."[17] Viewed up close, painting is like a form of writing that has revived the aural and visual origins of language, one in which the sentence has disintegrated into its components, those parts of the sentence that French also knows as its *membres,* members or limbs. And we know that the metaphor of dismemberment was particularly dear to Huysmans, as much in literature as in painting. The library of des Esseintes is a veritable freak show of anatomical curiosities in which the books stand on the shelves like so many rare species of a decomposition that transforms the literary text into a dismembered corpse; the sentences lose their limbs, their joints crack, their limbs rot or hang loose: "Des Esseintes's interest in the Latin language remained undiminished, now that it hung like a completely rotted corpse, its limbs falling off, dripping with pus, and preserving, in the total corruption of its body, barely a few firm parts, which the Christians took away to steep in the brine of their new idiom."[18]

This fascination with dismemberment carries over from the literary to the art critic. Huysmans similarly rejoices in the bluish flesh and disjointed bodies of Degas's women, who wash or dry themselves in strange and often very complicated postures, like disjointed mannequins, or the monstrous figures of Grünewald's Isenheim altarpiece with their rotting limbs and swollen flesh. Painting somehow places before his eyes the very metaphor of dismemberment that he tirelessly applied to literature. It brings the metaphor into existence, literally gives it body; the explosive color disintegrates the unity of plastic form and pictorial matter alike.

For Huysmans, artistic metamorphosis of the body was by no means the exclusive preserve of art. It could also be the aesthetically felicitous effect of painful natural processes such as illness. In tuberculosis, leprosy, and syphilis, the flesh decomposes and the body is invaded by flecks and patches. It is as if nature said, "Anch'io son pittore," as if it too had become a modern painter, a colorist. If art is a kind of antinature, illness is the only occasion when, in the eyes of the aesthete, nature finally turns to art, "working in the living flesh," to adopt the astonishing expression that van Gogh uses about Christ.[19] In *Manette Salomon*—in which the Goncourt brothers indulge their humorous streak, what they call *blague* or prankishness—the character Anatole is a parody, taken to the extreme, of this fundamental and enduring theme in the colorist aesthetic. He is a painter of considerable technique but without any particular talent other than that of imitation or pastiche (in short, a talent for *blague*). An allegory of the end of art, the last representative of a conception of mimetic painting now declining into comedy and derision, that "beast Anatole" as his friends call him, lives with an ape that he has dubbed "Vermillon" (vermilion). Vermillon is heir to an entire tradition that makes the ape emblematic of the painter. He loves painting; he loves it so much that he eats it, feeding from the tubes that lie scattered about Anatole's studio. He dies of the illness from which artists die, pneumonia. Down to his last penny, Anatole eventually accepts a job with an embalmer. His job is to paint the flesh of the corpses, which would otherwise take on a mummified color. In a parodic image of the colorist painter, Anatole literally paints flesh: applied to the dead, his paints restore the color of living flesh.

Flaubert, too, had noted that nature turns artist over the course of an illness. Visiting Damascus, he reported his experience of a leper house:

> Two or three days ago, we went to see the local lazar-house. It lay outside the town, near a marsh where crows and bearded vultures flew off as we approached. There they were, the poor wretches, men and women (perhaps a dozen) all together. — No harem here, no veils to hide the face, no distinctions of sex. — They are masked with purulent crusts, they have holes where their noses should be, and I had to use my lorgnette to make out on one of them whether it was greenish rags or hands hanging from the ends of his arms. They were hands. (O colorists, where are you? What idiots painters are.)[20]

Huysmans, too, thought most painters were idiots when it came to their pictorial achievements, though he granted some exceptions.[21] There were, in his view, colorists capable of painting the greenish rags or purulent crusts that Flaubert describes. But very few of them could be seen at the Salons or the Académie des beaux-arts. And what distinguished these colorists in Huysmans's view, setting them apart from the painters favored by the public and the Salon judges, was not the greater importance that they accorded to color but the different treatment they gave it. For Huysmans, the contrast was not between colorists and draftsmen, as it had been for Baudelaire when he compared Ingres and Delacroix;

it was between two ways of perceiving and treating color. The division that Huysmans perceived between colorists and non-colorists was no longer the traditional one between color and line but between two perspectives on color.

In Huysmans, color is always subject to a twofold specification, one that implies a positive or a negative evaluation. It is described either as a material property—a quality of the object perceived—or as a modification of perception and thus an act of the perceiving subject. In the former case, color is naturalized; in the latter, it is aestheticized. In the former, the effects and transformations of color are analogous to those resulting from natural processes. Here the mutability of color shares in the more general destiny of matter, whose vicissitudes it undergoes: decomposition, excretion, liquefaction, or petrifaction. Color thereby becomes animal, vegetable, or mineral. In a word, it becomes natural—that is, ignoble. These descriptions of the degenerative nature of color form part of the grand narrative of natural history, a history receding toward the prehistoric forms of matter, its ineluctable movement ending with a reversion to lava, magma, and chaos. It is a history not of sedimentation but putrefaction.

But color can also be considered as something that alters perception, as we said; in Schopenhauer's terms, as a mere "affection of the eye."[22] Des Esseintes finally decides not to paint the walls of his house violet since he has only to take a few drops of the drug santonin to see the entire world in that shade. From this second point of view, color is no longer a natural property inherent in matter but a purely subjective phenomenon, lacking any external correlate and corresponding to nothing in empirical reality or the so-called objective world. This color has only an aesthetic existence, in the strict sense of the word; it exists only in the sensibility of the individual. And it can be considered an "affection of the eye" twice over since it appears only in a gaze itself distorted, modified by physiological troubles that disorder the sensory apparatus. For Huysmans, as we shall see, this other kind of color originates in a whole series of malfunctions of the visual apparatus, ranging from blinking to color blindness and including retinal disorders, ophthalmia, and degeneration of the optic nerve. Their effect is to denature the gaze, or, to use a term then fashionable, to "hystericize" perception. This other process undergone by color—a pathological process—is radically different from the first. It partakes not of the regressive tendencies of nature but of the modern history of art. Huysmans thus contrasts the ailments of color with the ailments of the eye. The former made any visit to the Salons a "descent into pigment hell,"[23] while the latter opened the way to the paradise of art. Paradisiacal or hellish, their description invariably takes us back to the emblematic image of the hospital.

Baudelaire was probably the first to make the hospital one of the loci of painting. In the *Salon de 1846,* he assails Horace Vernet in no uncertain terms; he hates him "because his pictures are not painting but a sort of agile and frequent masturbation, an irritation of the French epidermis."[24] He goes on to say: "As you see, here we are in the infirmary of painting, with its sores and its ailments before us."[25]

In Huysmans, the description of these sores and ailments forms a veritable treatise on the pathologies of pictorial matter: an extremely detailed study of the symptoms of a retrograde process leading to the senescence and death of art. The main center of infection remained, of course, what he called the "daylight asylum in the rue des Beaux-Arts."[26]

In his view, pictorial color was threatened by many dangers, in particular a whole series of natural catastrophes from which only the great painters had contrived the means to escape. The first occurred when color took on the appearance of a liquid and began flowing like milk. This lactescent color, drooling and gloopy, abandoned all propriety and restraint, forming dirty mixtures with other colors. It bore the stigmata of the natural, whose social incarnation was the family and whose preeminent form of expression was, in the eyes of our bachelor artist, maternity. To put it in other terms, this color is not artistic but bourgeois. And if color should happen to flow, it was primarily because it had gone off. This deliquescence could often be blamed on the "villainy of our modern suppliers," who sold bad-quality paints.[27] Matter was inherently liable to putrefaction, and trade exacerbated its corruption. Huysmans describes Moreau's *The Apparition* (pl. 14) thus: "The crimsons were once like bared flesh but have declined into indeterminate browns; the yellows and pinks have vanished; it is a sorry fact, but this watercolor has gone off."[28]

This "turning" of color resulted from the distressing procedures and recipes known at the time as "painters' cuisine." But Huysmans saw it as symptomatic of painting's disastrous regression toward what one might call the infantile stage of aesthetic experience, an oral stage that reduces all objects to foodstuffs. Describing color in alimentary metaphors, he transformed the Salon into a market, a vast array of edibles in which vegetables are found side by side with dairy products, with lettuce next to butter, eggs, and cheese: "Vegetables, fruit, and flowers are now spread out in the aisles, corridors, and rooms from the banisters to the frieze. They grow pell-mell together in defiance of the seasons, for the most part bearing in minium letters the indication 'for Monsieur So and So' or rather 'for Madam So and So,' for it is mostly women who go in for this form of cultivation."[29]

From the descriptions in *L'art moderne* there emerges the outline of a naturalistic novel, one whose title might have been *Le ventre de Paris* (*The Belly of Paris*).[30] This market is only nominally artistic. The full range of provisions needed to satisfy the appetite of bourgeois families can be found there. Nourishment is available for the heads of families, their wives, and their children, as it is for soldiers and (of course) for the *peintres pompier,* who paint for their supper and whose paintings are therefore a dog's dinner. For food is a profoundly bourgeois pleasure and as such despised by the aesthete. The artist either does not eat or does so in reverse (*à rebours*), like des Esseintes, who is obliged by his lack of appetite to absorb through enemas the nourishment required to restore his depleted organs.

Here are some of Huysmans's culinary and alimentary metaphors: A still life by Monginot: "A sickly mush of overripe fruit," "his gooseberrys and raspberries on a cabbage leaf are vague and lacking in clear outline, seen as if through a muslin curtain. . . . His fruit are deliquescent." Gervex: a "stew of colors cooked up by a road mender in pea-green overalls." Dubufe: his "figures are gelatinous, like half-frozen cream." Berthe Morisot: "still these half-beaten egg-whites, vanilla-flavored relics of a meal of paint." Cabanel: "a confectioner of the fine arts." Ballavoine's picture: "painted with gooseberry juice and whey." Puvis de Chavannes's fisher boy: "lettuce-green soaked in milk." We note that the metaphor goes hand in hand with color symbolism. The whiteness of milk and more particularly of whey is regressive; green, the color of nature, corresponds to mindless bliss; while blue is often the expression of an inane spirituality. "The sin of the terrible blue has again been committed," Huysmans observes about a picture by Caillebotte.[31] This is contrasted with orange, an "irritating and sickly color of fictive splendor and acid fevers"—and the shade with which des Esseintes eventually decides to paint the walls of his house.[32] In one of the most nauseating transformations, the lactescent paint mutates into butter, mayonnaise, margarine, or lard. Roll: "it is a vinous, buttery mess";[33] Merson: "a mayonnaise Jesus"; Cormon: "margarine of colors"; Perugino's Messiah: "a lard figurine."

But color does not just turn. It can also harden. It can liquefy or solidify; it can become butter or crust, spreading out in nauseous secretions or hardening into frenzied retentiveness. Huysmans's alimentary and culinary metaphors are somewhat reminiscent of Céline's. The disastrous metaphors of color oscillate between the twin poles of diarrhea and constipation. The stiffer side of things includes Béraud's "leadenness" and "pastries," the "ivory" of Cabanel, the "smooth," "icy" surfaces of Bonvin, the "white stonework" of Descamps, and the "chalky white" of Rochegrosse. This solidifying tends toward petrifaction. It transforms flesh into stone. Here painting becomes mineral and borders on sculpture, reminding Huysmans of the appalling white-marble "bricklaying" of the "official plasterers" that he so detests. If liquefaction is described through gustatory metaphors, hardening, which can reach the stage of an atomized aggregate—solid rather than liquid decomposition—leads Huysmans toward tactile metaphors. Here we have the "marble specks" of Bracquemond, the "sequins all sticking one to another" of Fortuny's students, the sin of "strumming," the obsession with "arpeggiating" or "knitting." Even Renoir is sometimes accused of making "knitted" painting, while

Seurat's work is all "colored fleas," "mosaics of colored dots," or "knitting with tiny stitches." We seem to have left the market of les Halles for the Bon Marché department store. We are no longer in *Le ventre de Paris* but in *Au bonheur des dames* (*The Ladies' Paradise*).[34] The same kinds of disaster occur in literature. Language too can liquefy or harden like color. In the "humid language of Monsieur Renan," it "liquefies"; in the "grim, leaden style of the institutes," it is petrified. The nadir is attained when the two kinds of disaster combine in a regressive movement from hard to soft, from the mineral to the molluscan, as it does in the painter Bouguereau: "This is no longer even porcelain, it is the pulpy flesh of an octopus."

All these metaphors suggest a sort of alimentary cosmology, an apocalyptic vision of the world as a sort of enormous factory of foodstuffs in which the distinction between the raw and the cooked, between nature and culture, has been abolished. The characters in Huysmans's novels tread in "parfaits of filth," walk in "sorbets of snow," slip on the "dilute compote of earth," their boots spitting out the "milky coffee they have absorbed in the ponds." Everything rots, turns, and decomposes.[35] In *En route*, Huysmans remarks that women's voices "sour the psalms."[36]

No surprise, then, that the two most successful creations of nature's infernal kitchen are carnivores: forms of digestive life, cannibal flesh. The first is orchids, flowers that seem wholly artificial, as if "borrowing the long-lasting colors of… rotting flesh."[37] The second is Woman, the great devourer, nature's terrifying masterpiece made in its own image.

Huysmans contrasts this depraved color—this viscous by-product of matter—with what one might call artistic or "modern" color, the color employed by modern artists. Entirely a matter of subjective sensitivity, and thus aesthetic in the strict etymological sense, this form of color is completely alien to the nauseous world of nature and therefore resists all attempts at reification. Unlike the other kind, this one is (as we have seen) exclusively related to the eye of the painter. Describing it takes us into a strange universe of kinesthetic delirium in which vision escapes the category of common perception to become, in Taine's paradoxical expression, "true hallucination."[38]

This conception of color was widespread in Huysmans's time. It was the logical endpoint of the artistic and scientific changes that had, over the course of the nineteenth century, overthrown all previous notions of color vision. Huysmans's aesthetic in this respect illustrates the influence that these new analyses of perception—and more particularly of the perception of color—were having on the theory of art. Of course, this influence was for the most part indirect and exerted only through many displacements and reformulations.[39] Nonetheless, the connection is undeniable. The research taking place in physics, chemistry, and medicine, particularly in the field of psychiatry, resulted in the redefinition of a number of terms that played a fundamental role in the theory of painting. That research concerned the mechanism of the sensations. Above all, it concerned the mechanism of apparently aberrant sensations that cannot be related to a felt or perceived object, perceptions that had always been described as illusory or imaginary. Now it was discovered that although they seemed purely subjective, such perceptions obeyed laws, possessed what one might call objective reality, and occurred very frequently in color vision.

The existence of certain visual aberrations in the perception of color had been demonstrated as early as the eighteenth century by Buffon. He had observed the appearance of strange chromatic phenomena when one stared at a red form on a white background:

> When one stares long and hard at a red spot or figure on a white background, such as a little square of red paper on a piece of white paper, one sees a sort of crown of pale green around the little red square. If you then stop looking at the red square and turn your eye to the white paper, you very distinctly see a square of pale green tending toward blue. This appearance is more or less prolonged depending on the strength of the impression made by the red. The size of the imaginary green square is the same as that of the real red square, and the green does not vanish until after the eye has reassured itself by looking at a number of other objects in succession, whose images destroy the excessively strong impression made by the red.[40]

The existence of these "imaginary" colors obviously raises theoretical difficulties insofar as the laws of Newtonian physics cannot explain them. Buffon therefore suggested distinguishing "natural colors" that "depend exclusively on the properties of light" from those that "depend as much on our organ as on the action of light." He proposed calling the latter "accidental colors" because they appeared only "when the organ has been strained or subjected to too strong a commotion."[41] These phenomena of course underpinned the analysis of color developed by Goethe. But unlike Buffon, Goethe used them to argue against Newton's theory, which explained color as deriving from the decomposition of light. These subjective colors, which "belong altogether to the subject or in a great degree to the eye itself," wrote Goethe at the outset of his *Zur Farbenlehre* (*Treatise on Color*), "are the foundation of the whole theory." Until then they had wrongly been considered secondary, accidental, or illusory; they were caused by the very nature of the visual organ. This is why he decided to call them "physiological": "We have called them physiological colors because they belong to the sound eye; [and] because we consider them the necessary conditions of vision."[42]

Whether they were termed "accidental," "imaginary," "subjective," or "physiological," these colors that belong to the eye, as Goethe put it, were to become the subject of increasing interest throughout the nineteenth century on the part of scientists and artists alike. Thus Chevreul, for example, taking up Buffon's problem in the wake of several others, shows in his *De la loi du contraste simultané des couleurs* (*The Laws of Contrast of Color*) how a color can be created by the simple juxtaposition of two others. Delacroix, at exactly the same period, developed a theory of optical mixing based on a similar principle. Independent of any idea of influence,[43] a coincidence of this kind illustrates the convergence that may occur at a given moment between a scientific theory and an artistic theory born of an artistic experiment and worked out on the basis of artistic experience. On the back of a page in a book of sketches made in Morocco, Delacroix drew an optical triangle accompanied by these words:

> From the three primary colors, three binary colors are formed. — If you add the primary tone to the binary tone opposed to it, you annihilate it, i.e., you produce from it the half-shade required. — Thus, adding black is not adding the half-shade; it is just sullying the tone, whose true half-shade is in the opposite tone, as I have said. — Hence green shadows in red. — The head of the two little peasants. The yellow one had violet shadows. The ruddier, redder one had green shadows.[44]

Some ten years later, he noted in his *Journal:*

> The more I reflect on color, the more I discover how much the reflected half-tint affords us the principle that must dominate, because it is what gives the true tone, as a matter of fact, the tone that constitutes the value, and the one which counts in the object and causes it to exist. Light, to which the schools teach us to attach equal importance, and which they place on the canvas at the same time as the half-tint and the shadow, is only a pure accident: without understanding that, one can not understand true color, I mean color that gives the feeling of thickness and the feeling of that radical difference which should distinguish one object from the other.[45]

In *Manette Salomon,* Coriolis despairs of ever being able to "make light with colors" as Delacroix can.[46] The great lesson of Delacroix, Huysmans says in his turn, is to have taught artists to paint what he magnificently calls "absent color" or the "tone absent from the palette," that is, a color that exists neither on the canvas nor on the palette and which the spectator can nevertheless see: a color genuinely perceived where it is not — like the Mallarmean flower "absent from all bouquets."[47] Thus Huysmans writes about Degas:

> There have been many new applications since Delacroix of optical mixing, that is of the tone absent from the palette and obtained on the canvas by the vicinity of two others.

Here, in the portrait of Duranty, are patches of almost bright pink on the forehead, green in the beard, blue on the velvet of the suit collar. The fingers are done with yellow flanked by episcopal violet.... No painter since Delacroix, who Monsieur Degas has long studied and who is his true master, has understood so well the marriage and adultery of colors.[48]

The painters were not alone in learning from Delacroix. George Sand tells of a soiree when the painter explained the "mystery of reflections." Having listened "eyes wide with surprise," Chopin began to improvise:

Chopin had withdrawn from the conversation. He was seated at the piano, unaware that we were listening. He improvised as if at random. He stopped:

"Well?" exclaimed Delacroix, "That's not the end of it!"

"It's not even the beginning." "Nothing's coming.... Nothing but reflections, shadows, contours that won't stay still. I'm looking for color, and I can't even find the drawing."

"You won't find the one without the other," Delacroix replied, "and both will come."

"What if I find nothing but moonshine?"

"Then you'll have found the reflection of a reflection." ...

That idea pleased the divine artist. Chopin restarted without appearing to begin again; his intentions were vague and uncertain-seeming. Our eyes gradually filled with soft color matching the smooth modulations entering our ears. Then the blue note sounded, and we were transported into the azure of transparent night.[49]

As to the poets, we have only to remind ourselves of the lines by Verlaine so close to des Esseintes's heart:

For we want the nuance again,

Not the color, the nuance alone

....

And the rest is literature, literature.[50]

It seems likely that Delacroix's ideas about optical mixing were worked out mainly on the basis of his own observations and owed little if anything to Chevreul's research of the same time. But their diffusion and application in painting elicited ever greater interest on the part of the scientists, who sought to understand the physical and physiological mechanism of these colors that existed only in the eye. The extraordinary scientific curiosity exhibited in the later decades of the nineteenth century in regard to the pictorial treatment of color in modern painters ought to be sufficient to refute, if need were, the simplistic vision generally entertained of the relations between the arts and science. Those relations are for the most part considered from a unilateral perspective, through the influence exerted on art by the transformations of science, as if the relation were exclusively one way and the evolution of art never had any influence on science. The only relation working in the other direction is, on this account, an aesthetic one. And that too is a relationship usually perceived as unilateral, as an expression of sensibility devoid of cognitive content. Scientists can be art lovers and often are — they may even be connoisseurs — but the idea that they might be interested in art as scientists and from a scientific point of view is not generally entertained.[51] Yet in the second half of the nineteenth century, that was exactly the kind of interest shown by physicists, doctors, neurologists, psychiatrists, and philosophers. The lecture given at the Académie des sciences by Paul Bert, which dealt with the persistence of distant colors, is particularly interesting in this respect.

According to the summary published early in 1878 in the science column of a newspaper, Bert had observed that a green light, formed by the combination of blue and yellow rays, was perceived as being bluer the farther away it was; that orange seemed at a distance to grow increasingly red; and that in violet the red predominated over the blue. He had compared these observations with those that could be made by examining pictures:

It is well known that certain painters, and by no means the least exceptional, allow their favorite colors to predominate in their paintings, sometimes to an exaggerated degree. For one, it is yellow; for another, violet, and so on. They are commonly said to "see yellow," "see violet," and so on. The favored color sometimes varies over the stages of a painter's life. Thus Descamps painted lilac during the last few years of his life and one was bound to infer that the cause was a physical modification of his visual apparatus.

To find out about this point, which is of interest to both physiology and the history of art, Monsieur Paul Bert painted a large number of patches of flat, even color on a canvas; then he asked one of his friends, a painter by profession, to copy the patches, after having first put before his eyes a number of glass lenses of various colors. As a further precaution, the colors had been placed on the palette by a third person, so that the painter, no longer recognizing their habitual layout, was obliged to examine with care the composition of the mixtures that he used in his copy.

The experiment produced the result that its author had expected a priori. The painter, seeing with the same lens the patch on the picture and the colors on the palette, made the same mistake in assessing the patch and the mixture of colors. Consequently he was not satisfied with his work till the representation was really similar to the model. Seeing through the colored lens had increased the difficulty of imitation but had not affected it as such.

But two exceptions must be made to this rule. Suppose the lens of the glasses to be green. If the painter uses them to examine the nuances of green, he will not assess them with his habitual accuracy, which is understandable, since they will all be as it were washed over with green; the representation of the nuances of green will therefore suffer in the copy. But the mistakes will be even greater for the various nuances of red. Since this color is complementary to green, it tends to veer toward the black when seen under red lighting. The result is that the composite colors in which red predominates will be brown; they will be killed; their delicate differences will not be perceived. With blue-lens glasses, it is the nuances of blue and above all of orange that will suffer and, overall, the errors in the copy will center on the nuances of the color used and more particularly on the nuances of its complementary.

If, then, we suppose that a painter genuinely sees violet through an original predisposition or through an alteration of his sight, his infirmity would not, as most people might expect, be identifiable through an excessive predominance of violet but through the insufficient variety and delicacy exhibited in the nuances of violet and more particularly of yellow. If he saw red and had to represent a nude figure in a landscape, there would be an unhappy monotony both in the flesh tones, of which red partakes in proportions that the painter would be unable to judge with precision, and above all in the very various nuances of green in the landscape.[52]

But for the difference in style, one might almost be reading Huysmans. Bert draws two conclusions from these observations, each of which corresponds to one of the two aspects of Huysmans's descriptions. The first is that the preference for certain colors exhibited by contemporary painters is motivated by "reasons of intellectual kind," that is, by conscious and deliberate artistic choices. The second is that the strange ways in which certain painters represent nuances — ways inaccurate from a scientific point of view — should be attributed to a distortion of their sight, that is, to pathological causes: "The experiments that we have reported further indicate how interesting it would be to examine painters' works from this new point of view. If there are some who err in the representation of two orders of nuances derived from complementary colors, this flawed execution should indeed be attributed to a distortion of their sight."[53]

The second conclusion is undoubtedly reminiscent of Huysmans's clinical descriptions. The convergence of the scientist's and the writer's points of view is the more striking since in Bert we come across an example familiar to readers of *À rebours,* one that we cited earlier in this chapter, that of the effects of santonin: "It would, incidentally, be very interesting to see what a painter who had ingested a certain quantity of santonin, a substance that makes one see everything in shades of violet, would produce when copying either from nature or a picture."[54]

This is precisely what des Esseintes envisages doing after having rejected violet as the color with which to paint his house, giving as his reason that, in the evening, violet becomes red — "and what a red!" Huysmans continues, "In any case he thought it quite pointless to make use of this colour, since by ingesting santonin in the appropriate dosage, everything looks violet and it is then easy to change the hue of one's wall hangings without so much as touching them."[55]

It is unlikely that Huysmans had read Bert. But he had read Véron, who cites the summary of Bert's lecture in a note, after mentioning the observations made by psychiatrists, and Charcot in particular, on the distortions in color perception found in cases of hysteria.[56] Their observations, Véron notes, afford scientific confirmation of Delacroix's optical triangle and prove that the "aureole of which Chevreul speaks really exists."[57] The effects produced by the ingestion of santonin evidently made a considerable impression on all those who were interested in color-vision: physicists, doctors, writers, art critics, and philosophers alike. In *De l'intelligence,* Taine too remarks that "after taking *santonine,* the sensation of violet is lost for some hours," citing in a note the many observations made on this subject by Helmholtz. Véron also mentions these, though in more vague and allusive fashion.[58]

The theory of sensation developed by Taine in *De l'intelligence* was based on an immense scientific literature. In a philosophical argument of almost unparalleled breadth and rigor, it offered a summary of all the scientific research on sensation conducted at that period.[59] Taine brought together not only the physicists but the doctors, citing, discussing, and analyzing their work on sensory phenomena and in particular on the aberrant sensations observed in amputees, hysterics, and the color-blind. All these observations and medical experiments coming thick and fast in the late nineteenth century showed that sensations— sometimes very vivid ones—could exist in the absence of external stimuli, as in the case of the phantom limb of the amputee. In short, there is such a thing as "subjective sensation":

> Hence it follows that all external excitants may be absent; if the nerve enters into action of itself, we should have the same sensation in their absence as in their presence.... In short, the direct condition of sensation is the action or molecular motion of the nerve; neither external events nor the other internal events of the living body matter much; they only act by means of the movement they excite; in themselves, they do nothing; they may be dispensed with. If the action of the nerve were always spontaneous, as indeed it sometimes is; if this action were still produced according to the ordinary order and degree, the external world and all within us excepting the nervous system might be annihilated, we should still have the same sensations and consequently the same images and the same ideas.[60]

It was already known that amputees could feel the limb of which they had been deprived. Taine moreover cited a number of cases studied by Esquirol proving that the blind could see and the deaf hear. How then is it possible to distinguish dreams from waking life, hallucination from true perception, and madness from normal mental states? How do we know that our sensations are not illusions, that they have a correlate in empirical reality? Effectively, Taine did no more than place on new foundations the question that Descartes had asked in his *Meditationes de prima philosophia*. And Taine asked that question in the same terms, since he started from the same hypothesis or rather fiction, that of the abolition of the external world. His answer, however, is noticeably different from that of Descartes. In Taine's view, there is nothing in a false perception that inherently distinguishes it from a true one. Every image and every sensation is hallucinatory by nature: "a sensation…engenders by its presence alone an internal phantom which appears [to be] an external object."[61] The difference between these internal phantoms engendered during sleep or madness and those born of a waking state in normal subjects is that the latter dissolve on contact not with reality but with other sensations. They are stopped by contact with other phantoms or simulacra: "The state of our mind when we are awake and healthy may be defined as *a series of hallucinations which do not become developed.*"[62]

There are therefore no false or true sensations but only those that develop unchecked, without encountering obstacles, and that are thus distinguished from those whose development is impeded by other and contradictory sensations. Hallucination is not an illusion; it is a sensation that meets no resistance.[63] The true perception, the perception that chimes with the real, is merely a "hallucination thwarted" or "aborted" or "rectified," Taine says, by other perceptions that as it were oblige it to conform to external reality. Whence the famous definition of perception as a true hallucination: "external perception is an internal dream which proves to be in harmony with external things; and instead of calling hallucination a false external perception, we must call an external perception a *true hallucination.*"[64]

This definition perfectly matches how Huysmans describes the perception of the artist and aesthete alike. In him we find the same logic of sensation,[65] which blurs the traditional distinctions between the normal and the pathological, hallucination and perception, and illusion and truth. It also resists the philosophical distinction between materialism and idealism since it is both wholly realist and wholly subjectivist. This logic of sensation ultimately leads to a sort of aesthetic solipsism, which Huysmans makes the founding and federating principle of all forms of artistic modernity, especially of its pictorial forms.

As we saw above, Huysmans attributed most innovations in painting primarily to physiological conditions, to visual disorders and the modified perception that resulted. His artistic theory is in this regard perfectly consonant with the medical and philosophical thought of his time.[66] It is a sort of extension, admittedly somewhat comical and unexpected,[67] of the research on vision conducted in physics, physiology, and medicine, research that proved the existence of the "physiological colors" postulated by Goethe.[68] In modern painters' very particular treatment of color, Huysmans saw the effect of vision disordered by malady: the symptom of retinal anemia or a weakened optic nerve. This formed one of his interpretations of the early period of impressionism. He ascribed certain kinds of clumsiness or failure visible in the earliest exhibitions to the "ravages of color blindness":

> Now add insufficient talent, the brutal clumsiness of the brushwork, the ailment quickly brought on by the tension of the eye, by that very human insistence on reducing a particular tone that one has, one fine day, perceived and as it were discovered, to another tone that the eye eventually perceives elsewhere, as the will dictates — even where it no longer exists — because of the loss of sangfroid that comes in the constant grim struggle of experiment, and you have before you the explanation of the touching madness laid out before the public in the early exhibitions at Nadar and Durand-Ruel's. Study of these works was primarily the province of physiology and medicine. I do not wish to name names. It is enough to say that in most cases their vision had attained the monomaniacal. One of them saw wigmaker's blue throughout nature and consequently turned a river into a laundress's bucket. Another saw violet: land, sky, water, flesh, everything in his work was somewhere between lilac and aubergine. Most would have confirmed Dr. Charcot's experiments on the disordered color-perception that he has observed in many hysterics in the Salpêtrière and in many people afflicted with ailments of the nervous system.

But these early failures were soon left behind. Huysmans wrote: "As I have so often said, the retinal acuity of the impressionist painters had advanced. It could grasp all the modulations in the tones of light but could not express them and the nervous papillae had attained such a hypersensitive state that our hopes were low. In short, purely impressionist art was verging on aphasia when, by some miracle, it began to speak."[69]

Illness may be one of the conditions necessary to the invention of art. It is not, of course, a sufficient condition. The physiological disorder that makes the eye see the world in an unprecedented manner and in new colors must be accompanied by a mastery of artistic means; the pathological irritability of perception must be placed under the control of a craftsmanship that requires patient work and a will constantly bent toward the realization of its goals. Then and only then can an ailment give rise to real artistic innovations, as in Cézanne: "an artist with diseased retinae, who in the exasperated apperception of his sight, discovered the prodromes of the new art."[70]

Evidently the illness that makes an artist great is nervous shock, that extremely subtle wave-movement propagated into the retina and provoking what Laforgue called an "ocular spasm."[71] Huysmans detected the symptoms of a nervous ailment of this kind in all the true painters. He recognized them in Moreau's "sinister hieratic allegories," which were, he said "exacerbated by the uneasy perspicuity of an entirely modern nervous disorder"; in Odilon Redon, who painted "hallucinated visions," "a fantastic [world] of disease and delirium"; in Degas, a man of "such vibrant nervosism";[72] or again in Grünewald, that "barbarian of genius," whose work leaves viewers "permanently hallucinated" (fig. 21; pl. 15). The same fact had struck the Goncourt brothers in regard to Degas. They noted in their *Journal* entry for 13 February 1874: "An original young fellow, this Degas: sickly, neurotic, his ophthalmia so severe that he fears he will lose his sight. But precisely on those grounds, an eminently sensitive being."[73]

The spiritualization of sensation that characterizes the artistic gaze is the aesthetic endpoint, as it were, of a nervous process. Hypersensitive, composed of filaments so tightly strained and of such delicacy that they seem always about to break, the eyes of the great painters have become wholly cerebral, that is, denatured. Through the nerves, man finally escapes from the ignoble material world of nature. And this nervosism (the term then current) has no less impact on the eye of the spectator. As unstable as color, as hypersensitive as the painter, and never long at a standstill, the lover of modern pictures shares all the attributes of modern painting. He is a modern spectator, a colorist, an agitated *flâneur* with an artistic eye; he hovers in front of the painting that has caught his fancy, now stepping close, now standing back.

For such is and has always been the distinctive mark of colorist painting, the fact that it is a mirage transformed by proximity: from the right distance, an image; from too close, a jumble of paint. Already in the seventeenth century, de Piles was insisting on the mobility of gaze required by Rubens's painting. And recall how Diderot described a still life by Chardin: "Move in and everything blurs, flattens itself out and disappears. Step back and everything re-creates and reproduces itself."[74] The gaze of Diderot's spectator already possessed an almost demiurgic power to make the forms of the painting vanish and come back to life in a sort of continuous re-creation that rehearsed and completed the artist's creative effort. In Huysmans, this re-creation is the effect of a hallucinatory perception, since it is accomplished under the same conditions as the original creation. And that creation was, as we have seen, the product of an eye that one might legitimately describe as hallucinated. Moreau's *The Apparition,* he tells us in *À rebours,* is "imperceptible to those of a precise, pedestrian cast of mind" and "accessible only to sensibilities that had been unsettled and sharpened, rendered almost visionary by neurosis."[75] When he approaches a modern picture, this more or less neurotic spectator undergoes a further nervous shock that completes his state of enfeeblement. Close up, his eye is assailed by a wave of chromatic sensations of such intensity that he is forced back.[76] Close up, he sees the "crush of

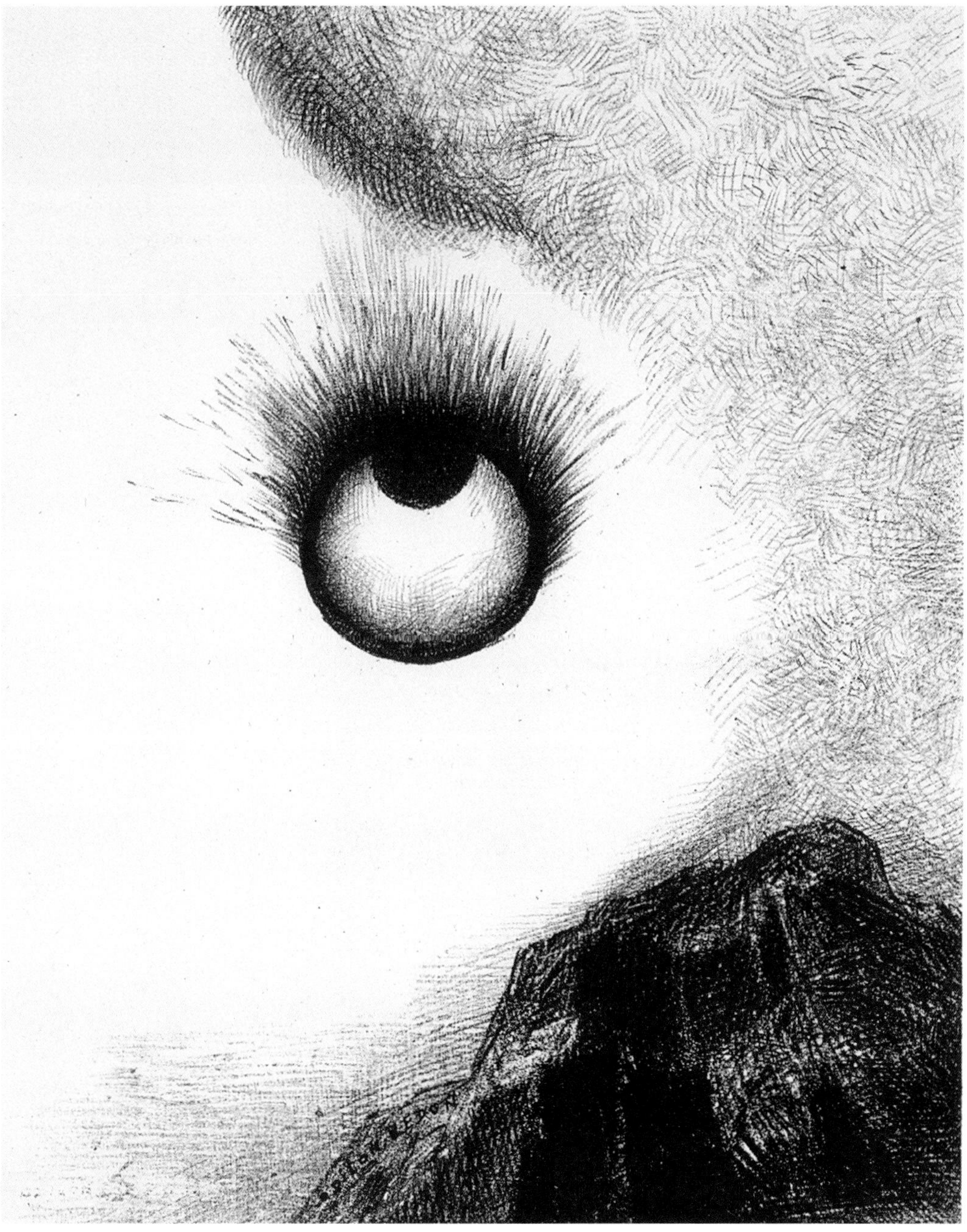

Fig. 21. **Odilon Redon (French, 1840–1916)**
Everywhere Eyeballs Are Aflame, pl. 9 from the *Temptation of Saint Anthony* series, 1888, lithograph,
20.5 × 15.9 cm (8 × 6¼ in.)
Chicago, Art Institute of Chicago

red, blue, and yellow," "wrinkled patches," a "mess" of colors rebounding off each other in the "wildest uproar." But from a distance, tranquillity is restored, as in the case of the Goya painting whose description we analyzed earlier in this chapter. The same thing happens when one contemplates a painting by Guillaumin, "who is also a colorist, and what is more, a ferocious one." Huysmans says, "At first glance, his canvases are a teeming mass of clashing colors and uncouth outlines, a congeries of stripes, vermilion, and Prussian blue. Step back and blink: everything falls back into place, the sense of space declares itself, the shrieking tones calm down, the hostile colors are reconciled, and one stands astonished at the unexpected delicacy assumed by certain sections of his canvases."[77]

The same, of course, holds for Degas: "Close up, it is a mass of slashing strokes, a hatching of colors that pummel and seemingly encroach on one another. A few steps back and everything slides into harmony, melting into a precise flesh-tone: live, palpitating flesh such as no one in France can do any more."[78]

But for Huysmans, Degas is not only, like Rubens and Delacroix before him, a very great painter of flesh. He is above all the inventor of a new way of painting flesh, and this makes him the first and greatest of modern painters. Somehow integrating into the surface of the painting the two viewpoints of the spectator's gaze, Degas shows flesh—particularly female flesh—simultaneously from both perspectives. No need to back off or move closer: the flesh is simultaneously "seen from close up with its rasping grain and from a distance with its sickly sheen."[79]

Close up, or from a distance—since Plato and Horace, the question of the "right" distance of the spectator from the object has haunted all analyses of representation and of pictorial representation in particular. What position should the spectator take up relative to the picture? The problem arises with all paintings but is particularly acute relative to a colorist painting—one that, according to tradition, highlights the representation of flesh. In this case, reflection on the distance between the spectator and the painting raises a much more fundamental question, one that completely transcends the restricted context of painting. This concerns the position of the eye no longer simply relative to color but to flesh in general: the relation of desire to its object, of man to woman or indeed femininity. Flesh itself has always been designated (in its essence, or rather its lack of essence) as feminine; and so has color, the sole means by which the texture of flesh can be represented in paint. In the tight network of images that make up the weave of our representations, men have no flesh—though there is, as Huysmans realized, one notable exception: Christ. But Huysmans was not content simply to revive a very old topos that the colorists had used before him. He transformed it by inscribing it into a new system of distinctions appropriate to the thinking of the nineteenth century. Huysmans reconceived the traditional identification between flesh, color, and femininity in terms of a contrast or opposition amounting almost to a principle: the opposition between flesh and nerves. This opposition affected the full range of his aesthetic assessments and completely determined the way in which he described the position of the spectator relative to the picture. If painting was flesh, the spectator, by contrast, was nothing but nerves. For Huysmans, aesthetic perception necessarily supposed a bloodless body. It is as if sensation battened onto the body like a vampire. Of des Esseintes he says: "the enormous strain to which his brain had been subjected had... further weakened the already exhausted blood of his stock."[80] The spiritualization of sensation effaces all the colors of the complexion. In this increasing tension of the nerves, flesh and blood eventually disappear. The body of the aesthete who scorns nature, is disgusted by meat, and loves flesh only in painting has itself been completely denatured.[81]

The polar opposite of the aesthete's emaciated body is that of woman: a body all flesh and blood, a body to be painted. It is the true "material for masterpieces," as the Goncourt brothers observe when explaining why Coriolis fell in love with his model Manette:

> The artist loved her no less than the man. He loved this woman for her body, for the lines that she made, for a particular shade in one place on her skin.... He loved her because she inspired him, as if through her his talent were revealed. He loved her because she placed before his eyes that Ideal of nature, that material for masterpieces, the real and living presence of Beauty that her charms embodied.[82]

When Manette's body is transformed by marriage and maternity, when her flesh no longer exhibits those delicate tones that remind him of Rubens and Titian, Coriolis predictably falls out of love with her. In Zola's *L'oeuvre,* Claude likewise loses interest in Christine when her body is no longer a body to be painted. This was a body that he had longed for, yearning to extract its secret—the secret of her magnificent flesh—and put it into his painting. For if woman is flesh and painting is color, no one can uncover the secret of painting—the art of color—without the closest possible investigation of woman's secret: the secret of her flesh. This is the double secret that Frenhofer claims to have penetrated when completing his portrait of Catherine Lescault in Balzac's *Le chef-d'oeuvre inconnu* (*The Unknown Masterpiece*). Where his two incredulous visitors see only "a wall of paint," a "chaos of colors, shapes and vague shadings, a kind of incoherent mist," Frenhofer sees a woman: "Here's true form—the very form of a girl. Haven't I captured the color, the energy of the line that seems to bound her body?... And that hair! You see how the light glows through it.... You see that breast?... The flesh throbs."[83]

And to share the secret of this flesh, Frenhofer asks Poussin and Porbus to move closer to the canvas and see how he has shaped the figure, trapped the light "by a series of brushstrokes and by accents applied with a full brush," or blurred the outlines: "Come closer, you'll see better how it's done. At a distance, it vanishes."[84]

The issue of the distance of the spectator from the picture thus conceals another, one that raises questions of perspective infinitely more formidable than those to which geometry has accustomed us. What distance from the flesh should a man maintain? Where must he be, to lovingly contemplate in the image the flesh that he cannot bear in fact? At the turn of the nineteenth century, many thought one should never come too close to the flesh, that is, to woman. From a distance, woman was beautiful, harmonious, and full of life. Close by, she was mortal and gave off an odor of putrescence. "Everything comes down to syphilis," says des Esseintes.[85]

In Huysmans's view, two painters knew how to paint the flesh in what he considered its hidden, intimate truth; two painters had homed in on flesh and represented it in all its magnificent, sumptuous horror. These were Degas, the painter of the girls and women of modern life, and Grünewald, the painter of Christ. For Christ's flesh-and-blood body is the only male body that can compete with the body of women, at least as regards color — that color by which painting is defined. Christ's is the other body to paint.

Huysmans's most astonishing text is the one he wrote about the series of pastels exhibited by Degas in 1886 in rue Laffitte. They represented women at their *toilette,* washing and drying themselves. Huysmans has been criticized for his profoundly misogynistic — and to that extent disputable — interpretation of these works. The first part of this criticism is undoubtedly true. You would have to be blind not to comprehend the image of woman presented when Huysmans tells us that Degas, "exasperated by the vileness of his surroundings," sought "with attentive cruelty and patient hatred" to "cast in the face of his century the greatest imaginable affront, upending the idol to which everyone always defers, woman, whom he here demeans by representing her plunk in her tub in the humiliating poses of her intimate ablutions."[86] But the violence of these observations also results from genuinely artistic determinants. That same violence is at the heart of Huysmans's productivity as a writer, and it is precisely that violence (and none other) that concerns us here. It is striking that Huysmans here uses the very word, *culbuter* ("upend," "overthrow"),[87] that he had used of Degas's sculpture in his review of the Exposition des Indépendants in 1881. In Huysmans's words, Degas had "at his first attempt…overthrown the traditions of sculpture."[88] So this affront to womanhood arose, in Huysmans's view, from the same iconoclastic purpose that had animated Degas in his sculptures. It was simultaneously an affront to the conventions of representation. By "upending the idol to which everyone always defers,"[89] Degas was overthrowing the traditions of painting as he had done those of sculpture.

And this iconoclastic vision is in close-up; it focuses right in on both art and women. For Huysmans, these nude studies represented woman seen very close up, that is, by the woman herself, when she believed herself free of the male gaze.[90] She was no longer a hieratic figure like Moreau's, her arm extended to keep the spectator in his place (see pl. 14). This was woman abandoned to her own concerns, caught in the most intimate poses, busy washing herself, turned in on herself, impenetrable in either sense of the term, like the woman pictured in *After the Bath: A Woman Drying Her Feet,* whose position leaves no interstices through which the male gaze or organ might reach (pl. 16). It was woman in the absence of the other, relating only to herself, closely communing with the sex whose secret Degas thus reveals — the fatal secret that Salomé conceals beneath her veils. From Huysmans's point of view, Moreau and Degas could be said to paint the same woman in her twin aspects. Moreau paints woman seen from afar: the Baudelairean idol "adorning herself in order to be adored,"[91] a woman to be gazed upon but never touched. Degas paints her in close-up, as she truly is, "natural, therefore, abominable," as Baudelaire also said,[92] a woman one can come so close to only because she does not see you. In both cases, Huysmans is clearly fascinated by a representation of the female body that implies the exclusion of the Other. Man is excluded either because the woman rejects him, as if she were saying, "Do not touch me," or because she ignores him, as if she were saying, "I don't see you." He writes, "In these pastels there is something of the cripple's stump, the beggar-woman's breast, the rocking hand-to-hand gait of the legless: a whole series of postures that even a pretty young woman must sometimes assume, adorable as she is while lying or standing but frog-like or simian when she must, like this woman, stoop to bind up her decay."[93]

But the way that Degas here depicts woman is in Huysmans's eyes an exemplary piece of great painting. He immediately goes on to say: "But in addition to the very particular tone of scorn and hatred, we should see in these works the unforgettable veracity of these specimens brought off with a broad, comprehensive line, with lucid and masterful spontaneity and a cold fervor; we should see the matte glow of the colors, the mysterious, opulent tone of these scenes; the supreme beauty of this flesh tinged blue or pink by the water and lit through closed, muslin-curtained windows in dark rooms."[94]

In addition to the image, we should see the paint, that is, move in closer to see the art, after which one can stand back and see the woman. But by then, what one sees will not be an image; it will be a picture. And this is something that Huysmans knows perfectly well, coming back to women as he does at the end of his description: "And there is more to it again, for this is not a man's scornful judgment, such as he might one day go back on. Rather it is the confident, penetrating hatred felt by certain women for the perverted joys of their own sex, an execration that makes them abound in hideous excuses and sully themselves by avouching out loud the damp horror of a body that no lotion can cleanse."[95]

Turning in on itself like these bodies with which Huysmans is so fascinated, the text comes to resemble the picture that it describes. And this correspondence, in the Baudelairean sense of the word, is so perfect that the description of the picture can without any difficulty be applied to the text that describes it. The deeper the description plunges into horror and abomination, the more those same glowing colors enter the writing, culminating in the extraordinary delicacy of the final touch, which is as transparent as a glaze. "In addition to the very particular tone of scorn and hatred," to apply to Huysmans the words that he uses about Degas, what we should take from "the damp horror of a body that no lotion can cleanse" ("l'humide horreur d'un corps qu'aucune lotion n'épure") is the "supreme beauty" of the phrase, the very same beauty that we find in "the bars are gaping mouths" ("ces barres, des bouches qui béent") of the text on Goya: a beauty for the ear, which is immediately understood when the phrase is read out loud and which has obvious analogies with Mallarmé's "vanished trinket of sonorous inanity" ("aboli bibelot d'inanité sonore").[96]

The cripple's stump, the beggar-woman's breast, the rocking hand-to-hand gait of the legless, and the living flesh returned to haunt Huysmans after his conversion to Catholicism; he rediscovered them in Grünewald's Isenheim altarpiece, in the bodies of Christ and Saint Anthony eaten away by some strange malady and covered with pustules and abscesses. During the same period, Charcot and Richet had both been fascinated by this picture, and Huysmans cites the clinical observations of the two psychiatrists, who diagnosed in the two figures — more particularly in the Christ — the symptoms of gangrenous ergotism and probably of syphilis too (see pl. 15).[97] Huysmans was especially interested in gangrenous ergotism, then also known as *ignis sacer,* "holy fire," or "Saint Anthony's fire." The illness ravaged Europe in the tenth century, showing itself in "apostemes and abscesses, gradually attacking every limb, and after consuming them, little by little detaching them from the trunk."[98] The newly converted Catholic did not go back on his taste for the putrefaction and dismembered forms that des Esseintes so admired in the "old carcass" of the Latin language.[99] But never did Huysmans so jubilantly sound the depths of horror, never plunge with such exhilaration into what the Goncourt brothers called the "charnel house of truth"[100] as when he wrote about Grünewald, that "maniac," the "Orlando furioso of modern painting," "the man who anticipates modern painting." Here again it was the supreme pictorial beauty of a putrefying corpse that triggered his enthusiasm: "Never has painting dared go so far in the rendering of putrefaction. Not even in the medical treatises on dermatological maladies are there plates so repellent. Imagine a swollen body modeled in fatty white *savon de Marseille* marbled with blue, on which pustules rise like foothills and nails pierce the flesh. It is the hosanna of gangrene, the triumphal chant of decay."[101]

This gangrenous and syphilitic Christ brings together all the components of Huysmans's imagination. He was overwhelmed by the Isenheim altarpiece not least because in these monstrous bodies so admirably delineated and colored, he saw a representation of his own conception of both art and the aesthetic experience. Had he not, even before his conversion to Catholicism, viewed painting as a form of the Eucharist, an aesthetic transfiguration of the ailing flesh and corruptible blood?

The old romantic hatred of achieved, classical form reached its culminating point in Huysmans's progressive identification of *colorisme* with the pathologies of vision in particular and the body in general. It is as if he wished to demonstrate the impossible truth of Goethe's observation to Eckermann, which equated classicism with health and romanticism with disease.[102] The condition of modernity in art is, in this view, the continuous re-creation of a color accurately representing putrefied flesh. What now inspired horror was the ideal beauty imposed by classical tradition, thus ensuring an ever more categorical rejection of sculpture.

Notes

1. Charles Baudelaire, *Salon of 1859,* in idem, *Selected Writings on Art and Artists,* trans. P. E. Charvet (Harmondsworth: Penguin, 1972), 324.

2. Edmond de Goncourt and Jules de Goncourt, *Journal: Mémoires de la vie littéraire* (Paris: Robert Laffont, 1989), entry for 18 September 1860, 1:613.

3. Pierre Brunel and André Guyaux, eds., *Joris-Karl Huysmans* (Paris: Éditions de l'Herne, 1985), 25.

4. Joris-Karl Huysmans, *Lettres inédites à Arij Prins, 1855–1907* (Geneva: Droz, 1977), 36.

5. François de Salignac de la Mothe-Fénelon, *Oeuvres,* ed. Jacques Le Brun (Paris: Gallimard, 1983), 1:535.

6. Quoted by Noël Richard in idem, *Profils symbolistes* (Paris: Nizet, 1978), 161. See the introduction by Mireille Dottin in idem, ed., *Jules Laforgue: Textes de critique d'art* (Lille: Presses universitaires de Lille, 1988).

7. Gustave Kahn, "Jules Laforgue," special issue, *Les hommes d'aujourd'hui,* no. 298 (1887); quoted in Mireille Dottin, ed., *Jules Laforgue: Textes de critique d'art* (Lille: Presses universitaires de Lille, 1988), 14.

8. Baudelaire, *Salon of 1859* (note 1), 303.

9. Charles Baudelaire, *Intimate Journals,* trans. Christopher Isherwood (London: Pan, 1990), 49. Translator's note: Isherwood in fact translates *images* as "pictures."

10. Charles Baudelaire, *The Flowers of Evil,* trans. James McGowan (Oxford: Oxford Univ. Press, 1993), 21: "Rubens, fleuve de l'oubli, jardin de la paresse."

11. "Lord, how many lances I broke for the triumph of the dash [*tache*]," wrote Zola in *Le figaro,* 2 May 1896, emerging from a twenty-year silent abstention from art criticism to deplore the state of contemporary painting. See Émile Zola, *Écrits sur l'art,* ed. Jean-Pierre Leduc-Adine (Paris: Gallimard, 1991), 469.

12. Translator's note: In her fine version, Margaret Mauldon translates these words as "the many-faceted, magnificent language that came from the pens of Claudian, of Rutilius and of Ausonius"; Joris-Karl Huysmans, *Against Nature,* ed. Nicholas White, trans. Margaret Mauldon (Oxford: Oxford Univ. Press, 1998), 29.

13. Translator's note: Mauldon translates the text as: "the variegated, magnificent style

14. Joris-Karl Huysmans, "L'exposition des Indépendants en 1880," *L'art moderne, Certains* (Paris: Union générale d'éditions, 1975), 130.

15. Paul Bourget reflected on a description in Huysmans's novel *En ménage:* "Examine this sentence. Is it not true that the writer has seen objects and no longer just their outline but the patch that they form, the sort of garish void that they make in the uniform background of light? Then the almost barbarous decomposition of adjective and noun happens all by itself: 'the peaked-cap blacks…the waistcoats like glasses of wine'"; Paul Bourget, "Paradoxe sur la couleur," in *Le parlement,* 14 May 1881, collected in idem, *Études et portraits: Portraits d'écrivains et Notes d'ésthetique* (Paris: Plon-Nourrit, 1919), 271.

16. Joris-Karl Huysmans, "Goya et Turner," in *Certains,* in idem, *L'art moderne, Certains* (Paris: Union générale d'éditions, 1975), 421–22.

17. Joris-Karl Huysmans, *Les Grünewald du musée de Colmar: Des primitifs au retable d'Issenheim,* ed. Pierre Brunel, André Guyaux, and Christian Heck (Paris: Hermann, 1988), 50.

18. Huysmans, *Against Nature* (note 12), 31.

19. Vincent van Gogh, *The Letters of Vincent van Gogh,* ed. Ronald de Leeuw, trans. Arnold Pomerans (London: Penguin, 1997), 369.

20. Gustave Flaubert to Louis Bouilhet, 10 September 1850, in Gustave Flaubert, *Correspondance,* ed. Jean Bruneau (Paris: Gallimard, 1973), 1:683.

21. What one might call pictorial idiocy has nothing to do with the stupidity of the painter. An intelligent painter can make stupid paintings, as Baudelaire and Huysmans knew. That painting can be stupid is an idea that seems entirely to elude philosophical analysis, and only art criticism seems to have any purchase on the meaning and appropriateness of the term.

22. Arthur Schopenhauer, *On Vision and Colors: An Essay,* ed. David E. Cartwright, trans. E. F. J. Payne, 2nd ed. (Oxford: Berg, 1994), 21.

23. Jacques Dupont, "La couleur dans

(presque) tous ses états," in André Guyaux, Christian Heck, and Robert Kopp, eds., *Huysmans: Une esthétique de la décadence: Actes du colloque de Bâle, Mulhouse et Colmar des 5, 6 et 7 novembre 1984* (Paris: H. Champion, 1987), 155–66. My own remarks are inspired by Dupont's remarkable analysis.

24. Charles Baudelaire, *Salon of 1846,* in idem, *Selected Writings on Art and Artists,* trans. P. E. Charvet (Harmondsworth: Penguin, 1972), 87

25. Baudelaire, *Salon of 1846* (note 24), 89.

26. Joris-Karl Huysmans, "La genèse du peintre," *La revue indépendante,* 1st ser., 1, no. 1 (1884), 25.

27. Joris-Karl Huysmans, *De tout* (Paris: P.-V. Stock, 1902), 68.

28. Huysmans, *De tout* (note 27), 68.

29. Joris-Karl Huysmans, "Le Salon officiel en 1880," in *L'art moderne, Certains* (Paris: Union générale d'éditions, 1975), 154–55.

30. Translator's note: *Le ventre de Paris (1873)* is Zola's novel about le marché des Halles, the central food market in Zola's Paris.

31. Caillebotte was moreover, in Huysmans's view, a typical case of a painter afflicted with "indigomania," a form of chromatopsia with which the impressionists were often diagnosed at this period.

32. This contrast between orange and blue relates to Delacroix's optical triangle. See note 44 below.

33. *Butter* and the nouns and verb derived from it (*beurrage, beurrer*) were terms commonly used by the critics at this time and are not necessarily pejorative. Describing Rubens's *The Fall of the Damned,* which overwhelmed them when they saw it in the Munich Pinakothek, the Goncourt brothers wrote: "Never has a paintbrush so frenziedly rolled and unrolled heaps of flesh, tied and untied clusters of bodies, never so frenziedly buttered fat and guts"; Goncourt brothers, *Journal* (note 2), entry for 18 September 1860, 1:613. In a less complimentary usage, in his "Notes sur le musée du Luxembourg en 1866," Laforgue makes fun of the "luxurious bread-and-butter" of Roll. See Jules Laforgue, "Notes sur le musée du Luxembourg en 1886," *La revue blanche,* 15 June 1895, in Mireille Dottin, ed., *Jules Laforgue: Textes de*

critique d'art (Lille: Presses universitaires de Lille, 1988), 126.

34. "Ah, the influence of the Louvre and the Bon Marché on our painting and literature!" wrote Laforgue about some still lifes by the nineteenth-century Middle Eastern artist Zacharie Zakarian. See Jules Laforgue, "Souvenirs d'un Salon" (1886, published posthumously in 1903), in Mireille Dottin, ed., *Jules Laforgue: Textes de critique d'art* (Lille: Presses universitaires de Lille, 1988), 121. Translator's note: Zola's *Au bonheur des dames* (1883) is the story of the rise of the modern department store, based on the two largest stores of Zola's time, those cited by Laforgue—Au Louvre and Le Bon Marché.

35. Jean-Pierre Richard writes "To 'turn' happy situations, to make them turn out badly like a failed mayonnaise, such is the principal and perhaps only driving force of Huysmanian narrativity"; Jean-Pierre Richard, *Pages paysages: Microlectures II* (Paris: Seuil, 1984), 105.

36. Joris-Karl Huysmans, *En route* (Paris: Plon-Nourrit, 1923), 66.

37. Huysmans, *Against Nature* (note 12), 77.

38. Hippolyte Adolphe Taine, *On Intelligence,* trans. T. D. Haye (London: L. Reeve, 1871), 224.

39. Thus the influence of Chevreul on the artists of the late nineteenth century was exerted through the lens of Charles Blanc. Few artists had read *De la loi du contraste simultané des couleurs* (*The Laws of Contrast of Color*) of 1839, but all of them knew Blanc's *La grammaire des arts du dessin* (1867), which was substantially based on Chevreul's ideas. On this point, see the remarkable work (to which I am much indebted), Georges Roque, *Art et science de la couleur: Chevreul et les peintres de Delacroix à l'abstraction* (Nîmes: Jacqueline Chambon, 1997).

40. George-Louis Leclerc, comte de Buffon, "Observations sur les couleurs accidentelles et sur les ombres colorées," in *Mémoires de l'Académie royale des sciences,* 1743, reprinted in idem, *Un autre Buffon* (Paris: Hermann, 1977), 142.

41. Buffon, "Observations" (note 40). Here again I follow the analysis of Roque, *Art et science de la couleur* (note 39), 13–16.

42. Johann Wolfgang von Goethe, *Goethe's Colour Theory,* ed. Rupprecht Matthaei, English translation trans. and ed. Herb Aach (London: Studio Vista, 1971), 78.

43. Blanc spread the idea that Delacroix had read Chevreul's book. There is no evidence to support this. On this question, see Roque, *Art et science de la couleur* (note 39), 197–200.

44. Eugène Delacroix, *Album de voyage Espagne, Maroc, Algérie,* 1832, MS, Musée Condé, Chantilly. The triangle and the note that accompanies it are analyzed in Kurt Badt, *Die Farbenlehre Van Goghs* (Cologne: DuMont Schauberg, 1961); and Lorenz Dittman, *Farbgestaltung und Farbtheorie in der abendländischen Malerei* (Darmstadt: Wissenschaftliche Buchgesellschaft, 1987).

45. Eugène Delacroix, *The Journal of Eugène Delacroix,* trans. Walter Pach (New York: Grove, 1961), entry for 29 April 1854, 381. To cite another example from the *Journal,* here is the entry for 7 September 1856: "From my window, I see a man at work laying a floor in the gallery; he is nude to the waist. When I compare his color with that of the outer wall, I notice how colorful are the half-tints of the flesh, compared with those of inert matter. I noticed the same thing, the day before yesterday, at the Place Saint-Sulpice, where a scalawag had climbed on the statues of the fountain; I saw him in full sunlight: dull orange in the light, very lively violet tones for the passage from the shadow, and golden reflections in the shadows turned toward the ground. The orange and the violet dominated alternately or mingled. The golden tone had a tendency toward green"; Delacroix, *Journal* (this note), 516–17.

46. Edmond de Goncourt and Jules de Goncourt, *Manette Salomon* (Paris: Union générale d'éditions, 1979), 25.

47. Stéphane Mallarmé, *Poésies, Anecdotes ou poèmes, Pages diverses,* ed. Daniel Leuwers (Paris: Le Livre de Poche, 1977), 207: "Crise de vers."

48. Huysmans, "L'exposition des Indépendants en 1880" (note 14), 131. Huysmans's definition of optical mixing is very close to that of Véron, from whom he perhaps borrowed it: "This production of a third color by the simple collocation of two tones is what painters call optical mixing. It is a very useful resource, since the artist can impart the sensation of a color that never yet featured on his palette. Delacroix made great use of optical mixing and his paintings are consequently the despair of copyists, who try to place directly on their canvases the colors that they believe they see in his"; Eugène Véron, *L'esthétique* (Paris: Alfred Costes, 1921), 282.

49. George Sand, *Impressions et souvenirs* (Paris: Calmann Lévy, 1896), 85–86.

50. Paul Verlaine, "Art poétique," in *Jadis et Naguère* (1884), in idem, *Oeuvres poétiques complètes,* ed. Yves-Gérard Le Dantec and Jacques Borel (Paris: Gallimard, 1962), 326–27.

51. Scientific interest in painting is beginning to revive among cognitivists and specialists of the neurosciences. But compared to that of the nineteenth-century scientists, their analyses of painting are generally pitiful for their poverty and their naïveté, not to mention exceedingly reductive. Moreover, they testify to a broad ignorance of all the other approaches to a work of art — literary, historical, and philosophical — and for the most part justify this position dogmatically, making a virtue of necessity by disguising their ignorance as rejection. My observations on this point do not arise from a principled opposition. On the contrary, it would be interesting if some kind of bridge could be built between neuroscientific research on the one hand and aesthetics, art history, and other such disciplines on the other. This might give a new impulse to thinking about art.

52. Paul Bert, résumé, *République française,* 29 January 1878, quoted in Eugène Véron, *L'esthétique* (Paris: Alfred Costes, 1921), 277.

53. Paul Bert, résumé (note 52).

54. Paul Bert, résumé (note 52).

55. Huysmans, *Against Nature* (note 12), 13. The entire passage describing how des Esseintes "again, and at considerable length, examined the whole range of colors and their gradations" (p. 12) should be analyzed in relation to the scientific theories of color developed at the time. To take just one example, the reason given by des Esseintes for eliminating the color violet coincides with Bert's observation concerning the persistence of red, which dominates blue in violet.

56. Véron, *L'esthétique* (note 48), 277. This is the source from which the résumé is quoted.

57. Véron, *L'esthétique* (note 48), 277.

58. Taine, *On Intelligence* (note 38), 120. The recurrence of the example of santonin in the most diverse authors illustrates the way in which ideas circulated among science, art, and philosophy at this period. It must be said that there is little or no equivalent today. Moreover, ideas moved very rapidly from one field to another. The first volume of Helmholtz's *Handbuch der Physiologischen Optik* was published in 1850; it was translated into French in 1867 and analyzed at length by Taine in *De l'intelligence* (1870). Véron's *L'esthétique,* which often refers to Helmholtz, appeared some years later in 1878.

59. It is hard to understand the oblivion into which this difficult but fascinating work has fallen. It is now rarely read by philosophers but affords a remarkable example of what can and should be the relationship between philosophy and science.

60. Taine, *On Intelligence* (note 38), 154–55.

61. Taine, *On Intelligence* (note 38), 264.

62. Taine, *On Intelligence* (note 38), 233.

63. Taine, *On Intelligence* (note 38). One might here perceive an analogy between Taine's definition and Bichat's celebrated definition of life as "the set of functions that resist death"; Marie-François-Xavier Bichat, *Recherches physiologiques sur la vie et la mort* (Paris: Brosson, Gabon, 1800), 1. For Taine, true perception is basically nothing more than the set of sensations that resist hallucination.

64. Taine, *On Intelligence* (note 38), 226. At the end of the chapter "La perception extérieure et l'éducation des sens" ("External Perception and the Education of the Senses"), Taine recapitulates his series of analyses and conclusions thus: "We have found out that the objects that we call bodies are but internal phantoms, that is to say, fragments of the Ego, detached from it in appearance and opposed to it, though fundamentally they are the Ego under another aspect; that, strictly speaking, this sky, these stars, these trees, all this sensible universe which each of us perceives, is the work of each of us, or rather his emanation, or rather his creation, an involuntary creation, effected by him spontaneously without his consciousness of it, and extended to infinity around him like the shade of a little body whose outline goes on increasing in proportion as it becomes distant, and ends by covering the whole horizon with its immensity. — We have then found that no one of our sensations is situated in that part of the body in which we place it, that many of them, though belonging to us, appear as foreign to us, that, among these, some appear as permanent qualities of a being other than ourselves, while they are in fact transient moments of our being"; Taine, *On Intelligence* (note 38), 350.

65. I have of course borrowed this expression from Gilles Deleuze and his book on the painting of Francis Bacon, *Francis Bacon: The Logic of Sensation,* trans. D. W. Smith (London: Continuum, 2003). His arguments have often inspired my own reflections, particularly in this chapter.

66. The theme of the sick artist frequently recurs in Nietzsche and bears the mark of Schopenhauer's influence. But illness does not always have a positive connotation, as his critique of Wagner shows: "*Wagner est une névrose* (Wagner is a neurosis [in French in the original])…. In Wagner our medical men and physiologists have a most interesting case, or at least a very complete one. Owing to the very fact that nothing is more modern than this thorough morbidness, this dilatoriness and excessive irritability of the nervous machinery, Wagner is *the modern artist par excellence,* the Cagliostro of modernity…. Wagner is a great corrupter of music"; Friedrich Wilhelm Nietzsche, *The Case of Wagner,* in idem, *The Complete Works of Friedrich Nietzsche,* ed. Oscar Levy, trans. Anthony Mario Ludovici (Edinburgh: T. N. Foulis, 1911), 8:13–14. And in the epilogue to this work he adds, "One cannot refute Christianity: it is impossible to refute a diseased eyesight"; Nietzsche, *The Case of Wagner* (this note), 49.

Similarly, when Nietzsche talks about the color blindness of the philosophers, the word is used in an entirely pejorative fashion as a synonym for blindness, mendacity, and the refusal to see: "He who lives among the Germans should consider himself fortunate if he can find anyone who knows how to defend himself against the lies that the idealists tell themselves and against their color blindness, which Germans like and respect as they do virtue itself"; Friedrich Wilhelm Nietzsche, *Fragments posthumes (été 1882–printemps 1884)*, vol. 9, *Oeuvres philosophiques complètes,* ed. Giorgio Colli and Mazzino Montinari, trans. (German to French) Anne-Sophie Astrup and Marc de Launay (Paris: Gallimard, 1997), 254. However ambiguous Nietzsche's position on this issue, it must be acknowledged that it derives from a point of view profoundly alien to that of most French artists and authors of the late nineteenth century, who tend on the contrary to valorize illness and all forms of nervous degeneration. The same clinical vision produces a radically different aesthetic conclusion in France than in Germany. This divergence was to widen still further during the twentieth century, when in Germany there arose a notorious discourse about degenerate art. On this subject, see Jacqueline Lichtenstein and Jean-François Groulier, "'L'art dégénéré' ou la logique des exclusions," in *Traverses,* no. 3 (1992), 60–75.

67. Zola was struck by the comical aspect of Huysmans's descriptions. "There is a special comedy in your more outrageous effects that I find in no one else and which constitutes, in my view, one of your greatest originalities," he told Huysmans in a letter.

68. This research also supplied a scientific confirmation of Schopenhauer's theory of color, which was inspired by Goethe's. In a letter to Carl von Gersdorff, dated 1 November 1870, Nietzsche writes: "I recently had a very rejoicing experience when I discovered in the proceedings of the Vienna Academy of Sciences a study by Pr. Czermack on Schopenhauer's theory of color. He states that Schopenhauer, independently and by his own, original route, arrived at the very doctrine now designated as the Young-Helmholtz theory. There is a striking concordance between the two theories, precise to several orders of decimals. The entire point of departure, the idea that color is above all a physiological product of the eye, was, he says, first explicated by Schopenhauer. The author strongly regrets that Schopenhauer proved unable to free himself from Goethe's scientific principle, which is scientifically absurd, and from his anti-Newtonian furor"; Friedrich Wilhelm Nietzsche, *Correspondance,* vol. 2, *Oeuvres philosophiques complètes,* ed. Giorgio Colli and Mazzino Montinari, trans. (German to French) Henri-Alexis Baatsch, Jean Bréjoux, and Maurice de Gandillac (Paris: Gallimard, 1986), 150ff. The passage is quoted in Jacques Le Rider, *Les couleurs et les mots* (Paris: Presses universitaires de France, 1997), 121.

69. Joris-Karl Huysmans, "L'exposition des Indépendants en 1881," in idem, *L'art moderne, Certains* (Paris: Union générale d'éditions, 1975), 253.

70. Joris-Karl Huysmans, "Cézanne," in idem, *Certains,* in idem, *L'art moderne, Certains* (Paris: Union générale d'éditions, 1975), 309.

71. "Painting without ocular spasm," writes Laforgue, "is for me like Platonic, sentimental, castrated love, a love without localization"; Jules Laforgue, "Notes d'esthétique," *La revue blanche,* 1 December 1896, in Mireille Dottin, ed., *Jules Laforgue: Textes de critique d'art* (Lille: Presses universitaires de Lille, 1988), 159. Baudelaire had already written in his *Fusées* (*Squibs*): "There is, in the creation of all sublime thought, a nervous concussion, which can be felt in the cerebellum"; Baudelaire, *Intimate Journals* (note 9), 46.

72. Translator's note: The French *nervosisme* is defined by the *Dictionnaire de la Académie française* (8th ed., 1932–35) as a "morbid state characterized by disturbance of the nervous system" (2:228). It was translated as "nervosism" or "nervous diathesis."

73. Goncourt brothers, *Journal* (note 2), entry for 13 February 1874, 2:570.

74. Denis Diderot, *Salon de 1763,* in idem,

Arts et lettres (1739–1766), ed. Jean Varloot, vol. 13 of idem, *Oeuvres complètes* (Paris: Hermann, 1980), 380.

75. Huysmans, *Against Nature* (note 12), 46.

76. Philosophical aesthetics is by and large dominated by the Kantian tradition, that is, by a theory that closes off the question of sensory experience and affirms the primacy of imagination over sensation. It is therefore striking to note that art criticism is alone in giving a proper account of *aisthesis.*

77. Huysmans, "L'exposition des Indépendants en 1881" (note 69), 238.

78. Huysmans, "L'exposition des Indépendants en 1880" (note 14), 132. He is talking about Degas's portrait of the critic Louis Edmond Duranty.

79. Joris-Karl Huysmans, *Salon de 1879,* in idem, *L'art moderne, Certains* (Paris: Union générale d'éditions, 1975), 27.

80. Huysmans, *Against Nature* (note 12), 70.

81. Des Esseintes, Huysmans tells us, experienced the "dislike that meat inspires in those who have no appetite"; Huysmans, *Against Nature* (note 12), 171.

82. Goncourt brothers, *Manette Salomon* (note 46), 197.

83. Honoré de Balzac, *The Unknown Masterpiece,* trans. Richard Howard (New York: New York Review of Books, 2001), 39–40.

84. Balzac, *Unknown Masterpiece* (note 83), 42.

85. Huysmans, *Against Nature* (note 12), 77. On this subject, see Patrick Wald Lasowski, *Syphilis: Essai sur la littérature française du XIXe siècle* (Paris: Gallimard, 1982).

86. Joris-Karl Huysmans, *Certains,* in idem, *L'art moderne, Certains* (Paris: Union générale d'éditions, 1975), 294.

87. Translator's note: The term *culbuter* used in a sexual context has roughly the sense of "lay," probably better represented in this case by "upend" than "overthrow."

88. Huysmans, "L'exposition des Indépendants en 1881" (note 69), 228. Cf. chap. 4, nn. 71–73.

89. Huysmans, *Certains* (note 86), 294.

90. Degas said that he would like to represent women as though he were seeing them through a keyhole.

91. Charles Baudelaire, "Éloge du maquillage," in idem, *Curiosités esthétiques: L'art romantique et autres oeuvres critiques,* ed.

92. Baudelaire, *Intimate Journals* (note 9), 25.

93. Huysmans, *Certains* (note 86), 295.

94. Huysmans, *Certains* (note 86), 295–96.

95. Huysmans, *Certains* (note 86), 296–97.

96. Mallarmé, *Poésies* (note 47), 76: "Ses purs ongles très hauts dédiant leur onyx," (line 6).

97. On Huysmans's sources, see the excellent critical edition established by Pierre Brunel, André Guyaux, and Christian Heck: Huysmans, *Les Grünewald du musée de Colmar* (note 17).

98. Huysmans, *Les Grünewald du musée de Colmar* (note 17), 45.

99. Huysmans, *Against Nature* (note 12), 33. "The religious conversion undergone by the author of *En ménage* failed to produce an equivalent literary conversion," as Remy de Gourmont rightly observed. See Remy de Gourmont, "M. Huysmans, écrivain pieux," in idem, *Promenades littéraires* (Paris: Mercure de France, 1963), 3:73.

100. Edmond de Goncourt and Jules de Goncourt, *Journal des Goncourt: Mémoires de la vie littéraire,* vol. 3, *1866–1870* (Paris: G. Charpentier, 1888), entry for 25 February 1867, 106.

101. Huysmans, *Les Grünewald du musée de Colmar* (note 17), 43. This description bears comparison with that of Zurbarán's *Saint Francis Standing:* "The face is as if molded, excavated from ash, and the mouth hangs open beneath the ecstatic eyes, all white, as though blinded.... This painting is clearly a product of the harsh and terrible mysticism of Saint John of the Cross; it is the art of the Torturer, the delirium tremens of divine ecstasy in this nether world; ah yes, but what a pitch of adoration bursts out of this canvas, what an outburst of love suffocated by anguish"; Joris-Karl Huysmans, *L'écho de Paris,* 2 February 1898.

102. Johann Wolfgang von Goethe, *Conversations with Eckermann: Being Appreciations and Criticisms on Many Subjects* (New York: M. Walter Dunne, 1901; reprint, n.p.: Kessinger, 2000), entry for 2 April 1829, 302.

The Decline of a Paradigm

All the modes of aesthetic reflection practiced to date err in failing to highlight the different ways in which humans perceive works of art.

— Konrad Fiedler[1]

THE HISTORY that I have sought to analyze in this book ends with the advent of modernity, which is at once its fulfillment and conclusion. It sets before us an idea of art dominated by the double paradigm of painting and vision, one that has always relegated sculpture to second place. It is striking to observe that the development of certain controversies related to the sense of touch, far from improving the status of sculpture, merely reinforced the privileges of painting. In the second half of the nineteenth century, science in the form of physiology and psychology came to the assistance of the myth of the blind philosopher—a myth by then somewhat hoary—by validating the new concepts of optics and haptics. Theorists like Wölfflin and Riegl demonstrated the interpretative relevance of the bipolarity of these two values. But the area in which they were most fruitfully applied was the analysis of pictorial form. Haptics had originally been a category integral to all approaches to sculpture; diverted from its original field of application, it was now put to nearly exclusive use exalting the powers of painting.[2] The concepts of plastic and tactile value came to serve discourses on painting, to the clear detriment of sculpture. The property of plasticity was attributed primarily to the picture, while tactile values were ascribed to line and color. The preeminence of the pictorial paradigm was constantly reasserted and reaffirmed on the basis of implicit evaluations. Although it was never formally recognized, a theoretical hierarchy grew up; it favored painting at the cost of real ignorance of the other arts in general and of sculpture in particular. To take just one example of the dissymmetry in our relationship with painting and sculpture, consider how the attention given to Matisse's sculpture—especially by art critics—long remained exiguous while his pictorial works were fervently praised. This suggests that indifference to sculpture was not merely a cultural symptom or the product of a more or less consistent aesthetic attitude but a constitutive trait of our relationship to art. And this relationship was inherited by modernity. When Ad Reinhardt defined sculpture as "something you bump into when you back up to look at a painting,"[3] he was merely fueling a tenacious prejudice, one that the silence of the theoreticians over three centuries had done nothing to dispel. Caylus long since condemned this silence. Should we not reverse the poles of Reinhardt's dictum, and say that, for many critics and theorists, painting has too often been the obstacle that prevented them from seeing sculpture?

We have attempted to explain the reasons behind this indifference, indeed this reticence. For several centuries, sculpture was forced to bear as a stigma its excessively substantial and solid reality and its manifest adherence to classical antiquity. Sculpture could not attain recognition while painting was so exclusively identified with modernity nor while it was itself perceived through literary schemata and sterile comparisons. Hegel had long since criticized this inability to perceive sculpture in its singularity, touching on the issue in relation to the disputes about Lessing's *Laocoon:* "Previously there was much preoccupation with such matters of psychological importance because Winckelmann's enthusiasm and genuine artistic sense had not yet sunk in, and, besides, such bookworms were the more disposed to indulge in such discussions because frequently they had neither the opportunity to see actual works of art nor the ability to understand them if they had seen them."[4] Above all, it was not possible to apprehend sculpture in all its specificity when it was considered in relation to painting, when it was judged according to categories that had not been developed for or grown out of the practices of sculpture, and when it was constantly being evaluated on the basis of heterogeneous criteria that were alien to what one might call its essence.

The influence of theories of painting has, it is true, been very fertile in the history of sculpture. It several times enabled sculpture to liberate itself from traditional models, as we saw in the eighteenth century with the birth of Rubenist sculpture and in the late nineteenth century with the advent of what Huysmans calls modern sculpture. At the same time, these theories paradoxically helped to maintain the servitude of sculpture to the pictorial paradigm and more particularly to the colorist paradigm. As a result, the birth of modern sculpture has sometimes been perceived as the ultimate triumph of colorist ideas; it has been celebrated as a definitive and unprecedented victory of painting. In this version of events, colorism finally awoke sculpture from the long sleep into which it had been lulled by its obsession with the ancient model. This paradox goes a long way toward explaining the route taken by this book, which may at times seem to accord too great a prominence to the heterogeneous. I have found myself with no other choice than to interweave two issues, which, although mutually exclusive in theory, tend to merge in fact: that of color, which belongs to painting, and that of plastic form, which belongs to sculpture.

We have said that this route ends with the advent of modernity—modernity, that is, in the sense of Baudelaire and Huysmans. That modernity, as I have tried to demonstrate, still belongs to the history whose beginnings I have traced to the seventeenth century. It is, as it were, the final form taken by that history; it is the Hegelian moment when the circle is completed, when the circle closes in on itself to give birth to something else, in this case a new vision of modernity and more especially of sculpture. In this respect, Hildebrand's *Das Problem der Form in der Bildenden Kunst* (*The Problem of Form in Painting and Sculpture*), whose first edition dates from 1893, can be considered one of the foundational texts that completely turned its back on the history of the *paragone.* Hildebrand's work consisted of the reflections of a sculptor who was also a great theorist and constitutes a complete break with the pictorial paradigm. One reason for this is the aesthetic and metaphysical postulate common to Fiedler and the group of artists to which Hildebrand belonged, which stated that any genuinely achieved form necessarily obeyed a principle of autonomy.[5] The theory of sculpture thus conceived was first and foremost the theory of a specific art and ran counter to the old legitimating discourse of the traditional *trattati* (treatises) and academic lectures, which was for the most part intended to acknowledge or legitimate a particular status. It finally broke with the entire network of scholarly and literary references, rejected all colorist influence, and above all refused the topic of the arts such as it had been formulated for the previous few centuries. The question of plastic form, as treated by Hildebrand, appeals to a psychology of perception and to the concepts of space, volume, and plan. The first act of Hildebrand's artistic thinking is to return to the originating impulse, that is, to the perceptual experience of touch in the constitution of form: "All our knowledge concerning the plastic nature of objects is originally derived from movements which we make either with eyes or with hands."[6]

In this way a theory of sculpture again becomes possible and on entirely new foundations, namely the sensory data supplied in the second half of the nineteenth century by the physiology of Helmholtz and the psychology of Fechner. There is no room here to consider the theoretical content of that research. But it constituted such a decisive break that recourse to the old pictorial paradigm was effectively ruled out. To think about sculpture as Hildebrand did was to put the concepts of surface, volume, haptics, and optics to work. This in its turn meant that cosmetic expressivity—the colorist mask—was at last rejected in the quest for pure form. The theory of sculpture could now produce "pure" concepts— concepts destined primarily for the comprehension of plastic works. When Wölfflin applies the concept of haptics to the painting of northern Europe, he

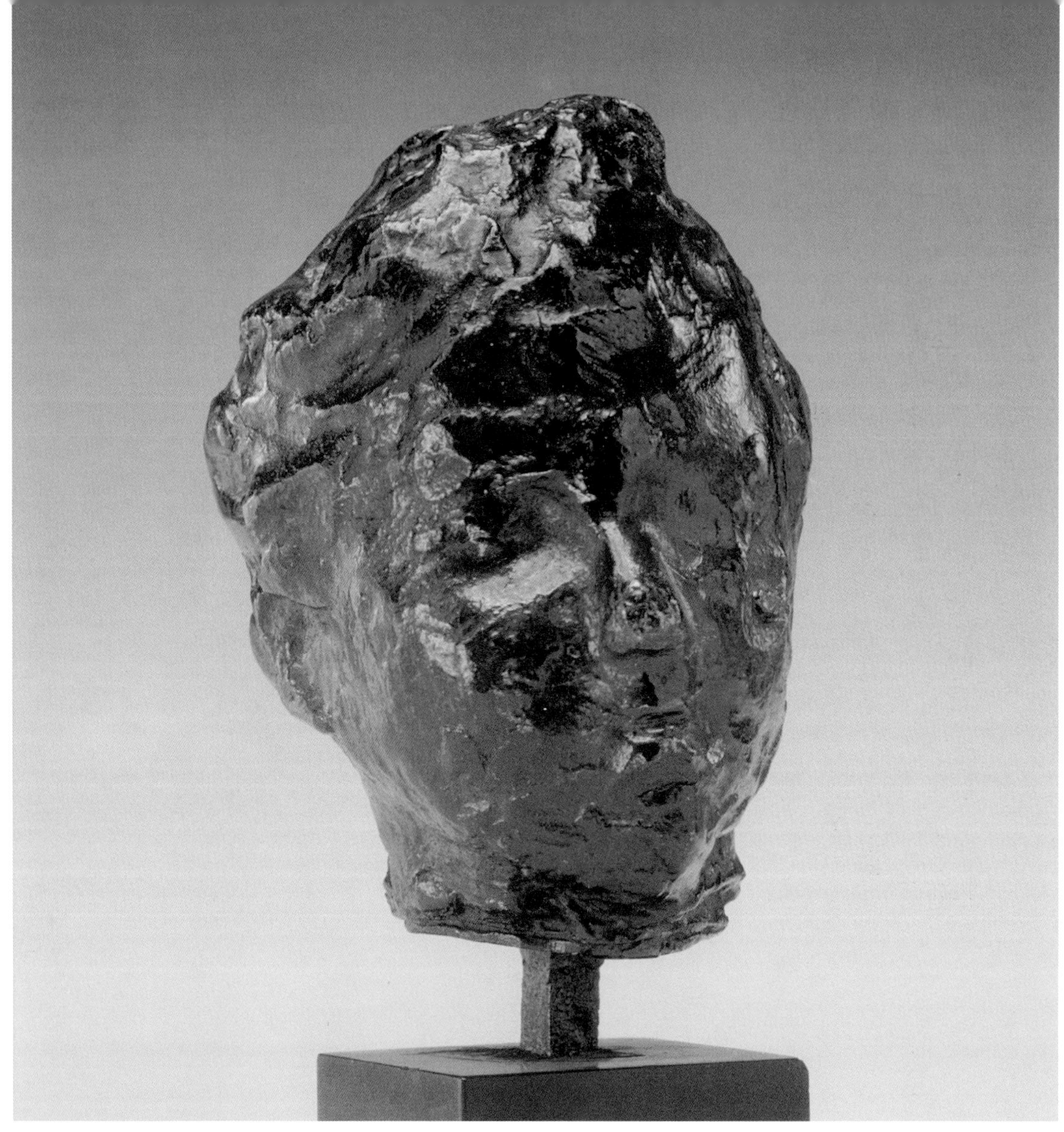

borrows from Hildebrand a notion originally created for the interpretation of sculpture. For the theory of plastic form, this transfer undoubtedly constitutes a reappropriation. But it seems unlikely to mark the end of the hegemony of the pictorial paradigm. Despite the best efforts of Hildebrand and others, sculpture struggles even today to become a theoretical object on a par with painting; that is to say, a theoretical object in its own right (fig. 22).

Notes

1. Konrad Fiedler, *Schriften über Kunst* (Munich: R. Piper, 1914), aphorism 29, p. 27.

2. On this subject, see Didier Ottinger, *Haptisch: La caresse de l'oeil,* exh. cat. (Les Sables d'Olonne: Musée de l'abbaye Sainte-Croix des Sables d'Olonne, 1993).

3. Quoted in Lucy R. Lippard, "As Painting Is to Sculpture: A Changing Ratio," in *American Sculpture of the Sixties,* ed. Maurice Tuchman, exh. cat. (Los Angeles: Los Angeles Country Museum of Art, 1967), 31.

4. Georg Wilhelm Friedrich Hegel, *Aesthetics: Lectures on Fine Art,* trans. T. M. Knox (Oxford: Clarendon, 1975), 2:769. Though Hegel does not name Lessing, he is here accused of being one of the theorists and scholars who, unable to truly see and understand works of art, lose themselves in "matters of psychological importance." Hegel's purpose is by no means to criticize scholarship, since he considers knowledge the principal pathway toward and an essential condition of our understanding of art. His objection is to a mistaken use of scholarship in our relationship with works of art.

5. Extracts from Fiedler and other theorists of plastic form and "pure visibility," such as Wölfflin, Hildebrand, Berenson, and others, can be found in Roberto Salvini, ed., *La critica d'arte della pura visibiltà e del formalismo* (Milan: Garzanti, 1977).

6. Adolf von Hildebrand, *The Problem of Form in Painting and Sculpture,* trans. Max Meyer and Robert Morris Ogden, 2nd ed. (New York: G. E. Stechert, 1932), 23–24.

Epilogue

More than three centuries after Varchi's survey, the early-twentieth-century critic Edmond Claris asked artists, critics, and collectors to give their views on Baudelaire's critique of sculpture, along with a reply to the question: "Can and should sculpture compete with painting?" He published the replies in a work entitled *De l'impressionnisme en sculpture.*[1] Claris considered this "a major question that seems to hold within it the entire genesis of future art." He thought that a "manifestation like that set off by Monet, Pissarro, Raffaëlli, Renoir, and Degas" had occurred and that, with artists such as Auguste Rodin and Medardo Rosso, sculpture was entering upon "a period of pure creation" (fig. 23). Compared to the answers to Varchi's survey, those elicited by Claris were very disappointing. The issue of the *paragone* had clearly lost its relevance, at least for the artists. We will confine ourselves to citing Claude Monet's reply: "Let me tell you frankly that I have no interest whatever in this sort of thing. My trade is painting and I think that this sort of discussion should be left to those fascinated by such things, those whose trade is writing."

Note

1. Edmond Claris, *De l'impressionnisme en sculpture* (Paris: La nouvelle revue, 1902). The text has been republished in Luciano Carmel, ed., *L'impressionismo nella scultura,* exh. cat. (Milan: Electa, 1989), 79–91.

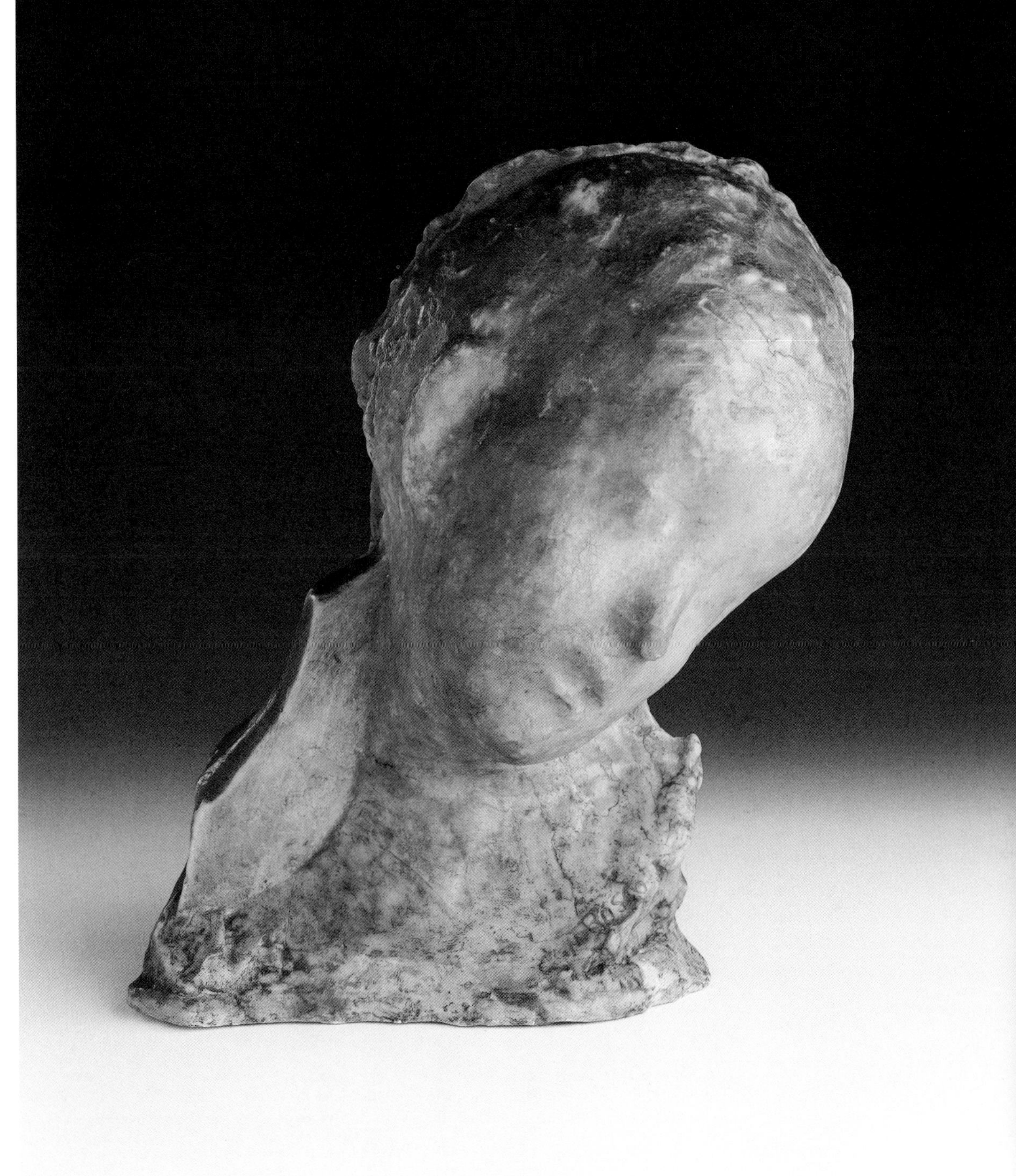

Fig. 23. **Medardo Rosso (Italian, 1858–1928)**
Sick Boy, 1893, wax and plaster, 26.7 × 23.8 × 17.8 cm (10½ × 9⅜ × 7 in.)
Middlebury, Vt., Middlebury College Museum of Art

Illustration Credits

<table>
<tr><td>Fig. 1</td><td>Photo: Hervé Lewandowski, courtesy Réunion des musées nationaux/Art Resource, New York</td><td>Fig. 15</td><td>Photo: Gérard Blot, courtesy Réunion des musées nationaux/Art Resource, New York</td></tr>
<tr><td>Fig. 2</td><td>Photo: Timothy McCarthy/Art Resource, New York</td><td>Fig. 16</td><td>Photo: G. Blot/C. Jean, courtesy Réunion des musées nationaux/Art Resource, New York</td></tr>
<tr><td>Fig. 3</td><td>Photo: Réunion des musées nationaux/Art Resource, New York. Droits réservés.</td><td>Fig. 17</td><td>Photo: Erich Lessing/Art Resource, New York</td></tr>
<tr><td>Fig. 4</td><td>Photo: Erich Lessing/Art Resource, New York</td><td>Fig. 18</td><td>The State Hermitage Museum, St. Petersburg</td></tr>
<tr><td>Fig. 5</td><td>Getty Research Institute, Research Library, 85-B16841. Photo: © 2008 J. Paul Getty Trust</td><td>Fig. 19</td><td>Courtesy of Académie des sciences, belles lettres et arts de Lyon</td></tr>
<tr><td>Fig. 6</td><td>Photo: Alinari/Art Resource, New York</td><td>Pl. 1</td><td>Photo: Erich Lessing/Art Resource, New York</td></tr>
<tr><td>Fig. 7</td><td>Photo: Louis Deschamps, courtesy Réunion des musées nationaux/Art Resource, New York</td><td>Pl. 2</td><td>The Norton Simon Foundation</td></tr>
<tr><td>Fig. 8</td><td>Photo: Hervé Lewandowski, courtesy Réunion des musées nationaux/Art Resource, New York</td><td>Pl. 3</td><td>Photo: Michele Bellot, courtesy Réunion des musées nationaux/Art Resource, New York</td></tr>
<tr><td>Fig. 9</td><td>Photo: Réunion des musées nationaux/Art Resource, New York</td><td>Pl. 4</td><td>Photo: Franck Raux, courtesy Réunion des musées nationaux/Art Resource, New York</td></tr>
<tr><td>Figs. 10, 11</td><td>Photo: C. Jean, courtesy Réunion des musées nationaux/Art Resource, New York</td><td>Pls. 5, 6</td><td>Photo: Gérard Blot, courtesy Réunion des musées nationaux/Art Resource, New York</td></tr>
<tr><td>Figs. 12, 13</td><td>Photo: Scala/Art Resource, New York</td><td>Pl. 7</td><td>Photo: Franck Raux, courtesy Réunion des musées nationaux/Art Resource, New York</td></tr>
<tr><td>Fig. 14</td><td>Photo: © H. H. Arnason</td><td>Pl. 8</td><td>Photo: Thierry Le Mage, courtesy Réunion des musées nationaux/Art Resource, New York</td></tr>
</table>

Pl. 9	Purchase, special contributions and funds given or bequeathed by friends of the Museum, 1961 (61.198). Photo: © The Metropolitan Museum of Art/ Art Resource, New York

Pl. 10	Hood Museum of Art, Dartmouth College, Hanover, New Hampshire; purchased through the Mrs. Harvey P. Hood W'18 Fund, the Florence and Lansing Porter Moore 1937 Fund, and the Hood Museum of Art Acquisitions Fund

Pl. 11	Photo: Scala/Art Resource, New York

Pl. 12	Photo: Erich Lessing/Art Resource, New York

Pl. 13	H. O. Havemeyer Collection, Bequest of Mrs. H. O. Havemeyer, 1929 (29.100.370). Photo: © The Metropolitan Museum of Art/Art Resource, New York

Pl. 14	Photo: Jean-Gilles Berizzi, courtesy Réunion des musées nationaux/Art Resource, New York

Pl. 15	Photo: Bridgeman-Giraudon/Art Resource, New York

Pl. 16	Photo: Jean Schormans, courtesy Réunion des musées nationaux/ Art Resource, New York

Fig. 20	Getty Research Institute, Research Library, acc. no. 920048* (box 2). Photo: © 2008 J. Paul Getty Trust

Fig. 21	Photography © The Art Institute of Chicago

Fig. 22	© 2007 Board of Trustees, National Gallery of Art, Washington, D.C. Collections of Mr. and Mrs. Paul Mellon

Fig. 23	Collection of Middlebury College Museum of Art. Purchase with funds provided by the Christian A. Johnson Memorial Fund, 1979.036. Photo: Ken Burris

Page references to illustrations are in italic.

portrait of (Fragonard), *110;* on relationship
of art and literature, 138–39; on relationship
of sight to touch, 68; on Rubens, 9; *Salon
de 1759,* 56; *Salon de 1763,* 55, 63–64, 72–73,
75–76; *Salon de 1765,* 82–83, 84; *Salon de 1767,*
138; *Salons,* 55; sculptural depictions of, *89;*
on sculpture, 70, 72–84, 86, 91–92, 96n79,
96n83, 135, 137–38, 145, 150; self-description,
85; on senses, 3; on touch, 84; on van Dyck,
77; on van Loo, 74, 94n69; on Vernet, 75;
Winckelman and, 82–83, 97n86, 139. *See also
Encyclopédie*
"Dioptrique" (Descartes), 3, 64, 68
Discours sur la poésie dramatique (Diderot), 85
Discus Thrower (sculpture), 155
Dorcy, Pierre, *A Hunter and His Mistress by the
Tomb of Two Lovers,* 132n8
Le drageoir aux épices (Huysmans), 165–66
Dubos, Jean-Baptiste: on pictorial illusion,
59–60, 61, 93n10; on poetry and sculpture,
136–37; *Réflexions critiques sur la poésie et sur
la peinture,* 59–60
Dubufe, Edouard, 172
Du Laurens, André, *Histoire anatomique,* 29
Düsseldorf school, 160n9

École des beaux-arts, pedagogical philosophy,
119–20
Elsen, Albert E., 162n32
Encyclopédie (Diderot): *Borghese Gladiator* in,
30; Encyclopédie project described in, 85;
Marmontel on pictorial illusion in, 60–61. *See
also Supplément à Encyclopédie*
En ménage (Huysmans), 190n15
The Enneads (Plotinus), 97n94
Entretiens sur le fils naturel (Diderot), 3
Esquirol, Jean-Étienne-Dominique, 179
Essay Concerning Human Understanding
(Locke), 65, 70
L'esthétique (Véron), 155, 163n65
Everywhere Eyeballs Are Aflame (Redon), *183*

Falconet, Etienne-Maurice: aesthetic of, 123;
on Bernini, 96n82; Diderot and, 8, 55, 75–76,
85, 138; influence of, 71; on nature of art, 141;
on *paragone* debate, 3; on Poussin, 53n53; on
Puget, 79; *Pygmalion and Galatea,* 75–76,
76; Réflexions sur la sculpture, 53n53, 71; on
sculpture, 53n53, 79–82, 96n81, 96n82
The Fall of the Damned (Rubens), 191n33
Farnese Herakles: in Académie instruction, 29, 47,
50n19; Anguier lecture on, 31–32; copies of, 25
Fechner, Gustav Theodor, 198
Félibien, André, on van Opstal, 25, 35–36, 38
Fénelon, François de Salignac de la Mothe, 165
Fiedler, Konrad, 197, 198
Le figaro (Zola), 190n11
Flaubert, Gustave: and modern man, 131; on
painting, 169; on poetry, 151
Les fleurs du mal (Baudelaire), 143, 147–48
Fragonard, Jean-Honoré: *Portrait of Denis
Diderot, 110; Study, 109*
François Girardon (Gabriel), *104*
François I, King of France, 51n22
Friquet de Vauroze, Jacques Antoine, 52n35
Froissac, Ernest, 166
Fusées (Baudelaire), 194n71

Gabriel, Revel, *François Girardon, 104*
Gautier, Théophile: biographical information,
165; on philosophical art, 140, 141; on sculpture,
135, 151, 152
Gayrard, Paul, Baudelaire on, 145
Gervex, Henri, 172
Geschichte der Kunst des Allerthums
(Winckelmann), 96n84, 128, 132n16, 133n34
Gilson, Étienne, 97n87
Giordano, Luca, *Carneades with the Bust of
Paniscus, 108*
Girardon, François: as inspector general of
sculpture, 122; *paragone* debate and, 122;
portrait of (Gabriel), *104*
A Girl with a Dead Canary (Greuze), 58–59, 91
Girodet de Roussy-Trioson, Anne-Louis: *The
Cairo Revolt,* 132n8; *The Deluge,* 132n8

**The Blind Spot: An Essay on the Relations between
Painting and Sculpture in the Modern Age**

Jacqueline Lichtenstein
Translation by Chris Miller

Jacqueline Lichtenstein is a professor of philosophy at the University of
Paris-IV-Sorbonne and has previously held positions at the University of Paris-
X-Nanterre and at the University of California, Berkeley. A recipient of numer-
ous research awards and grants, including a residential scholarship at the Getty
Research Institute in Los Angeles (2001–2), she specializes in the history and
criticism of art and aesthetics. Lichtenstein is the author of *La couleur éloquente:
Rhétorique et peinture à l'âge classique* (1989), translated as *The Eloquence of Color:
Rhetoric and Painting in the French Classical Age* (1993); the chief editor of the
series Essais d'art et d'esthétique, published by VRIN; and a contributing editor
to several prominent journals, such as *Les études philosophiques* and *Revue de
l'art*. She is currently working with Christian Michel on a ten-volume annotated
transcription of lectures given by artists at the Académie royale de peinture et de
sculpture from 1667 to 1792, the first three volumes of which are now in print.

Chris Miller, translator and editor, was born in Iraq and studied classics at
Oxford. He has lived and worked in Paris, Copenhagen, and Bogotá. A member
of the Institute of Translation and Interpreting (specializing in the fine arts), he
is a widely published literary critic, contributing editor of *The Warwick Review*,
cofounder and Member of the Board of the Oxford Amnesty Lectures, and member of the Editorial Board of *European Photography*. He lives in Oxford with his
wife and three children.

Carl Gustav Carus, *Nine Letters on Landscape Painting, Written in the Years 1815–1824; with a Letter from Goethe by Way of Introduction* (1831)
Introduction by Oskar Bätschmann
Translation by David Britt
ISBN 978-0-89236-674-3 (paper)

Karel Teige, *Modern Architecture in Czechoslovakia and Other Writings* (1923–30)
Introduction by Jean-Louis Cohen
Translation by Irena Žantovská Murray and David Britt
ISBN 978-0-89236-596-8 (paper)

Jean-Nicolas-Louis Durand, *Précis of the Lectures on Architecture* (1802–5) with *Graphic Portion of the Lectures on Architecture* (1821)
Introduction by Antoine Picon
Translation by David Britt
ISBN 978-0-89236-580-7 (paper)

Walter Curt Behrendt, *The Victory of the New Building Style* (1927)
Introduction by Detlef Mertins
Translation by Harry Francis Mallgrave
ISBN 978-0-89236-563-0 (paper)

Aby Warburg, *The Renewal of Pagan Antiquity: Contributions to the Cultural History of the European Renaissance* (1932)
Introduction by Kurt W. Forster
Translation by David Britt
ISBN 978-0-89236-537-1 (hardcover)

Sigfried Giedion, *Building in France, Building in Iron, Building in Ferroconcrete* (1928)
Introduction by Sokratis Georgiadis
Translation by J. Duncan Berry
ISBN 978-0-89236-319-3 (hardcover), ISBN 978-0-89236-320-9 (paper)

Hermann Muthesius, *Style-Architecture and Building-Art: Transformations of Architecture in the Nineteenth Century and Its Present Condition* (1902)
Introduction by Stanford Anderson
Translation by Stanford Anderson
ISBN 978-0-89236-282-0 (hardcover), ISBN 978-0-89236-283-7 (paper)

Friedrich Gilly: Essays on Architecture, 1796–1799
Introduction by Fritz Neumeyer
Translation by David Britt
ISBN 978-0-89236-280-6 (hardcover), ISBN 978-0-89236-281-3 (paper)

Nicolas Le Camus de Mézières, *The Genius of Architecture; or,*
The Analogy of That Art with Our Sensations (1780)
Introduction by Robin Middleton
Translation by David Britt
ISBN 978-0-89236-234-9 (hardcover), ISBN 978-0-89236-235-6 (paper)

Claude Perrault, *Ordonnance for the Five Kinds of Columns after the*
Method of the Ancients (1683)
Introduction by Alberto Pérez-Gómez
Translation by Indra Kagis McEwen
ISBN 978-0-89236-232-5 (hardcover), ISBN 978-0-89236-233-2 (paper)

Heinrich Hübsch, Rudolf Wiegmann, Carl Albert Rosenthal, Johann Heinrich
Wolff, and Carl Gottlieb Wilhelm Bötticher, *In What Style Should We Build?*
The German Debate on Architectural Style (1828–47)
Introduction and translation by Wolfgang Herrmann
ISBN 978-0-89236-199-1 (hardcover), ISBN 978-0-89236-198-4 (paper)

Otto Wagner, *Modern Architecture: A Guidebook for His Students to*
This Field of Art (1902)
Introduction and translation by Harry Francis Mallgrave
ISBN 978-0-226-86938-4 (hardcover), ISBN 978-0-226-86939-1 (paper)

In Preparation

Laurence Bertrand Dorléac, *Art of the Defeat, France 1940–1944* (1993)
Translation by Jane Marie Todd
ISBN 978-0-89236-891-4 (hardcover)

Régis Michel, *Ideal Beauty: A Western Phantasy* (1989)
Translation by Simon Pleasance and Fronza Woods
ISBN 978-0-89236-768-9 (paper)

Designed by Kurt Hauser

Production coordinated by Stacy Miyagawa

Type composed by Diane Franco in Minion and Antique Olive

Printed in China through Asia Pacific Offset, Inc., on Gold East Matte